VILAS CO.

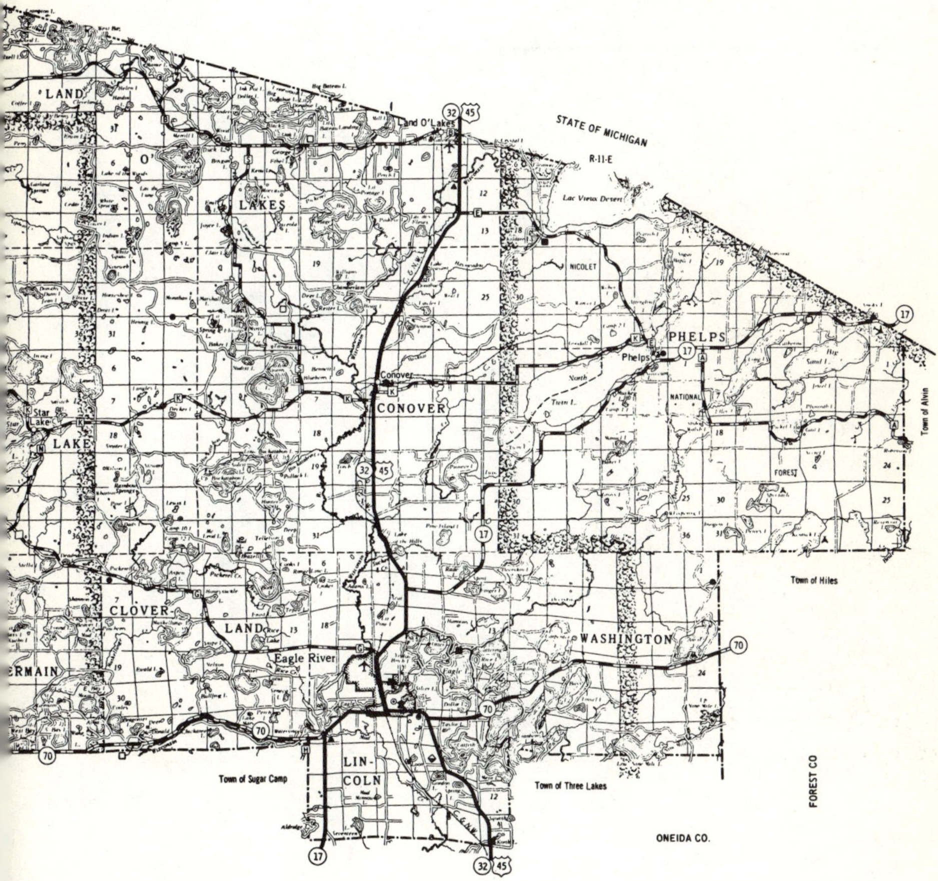
STATE OF MICHIGAN
R-11-E
Land O'Lakes
LAND
O'
LAKES
Lac Vieux Desert
NICOLET
PHELPS
Phelps
NATIONAL
FOREST
Conover
CONOVER
Star Lake
LAKE
CLOVER-
LAND
Eagle River
WASHINGTON
ERMAIN
LIN-
COLN
North Twin L.
Big Sand L.
Town of Alvin
Town of Hiles
Town of Sugar Camp
Town of Three Lakes
FOREST CO.
ONEIDA CO.

*To my mother and the
memory of my father, with
unbounded appreciation.*

Easy Going

Wisconsin's Northwoods
Vilas and Oneida Counties

Michael J. Dunn, III

Illustrations by William T. Pope

Tamarack Press
P.O. Box 5650
Madison, Wisconsin 53705

Easy Going
Text © copyright 1978 by Michael J. Dunn, III.
Illustrations © copyright 1978 by Tamarack Press. All rights reserved. No part of this book may be reproduced in any form or by any means without the written consent of the publisher.

Edited by Diana Balio.
Designed by Patricia Dorman.
Cover design by Dale Mann.
Typeset by Parkwood Composition Service, Inc.
Printed in the United States of America by George Banta Company, Inc.

First printing 1978.

Library of Congress Cataloging in Publication Data Dunn, Michael J. Easy Going—Wisconsin's Northwoods, including Vilas and Oneida Counties. (Easy Going)

Bibliography: p.
Includes index.
1. Vilas Co., Wis.—Description and travel—Guide-books.
2. Oneida Co., Wis.—Description and travel—Guide-books. I. Title. II. Series.

F587.V6D86   917.75'23'044   78-908

ISBN 0-915024-16-0

CONTENTS

Author's Note — 6

Introduction — 9

Vilas County

Lac du Flambeau — 21
Manitowish Waters — 27
Winchester and Presque Isle — 33
Arbor Vitae and Woodruff — 39
Boulder Junction — 46
St. Germain — 54
Star Lake and Sayner — 59
The Lost Region — 67
Eagle River — 70
Conover — 82
Land O'Lakes — 86
Phelps — 94

Oneida County

Minocqua — 101
Hazelhurst — 109
The Willow Region — 113
The Cassian-Nokomis Area — 116
Lake Tomahawk — 120
The Rhinelander Area — 125
Three Lakes and Sugar Camp — 136
Pelican Lake — 146

Index — 152

AUTHOR'S NOTE

Welcome to the northwoods of Vilas and Oneida counties—1,981 square miles that offer not only cranberries and potatoes for your table, the paper that wraps your candy bar and lines your cereal box, and perhaps even the factory-built home in which you live, but that also offer many of your favorite kinds of recreation. The good life in these counties is attracting not only vacationists but so many new permanent residents that Vilas County became the state's fastest-growing county between 1970 and 1977, and Oneida County was among the other leaders. In compiling this volume in the *Easy Going* series, I had two aims: to examine the two counties and their good life from my vantage point as historian and forty-year summer resident of one of their communities, and to weave my discoveries into a little book that could guide not only visitors but also summer residents and all-year citizens to a better understanding and greater appreciation of this northwoods.

Some topics are too extensive even for a book of this size to cover specifically or completely. One is boating opportunities and boat landings. The two counties have literally hundreds of public and commercial boat landings (allowing public access to more than 680 lakes in Vilas County alone, for example). The location of these access points on easily obtainable town and county maps obviates turning *Easy Going* into a repetitious catalog of boat landings. Fishing and hunting spots are another category risky for a book of this kind. Only local experts or specialized publications can give you the latest rundown on those ever-changing attractions.

Snowmobile trails are a third north-country institution that could easily turn *Easy Going* into a catalog and then quickly outdate it. Local snowmobile maps, issued annually in most communities, are your best index of current trails. It has been customary for regional snowmobile clubs, principally using their own equipment and volunteer labor, to groom their areas' snowmobile trails, with some state or county funding assistance. Recently, however, one of Vilas County's most influential clubs, after a 43-3 vote of members, served notice that it would discontinue its grooming services after the 1977–78 winter. If this becomes a trend, the trail-grooming arrangements reflected in this book may change, but you can be sure that snowmobiling itself will still be there.

Northwoods fun seekers have several special helps to supplement *Easy Going*. One is the telephone, not only for calls to chambers of commerce for information or to restaurants and motels for reservations, but also to special hotlines. The state transportation department, for instance, usually has a hotline number for recorded winter road-condition reports in the Rhinelander area, and Vilas County has had a snowmobile hotline. Check directory assistance for current numbers. The area code for both Vilas and Oneida counties is 715.

Two other aids are maps and local newspapers. Free county and local maps are adequate for most casual use. Specialized maps, however, can provide additional information. Lake maps can help any fisherman but are particularly useful in selecting ice-fishing spots. Snowmobile maps are indispensable for participants in that sport. Northern Highland State Forest maps cover canoeing and snowmobiling as well as routine recreational interests; Nicolet National Forest maps show that area in precise detail. Topographic maps are vital for any hiker or canoeist or cross-country ski explorer, but they also make the countryside much more meaningful for any visitor or resident. The Oneida County government has prepared a county road atlas showing every named road in the county. A check for four dollars sent to the county clerk's office at the courthouse in Rhinelander

54501 should cover the costs of obtaining a copy of this remarkably useful book. Plat books are another detailed and interesting guide to the face of both counties.

Newspapers and special supplements are helpful in keeping up with events, facilities, and attractions. The largest papers are the *Rhinelander Daily News,* whose summer *Fun Country* supplement is available free at many chambers of commerce, and the *Vilas County News-Review* (from Eagle River), whose very large *Vacation Week* supplement is available free throughout the county and in the Three Lakes area. Minocqua's weekly newspaper, the *Lakeland Times,* covers the western portions of both counties. From its vantage point in Presque Isle the *Walleye Street Journal* keeps up with its surrounding area. For winter fun seekers, the *News-Review* has begun a *SnoTIMES* supplement.

Personal testing or inspection is a conscientious travel writer's most valuable tool, one that I employed throughout preparation of this book (from scenic drives to canoe streams, bike trails to shops) and inflexibly in my dining and lodging investigations.

In dining my particular concern was not cafés or drive-ins but supper clubs and luxury dining places where a meal and drinks may represent a considerable outlay. My choices for a test meal were heavily advertised establishments or well-recommended local favorites that would naturally attract visitors—85 restaurants in all. In each case I dined anonymously and at my own expense, usually with a companion so as to double the variety of foods sampled and the judgment that went into each evaluation. This was my assurance that the impression I received would be similar to that of any *Easy Going* reader. Not all tested restaurants made the book; perhaps its most unusual contribution to Wisconsin travel literature is the idea of a one-authority evaluation of an entire region's dining possibilities.

Change is the inexorable foe of the travel writer, however, and this seems to be doubly the case in the northwoods. I tried to choose stable shops, dining places, and resorts and motels for listing or recommendation here, but a hint of the difficulty in doing so can be seen in the fact that one third of the first 51 dining places that I tested have either been for sale or changed hands during the two-year research time for the book! I wrote about my recommended places, then, as I found them on my visits. A change in owner or even just a change in chef or cook might turn any of them into a disaster; such a change might also turn into a fresh landmark some restaurant that I rejected for mention here.

Several criteria dictated the final choices of the lodging and camping establishments. The minimum resort size that I set for consideration was five lodging units (larger for motels). A resort of that size could promise enough activities for most visitors and would be equipped to handle the correspondence that mention in a book might bring. Also, as one writer could not possibly visit all 700 to 1,000 accommodations establishments scattered around an area equal in size to the whole state of Delaware, the five-cottage limit helped in narrowing the number down to about 400 places. These I visited in person, including every public and private campground in both counties. Other criteria for visiting were advertising, location, appeal, and local recommendation, the last of which led me to a few outstanding mini resorts that simply could not be ignored in the final compilation of the book's lodging sections. Only in the case of state and national forest campgrounds did I list every facility without discrimination. Space limitations prohibited including details of campgrounds, but, unless otherwise indicated, every one has a beach.

Important in my final judgment of resorts were such elements as grounds, beaches, activities, comfort, and attractiveness of cottages and rooms (the trend in housekeeping resorts is toward such pleasantries as carpeting, and such upgrading counted heavily in my evaluations). Also significant were the personalities and attitudes of proprietors, and the

7

professionalism that a guest might never see. Occasionally a bit of faded paint was overbalanced by the presence of an especially likeable host or an unusually charming location. Finally, I double-checked with local sources about intangibles that I could not personally examine, such as cleanliness, long-standing reputation, integrity, and hospitality. The choices here are entirely and absolutely my own, but they carry the most pleasant and valuable endorsement that resorts can have: the regard of their peers.

The business seasons and closed days of all listings are those that were usually observed in 1977; even year-round resorts and restaurants often close for personal vacations between the busy seasons of the year. The most common times for such closings are late fall and late winter (March and April). When used in this guide, the word *daily* means seven days a week, Sundays included. And the abbreviation *q.v.* refers readers to another mention of a topic.

The best counsel I can give to would-be resort guests is to use *Easy Going* principally as a preliminary guide, writing for folders from resorts that look appealing, and then visiting them in person on your next trip north. Meet the owners, see their cottages and facilities, check on their policies regarding pets and deposit refunds. Look at the resorts' style too. Some resorts, for instance, almost compel a high degree of socialization and participation in picnics or games; others hold a family's privacy sacred. The choice of the wrong style can ruin an eagerly anticipated vacation.

Local chambers of commerce can provide lists of smaller resorts, which often give guests excellent treatment, fine facilities, and very good value.

John Donne's assertion that no man is an island is to no one more meaningful than it is to a travel writer, and the debt of thanks that I owe to helpers and guardian angels is huge, especially to the resort people, listed or not, who kindly let me inspect their establishments, and to chamber of commerce personnel the counties over who patiently provided the aid and advice I requested.

Thanks are due also to Department of Natural Resources, Nicolet National Forest, Vilas County, and Oneida County employees, who were more than cooperative, like Floyd Reinemann, Fred Copp, James Kempinger, Richard Wendt, Chet Botwinski, Morse Reese, Carl Stein, Frank Sarkauskas, the Eugene Radloffs, Ken Anderson, Walt Mayo, Karen Parish, Werner Zimmer, Shirley Haney, and Dennis Harper; and to the University of Wisconsin-Extension's Herman Smith. To others whom I may have missed: Thank you, and forgive me.

A personal debt of thanks is also due to Laurie Graf of the Sylvia Graf Foundation, who has assisted me for several years in preserving western Vilas County history; to George LaPorte, without whom there would be much less history to record; to my brother and sister-in-law, David and Gretchen, for their unflagging interest and support; to two special mentors, Robert Hackett and Clarence Brown; and to my editors, Jill Dean and Diana Balio.

M. J. D.
Manitowish Waters, Wisconsin
Autumn 1977
AMDG

INTRODUCTION

GEOLOGY-GEOGRAPHY

Vilas and Oneida counties are located in what is called the Northern Highland. That is the name that geographers and geologists give to Wisconsin's and Upper Michigan's portion of the gigantic rock "shield" that extends northward to Hudson Bay and eastward to Labrador. The shield has variously been called the Precambrian Shield for one of the important geological periods of its formation, or the Canadian Shield for the area of its greatest extent, but the Canadian adjective took on new significance in the 1970s as mining company geologists made the same sort of discoveries in the shield's Wisconsin Highland that their predecessors had made in Ontario and Quebec years before. Important new mineral discoveries had been made in Oneida and adjacent Forest counties, and as this book went to press, exploratory drilling on promising Vilas County sites was in the negotiating stages.

The Northern Highland covers most of northern Wisconsin from Douglas County to Marinette County, except for a narrow coastal belt known as the Lake Superior Lowlands. From southern Douglas County it would be roughly delineated by a line drawn through Hayward, Chippewa Falls, Owen, Marshfield, Wisconsin Rapids, Stevens Point, Waupaca, Shawano, and Wausaukee.

The highland is arched along its backbone, or very gently domed, sloping, for example, from a height of 1,708 feet at Land O' Lakes to 1,500 near Merrill, 1,400 near Wausau, and 1,000 at Wisconsin Rapids. The shield is a region of igneous and metamorphic rocks that range in age from 600 million to almost 4,000 million years and is almost entirely buried, in its Wisconsin form, by glacial deposits of sand and gravel.

The history of the formation of the Northern Highland can be simplified for casual and vacation-minded readers by dividing into six periods the four-billion-year history since the hardening of the earth.

The first period was the 3,500-million-year Precambrian era, which saw the rocks deposited and folded in great earth-crust disturbances, forming mountains not unlike alps. In the second stage these mountains were eroded almost to a low plain, or peneplain.

Third in the stages was a time of sea submersion, perhaps several submersions, when the sea waters deposited layers of sediment (limestone and sandstone, for instance) upon future Wisconsin; this ended perhaps 200 million years ago. Fourth was another period of erosion by water, wind, and weather. The fifth epoch, the Pleistocene or glacial period, gave the Northern Highland most of its present distinctive terrain.

The glaciers grew from long accretions of unmelted snow thickening into ice in three centers in Canada. When these were thousands of feet thick, they became a plastic mass that spread out in all directions, especially southward, at a rate of anywhere from a few feet to a few hundred feet per year.

Some idea of the terrain-changing pressure of the moving glacier may be gleaned from the fact that a mile-thick glacier exerted a pressure of 1,250 tons per square yard, just standing still; complete the thought by considering its grinding movement over thousands of years and the volume of all that glacial water melting off in sheets. Then the surface transformation of a vast area is not at all surprising.

The Ice Age occurred in four distinct stages, separated by interglacial epochs totaling 700,000 years. The stages were named for the states where their differing effects were first significantly analyzed: Nebraska, Kansas, Illinois, and Wisconsin.

The important glacial stage in Vilas and Oneida counties was the Wisconsin stage, which overran and rearranged some of the earlier stages' contributions. Theorists now are not sure whether there were three complete and separate glacial stages in the Wisconsin period, or just three related advance-and-recession cycles over the period from 50,000 years ago to less than 10,000 years ago.

What they do know, though, is that the ice movement took the form of five important tongues of ice, or lobes, which slid side by side into Wisconsin, the Chippewa lobe overrunning the Vilas and Oneida area; just to its east was the smaller Langlade or Wisconsin Valley lobe. The glacier would pick up material in one area and drop it later in its movement or melting. Much of the sands deposited in Vilas and northern Oneida counties, scientists theorize, was brought in from the sandstone areas of northern Michigan, for hill forms tell us that the last glacier moved in the direction of south southwest.

The sixth period in the formation of today's Northern Highland has been the few thousand years—maybe as many as 9,000 or as few as 5,000—of glacial melting, natural erosion, drainage system development, and revegetation of the highland. This period has not obscured the basic glacial features that make the highland so interesting, so often attractive.

As the ice growled across the land, it left beneath it varying thicknesses of earth material. If the ice melted quietly, a veneer of more of this material, previously suspended in the ice, was deposited. This is called *ground moraine*. Twenty feet is a good average figure for the thickness of this sort of deposit, though in places it is over 100 feet thick and in others only inches thick. Bare bedrock appears where it is especially thin, but such outcrops—bits of the primeval mountains perhaps—are rare in Vilas County and only a little more common in Oneida County.

The leading edge of the glacier bore a heavy load of earthy debris and often pushed more ahead of it. Where it stopped advancing, it left ridges sometimes designated *shove moraines*.

Where the glacier halted, its nose melting at the same rate as the movement of the glacier mass behind it, large ridges would form from debris that moved to the front of the glacier and was then dropped. These are *recessional* or *end moraines*.

The heavy debris made up the end moraine. The lightest materials at the melting nose would be swept away by the torrential sheets of meltwater running from the glacier and washing across the landscape. When this floodtide of fine material had dried, there remained a smooth plain, called an *outwash plain*. Often huge chunks of ice were orphaned and buried in this flood, and where they melted, hollows and pits were formed. Much of Vilas and Oneida counties is designated as this sort of pitted outwash.

Buried blocks of ice melted in the end moraines too, forming the kettles that are so common there; in places in Vilas and Oneida the kettles and separating ridges are so steep that farmers could never work them, even if the soil were good, and loggers left them till the last. The two counties' outstanding end moraine, I think, is the massive Winegar moraine, from Winchester and Presque Isle almost to Land O'Lakes. Also interesting is the Muskellunge moraine near Sayner. An extensive moraine makes up much of the Town of Lac du Flambeau, and Highway 51 traverses extensive end moraine from Minocqua almost to Heafford Junction.

The glacier in Oneida and Vilas counties scooped out few lake beds or none at all from solid rock, but it did make possible the area's numerous lakes by accounting for floodable kettles and depressions in end and ground moraines. Depressions not completely evened out during outwash plain formation explain some lakes, and the kettle melting explains many others.

Lakes cover about one sixth of the two counties' surface area. The soil map of Oneida shows over 800 lakes, while county publicity claims 1,200. Claims for Vilas run as high as 1,300 lakes. While the statistics may vary, experts agree that nowhere else on earth, except in the Minnesota-Ontario boundary waters and in southern Finland east of the Gulf of Bothnia, are there equal concentrations of lakes.

Finally, the glacier left some special treats for people who are willing to go to the trouble of learning to identify and locate them, treats with the unusual names of drumlins, kames, glacial spillways, and eskers.

Drumlins resemble an inverted spoon with its tip toward the south. Their direction usually parallels the ice flow direction (south southwest), and they can be up to half a mile long and 150 feet high. There is a small drumlin school or swarm north and west of Trout Lake, near Boulder Junction, while east of Monico and Pelican Lake there is a series of parallel ridges that seem to be an extension of a drumlin swarm that begins across in Forest and Langlade counties.

Kames are rounded or conical hills formed by debris either washed through shaftlike holes in the glacier, held till melting in hollows atop the ice, or poured down in cone form by streams running off the ice edge in chute fashion. Muskellunge Hill, at 1,860 feet Vilas County's highest point, is considered to be a kame.

A *glacial spillway* looks like a big stream bed across a moraine or outwash plain, now dry or containing a stream too tiny to have eroded so large a valley. A remarkable hollow in the Partridge Lake Wilderness just west of Camp 2 Road—the only landmark of its kind I've seen in the two counties—appears to be such a spillway.

Eskers, however, are the biggest treat of all. When streams formed and flowed in tunnels within or under the ice, they dropped some of their debris. Melting of the glacier left those former stream courses as snaky ridges, sometimes very steep and narrow at the top. Local old-timers often referred to these as hogsbacks or razorbacks. The Willow Region of Oneida County has a concentration of these, some in contiguous or very closely related strings as long as four miles.

WETLANDS, FORESTS, FLOWERS, FOREST MANAGEMENT

The northwoods, as we casually call it, is not all woods by any means. In reality, it is a combination of wetlands, field openings, and forest.

Its wetlands include marshes and swamps, common elsewhere in the state too, plus a particularly northerly phenomenon, the northern bog.

To be a *marsh,* technically, a wetland must be treeless, dominated by grasses and sedges. Powell Marsh is a good example, though far larger than average. Its grasses used to supply hay for loggers' horses and raw materials for manufacture of grass rugs or wicker furniture downstate. Now the marsh is managed for wildlife control. Thunder Lake Marsh near Three Lakes was once the subject of a drainage scheme designed for farming its promising soils. It too is now a game area.

The plant communities of a wet marsh include tiny but lovely orchid types, water lilies, reeds, grasses, cattails, aquatic shortweed, duck potato, and wild celery. Sometimes a wet marsh or reedy lake shallow also contains wild rice beds. Vilas County authorities are now experimenting with seeding wild rice in locations from which it is known to have vanished.

A dry marsh, whose decayed vegetation has raised the growing level above the original water level, has grasses, sedges, iris, and shrubs like willow, leatherleaf, and alder.

A *swamp* is a wetland that hosts shrubs and such trees as tamarack, spruce, and cedar. The needles of the tamarack, interestingly, turn yellow in fall.

The *northern bog,* marked by dark, acid water, usually occurs in a motionless kettle area, where the vegetation at first rings the kettle pond shore, gradually encroaches outward around a diminishing central pond, and eventually chokes and overgrows the pond completely. In its oldest stages, near shore, the bog supports spruce and tamarack, but nearer its younger center it is a quaking bog of grass tufts, cranberry, and labrador tea, interlaced with the creeper known as sphagnum moss. Lending fascination are the insect-eating sundew and pitcher plant. Beware, though: quaking bogs will not usually support the weight of a trespasser.

The northwoods also contains many openings, most of them not of prairie origin but traceable to abandoned farming operations or logging camps, or to old forest fire burns. These have value as game openings, and those in hollows where cold air collects and tends to inhibit vegetation are likely to remain naturally in grasses. The natural plant communities in forest openings are grasses, bracken fern, blueberries, and blackberries. Wildflowers are heavy-stalked *compositae,* members of the daisy family like black-eyed susan, asters, or oxeye daisy.

Forests, of course, have been the major northern vegetation type for ages. The first surveyors, around the time of the Civil War, gave us an idea of the virgin growth they encountered as they listed section corners, bearing trees, and witness trees in their field notes. Though they encountered some large sedge meadows and pine barrens, most of the area was about evenly divided between great pine forests and northern mesic forests of maple, hemlock, and yellow birch. Oneida had a somewhat larger share of the pine forests, Vilas a larger area of the hardwoods.

Loggers with their "cut and burn" philosophy removed most of these forests, ninety to fifty years ago, and the forests are still trying to restore themselves. Thus we see woods in the north that are in any of three stages: the pioneer or early reestablishing stage; the subclimax stage with competing trees and brush; and the climax forest, usually hardwoods like maples, so dense and mature that their thick overhead canopy precludes any heavy understory of brush or plants on the ground below.

Climax forests, of course, are the loveliest, and perhaps the most magnificent climax forest in either county is a hemlock stand on end moraine ridges off Rearing Pond Road near the community of Star Lake. Subclimax forests can also be very beautiful, and they are much more common, especially on well-drained uplands. Predominant trees in these forests are maple, hemlock, yellow birch, and bass.

Pioneer forests are the early stage in forest regeneration. White birch and aspen (also known as poplar or popple) figure prominently in this forest type. Pine forests in Vilas and Oneida counties generally combine white pines, distinguished by black bark and short delicate needles in sets of five, with Norway or red pines, which have reddish-brown, scaly bark, long, coarse needles in pairs, and often a very tall, limbless profile. Jack pine barrens are ugly, sandy areas dominated by the scraggly jack pine with its short, coarse needles. Boreal forests of spruce and balsam are not very common in these counties. Where any especially attractive forest areas exist, I have listed them at their respective towns.

Woodland wildflowers are mostly spring varieties that flourish before the leafy canopy above closes over. Some are delicate white spring ephemerals like anemones. Others are the violet, the partridge berry and bunchberry, the bloodroot, the twinflower, and, most enchanting of all, the trillium. Among good trillium-viewing areas are Highway G south from Pelican Lake and Highway A east of Phelps.

Visitors in the Vilas-Oneida area can see evidence of forest management—trucks hauling pulpwood to paper mills or rail sidings, popple peelers stripping new-cut trees of bark in May, when bark peels easily (giving the pulpwood premium value at the mill), or just the sight of cutover lands.

Modern forest management focuses on three principal cutting practices. Selective cutting removes target species for their own value or to strengthen remaining valuable species in a tract. Clear-cutting removes all trees from a tract, much as a farmer might clear a woodland for cropping, but more crudely, since the slash may be left. The tract then usually regenerates in quick-growing popple. Popple is an even-aged species that cannot compete with other trees under a subclimax or climax canopy. When a tract grows up in popple, the trees all have equal sun and grow swiftly to maturity, a croplike harvest, and then another cycle of regeneration. A fresh clear-cut may look hideous for a few years, but it often represents good use of land as well as sound economics.

One new antidote to this ugliness of clear-cutting is corridor residual cutting, whereby loggers leave belts of trees along roadways and other natural barriers over perhaps 5 to 10 percent of the tract. These improve the esthetics, provide shelter to wildlife that need forest cover, retain seed trees, and leave slash-free corridors where fire protection plows can penetrate easily, should fire occur.

One procedure that should be mandatory after every day in the woods in spring and summer is a careful check for wood ticks on oneself and on children.

NATIVE ANIMALS AND HUNTING

Whether it is the high point of a vacationist's day or just happenstance in the routine of a local resident, contact with forest animals is an inescapable part of being in the northwoods.

There is no quick and easy guidebook formula for directing people successfully to wildlife, only the merest hints...like choosing early morning around daylight, especially in hot weather, or early evening as the ideal times for looking. Everything else depends on species, the time of the year, even the year itself.

The native animal that seems most to enchant observers is the whitetail deer. Does drop their tiny, spindly fawns during the last two weeks of May or the first one of June, about 200 days after their conception in late autumn. Twins are fairly common in whitetails over age two. The fawns move about with the mother almost constantly by summer's end, by which time they are losing their spots. Shortly all deer are changing to the "blue" winter coat with the shedding of the short red coat, which will now not recur till April or May.

Antlered bucks make up perhaps 25 percent of the population. Their annual horn change begins in November or December. Porcupines, mice, and other rodents like the dropped horns for the minerals they contain, so very few shed horn sets are ever found in the woods. New horns begin to appear as soon as the grass greens up, and they harden as the passing summer hardens the internal blood vessels. In early September, perhaps between the fifth and the fifteenth, the bucks will start rubbing off the velvet.

Unlike many other wild species, the whitetail has adjusted very well to the presence of humans in its environment. About the only time that the deer can become a threat is when it is along a roadside, grazing or crossing, for it is unpredictable and a dangerous object to hit. Bear its roadside grazing habits in mind, especially if you are driving at twilight or at night, and particularly in fall. Remember too that if one deer crosses, another may follow, and that a deer might suddenly turn back in the direction from which it came.

The woods abound in ordinary animals like the woodchuck or the porcupine. The latter has an appetite for salt that causes it to gnaw ax or shovel handles or a much newer craving that causes it to chew plywoods for their resins. In spring the porkie can be seen feeding on new shoots high in popple trees. Contrary to old wives' tales, it cannot shoot or eject its quills.

The skunk is chiefly nocturnal but can be active any time. It likes burrows under porches or crawl spaces, and its presence is one by-product of leaving garbage around. Rabid skunks have been rare in the northwoods. But in case of any animal bite, do not shoot the offending animal through the head but turn the carcass or head over to a veterinarian, health official, or Department of Natural Resources (DNR) facility for tests. With a skunk, or any other animal, the best advice is that *if it acts odd, stay away from it!*

Raccoons prove far more appealing than skunks, with their bewitching black eyes and sometimes playful antics. Nocturnal, they are found along creeks, rivers, and lakes and especially in campgrounds.

Probably the most endearing and most common little wild animals of all, however, are chipmunks. Not only are they numerous; they respond to people (I have two little beggars who will cross the yard at the call of their names). They live in tunnels or old cavities in locations like brush piles. As with so many other wild animals, a caution or two is in order here: feed them only sensible food, watch out for bites, and never pick them up.

In addition to these wild but quite visible animals, the northwoods is home to animals that I regard as elusive. The prize among these, for almost everyone no matter how jaded, is the black bear. Sheer serendipity is about the only way you will ever get to see one. Nighttime bear watching used to be popular at garbage dumps, but under new regulations that call for covering of dumps daily and gating them at night, this activity has become a quaint part of the northwoods's past.

The bear chooses the area where humans are fewest; man's moving into its habitat is the bear's greatest threat. In suitable surroundings, however (roadless areas with a good mixture of habitat types), northern Wisconsin has a good bear population.

Bears do not mate for life but breed in late June or early July, the sow doing so only in alternate years. A sow will choose a hibernation site more carefully than a male, who may simply curl up by a stump, under a windfall, or in a deep hole in December, with snow to help insulate him. She dens up earlier and more elaborately under windfall tops or in a dug den where, conscious but with a slowed metabolic rate, she will give birth around early February to a tiny cub weighing under one pound. The cub or cubs will remain with her into the next hibernation, to be chased out the second spring.

At that point the rivalry between male adults and subadults becomes the young bear's greatest threat; one of the main causes of young bear mortality is the adult males' picking on male subadults. Barring that, a bear may live to its mid twenties, for it has few natural enemies beyond disease and encroaching man.

The black bear, game experts remind you, is still a wild animal, a very fast one with a big mouth. Ninety nine percent of the time he will avoid you; you'd be wise to give him wide berth one hundred percent of the time!

An animal considered common but seldom visible is the beaver. While other species have diminished, this species has proliferated. In the early 1900s it was rare if not vanished from these two counties; in recent years trappers here have been taking from 500 to 750 beaver a year. Its trademark, of course, is its remarkable complex of dams and lodges and the conical stumps it leaves when it cuts nearby trees, especially popple, for food.

The red fox is found in places where there may have been some development, like abandoned farms, in areas of lighter soils where it can find its favored diet of rabbits, mice, and other rodents. This graceful animal is not as large as it looks, standing perhaps 16 inches at the shoulder and weighing 12 to 14 pounds.

The coyote or brush wolf is fairly common but less often seen than heard. On a calm evening, particularly in early fall, one can hear the yipping of the pack, resembling the squeak-squeal-yap of small puppies. Populations of coyotes and foxes are down, but these species are a sporty and resilient resource.

Rounding out the list are the seldom seen mink, muskrat, weasel, and otter. Mink are still numerous enough to be trapped. The muskrat is a shy stream or lake bank dweller, sometimes seen swimming home. Ounce for ounce, the white weasel, his nose and tail tipped in black, may be the toughest of all wild animals. It has been known to kill and drag away a cottontail many times its size. The otter is remarkably playful and is most likely to be seen, if at all, at its sliding sites along winter's ice.

Attempts have been made to restore species that are known or suspected to have roamed the region in the past, or to establish new ones. In the latter case, an elk herd was started in captivity near Trout Lake in 1913 and set free in 1932. It increased a bit, partly by feeding on area gardens or crops, but the animals were shot by angry farmers or were poached away by local residents.

The fisher, which vanished here around 1932, was reintroduced between 1956 and 1963. The little pine marten, gone since 1925, was restored in 1974 and 1976. A few timber wolves were released in 1975, but cars, guns, and traps got them all within the year; speculation is that there may be a few native timber wolves ranging the Wisconsin-Michigan boundary area.

Vanished species are the cougar (last killed in this area in 1909), moose (not seen since 1920), caribou and wolverine (not seen here since the 1800s), and perhaps the Canada lynx.

Among the most unusual and intriguing of northwoods birds are the eagle, osprey, great blue heron, and loon. Vilas County in recent years has had around 30 known, active bald eagle nests and Oneida about 17, while osprey nests were 8 and 15 in the respective counties in 1975-76. The shy birds avoid built-up areas but are seen soaring above fairly populous places like Manitowish Waters after the summer visitor surge has passed.

Herons nest in fascinating rookeries, colonies of huge but crude-looking treetop nests; the ground below looks almost whitewashed. Northwoods folks benignly conspire to keep the locations of these nest areas secret to spare the great birds unnecessary upset.

Loons are close to a "changing status" situation, not far short of being labeled an endangered species. They are found only on quiet lakes with some wild shoreline and some respite from constant water skiing and pleasure boating. No northwoods stay can be complete without the haunting cry of a distant loon or its lilting laugh. A parent loon will live up to the name if a trespasser approaches its primitive nest, trying all kinds of crazy antics to draw the visitor away.

Hunting in Vilas and Oneida counties probably centers most on deer and partridge, which are sought in almost every township. One recent season the take was 4,866 deer!

Worth considering for partridge are the large networks of seeded walking trails in the Oneida County Forest tracts (especially the Cassian-Woodboro unit and the Willow unit) and in the Nicolet National Forest's Kimball Creek area (just across the line into Forest County—45 miles of trails). The Wisconsin DNR has scattered gated and seeded hunter walking trails, just as it has many game openings as part of its program to have approximately three percent of all forest land in permanent grassy or seeded game openings.

Bear are hunted in some of the wilder areas like Winchester or Powell. Ducks are sought to some extent in potholes, along the Wisconsin River, and at the Rainbow Flowage, and geese near the Powell Marsh or around hay and potato fields where geese feed.

A book, however, can offer no more than general guidelines. Any good hunter knows the value of local advice.

FISH AND FISHING

For either the serious angler or the family just taking the kids out to humor them, the counties of Vilas and Oneida have the right fish and fishing.

An idea of the importance of fishing in the recreation picture can be gained just from the fishing contests in the area: season-long countywide contests, local competitions, individual sport shops' contests, even special promotions like the World Championship Musky Classic (Boulder Junction, Manitowish Waters, Presque Isle, Winchester) or the celebrity-starring World Musky Hunt. In a variation of the contest theme, St. Germain has a Muskies for Tomorrow program that rewards sportsmen who throw back their keeper muskies.

Another index of fishing's popularity is the abundance of bait and tackle shops, guides, and taxidermists. A good sport shop can be a big help to the fisherman for, in addition to offering equipment, it can also advise on conditions and recommend a guide and perhaps a taxidermist to mount a prize catch.

A day with a fishing guide can be a wise investment, particularly for fishermen with limited time. He offers good company, expertise, and a better chance for fishing success. One guide who keeps a journal recorded in a recent season's 1,087 hours of fishing a major strike every 40 minutes and a keeper musky every 11.3 hours.

The DNR helps ensure a supply of fish with both its fish plantings and its fisheries research. Each spring DNR personnel net walleyes and muskies in area lakes, gently milk them for milt and eggs, and return them to the waters. Freshly fertilized eggs thus obtained are incubated and reared over the summer in the Woodruff hatchery and outdoor ponds and then planted in lakes as fingerlings or even, in the case of muskies, eight- to 12-inch fish. Visitors are welcome to watch the milking from their own boats and to visit the hatchery and ponds.

The DNR has also operated, for over 20 years, a five-lake experiment station east of Trout Lake at Escanaba Lake. Here fishing with no bag or size limits is allowed all year, in return for a tally of each fisherman's catch. The project, formally entitled the Northern Highland Fishery Research Project, has helped study whether fishing pressure can "fish out" a lake, and has allowed the DNR to experiment with fish plantings under controlled conditions, including sterilizing lakes and replanting them with new species.

These five lakes are popular in winter, as are many other northland lakes whose ice on weekends is dotted with colorfully garbed fishermen huddled over their holes or little warming fires. Shacks are popular too.

The Vilas and Oneida fishery includes all the expected species along with a few offbeat surprises. Very popular are panfish like perch or crappies (less large here than in more fertile waters downstate); sporty fish like scrappy smallmouth bass (found also in streams like the Wisconsin, Pelican, and Tomahawk rivers) and the more common largemouth; and the northern pike.

Most prized are the walleye and the theatrical musky. The two counties contain 352 musky lakes, 203 of them classed by the DNR as prime (Class A). One notion of what lakes produce muskies is available through a glance at results of a dozen years of Vilas County's annual musky marathon, which in that time produced 16,000 registered fish aggregating 99 tons and almost 9.9 miles in length. The lakes that consistently produced the most Vilas County muskies were Little and Big Arbor Vitae, Lac Vieux Desert, and Little St. Germain; following these were such lakes as Muskellunge, Star, Plum, High, Big, and chains around Boulder, Manitowish, and Flambeau lakes. From 1947 to 1949 Vilas boasted the world's record musky, a 64-pounder from little Halfway Lake near Lac du Flambeau.

Brown or brook trout occur naturally or have been planted in 76 streams and four lakes in Oneida, 33 streams and 14 lakes in Vilas. Spring ponds are also possible trout spots, but

17

none are really accessible. (Rainbows occur only in the Deerskin River and 14 lakes in Vilas.) The speckled-lake trout hybrid splake has been planted in a few lakes like Little Bass in northern Oneida, while Stormy Lake (Vilas) has coho, and Trout, Crystal, and Black Oak lakes (all Vilas) have lake trout.

Benson Lake, a widening of Manitowish Waters's river of the same name, is popular for sturgeon during the early fall season; it gave up a 67-incher to an acquaintance of mine in 1977. As a contrast, smelt, among the smallest of catchable fish, recently turned up in Fence Lake, Lac du Flambeau.

The rare sportsman who would rather watch than catch fish can take pleasure in doing so with scuba gear in clear bodies like Crystal or Big Carr lakes.

The DNR has four publications that may aid anglers: booklets 9-3600, 1-3600, 3-3600, and 6-3600, on walleye, musky, and trout lakes, and trout streams, respectively.

EARLY HOSPITALITY

Hospitality is one of the most respected of northern Wisconsin traditions, from the time when lumber camp cooks delighted in sharing their famous cookies and doughnuts with children, from villages like Winegar, to today when a tourist can slip into bed by the glow of a fireplace right in his carpeted bedroom.

The many faces of modern hospitality are painted in the rest of this volume, but let us look briefly at early hospitality in the northwoods.

Trading posts and even saloons provided some of the first hospitality, before formal resorts had developed to accommodate guests. Early visitors were often transients moving about in connection with their work, and they expected little more than a bed in the rustic log loft or a jury-rigged sleeping room in the attic. Hi Polar, trader on Virgin Lake, for instance, offered sleeping space to passersby on what would eventually become the Military Road, beginning to do so in the 1850s. An example of the saloon-type inn was the one operated where the dam and boat landing at Manitowish Waters attracted transients; Peter Vance (a "squaw man") operated it, as did one of the McKinney brothers.

In small towns, little pitcher-and-bowl hotels developed near railroad stations. Almost invariably they had false fronts on one end of their gabled roofs, and transoms and wide openings above and below the doors to allow heat from big woodstoves in the hall to circulate into the sleeping rooms.

Hunting and fishing clubs were popular in early days. Many were membership clubs, but some were cooperative clubs with individual private residences on the grounds, like the Manitowoc Club near Boulder Junction. Famous old ones, like the Twin Lakes Hunting and Fishing Club, have vanished, but others have become more diversified, like Big Sand Lake Club or Dairymen's Country Club, near Phelps and Boulder Junction, respectively.

Motels have been the newest addition, growing out of just a handful of tourist cabin courts of pre-World War II years. Housekeeping cottages really appeared only in the early 1920s, and even into the 1940s all but the most sophisticated were still plain log cabins or frame cottages whose exposed rafters and wall studs showed the wood of the outer siding. Kerosene lamps and privies were not uncommon even in the forties, nor were woodstoves or smelly oil stoves.

It was lodge-type resorts, however, that played the most colorful and interesting role in developing northern hospitality, for even the pioneer summer-home owners usually got their northwoods initiation at such resorts.

It is surprising how much development took place even before 1900. The resort of the Thomas family on Lac Vieux Desert was probably the first lake resort in these northwoods, about 1882. John Mann began his resort (now Cardinal's) on Trout Lake in 1888, and before the Goodalls took it over as a resort in 1891, the Twin Lakes club had developed remarkably.

The 1890s saw a flurry of resorts like Benedict Gauthier's at Flambeau (1891); Sayner's Camp at what would become Sayner after the railroad arrived in 1894 (resort opened in 1892); Coon's on Trout Lake and Buck's at Divide, later Winchester (both in 1894 or soon after). Bents built their camp early enough (1896) to be able to name their own lake, I have heard, and the year 1897 saw Oxley's Camp McKinley, near Boulder Junction and named for the president then in office, and LaFave's Resort at Manitowish Waters. The Everett Resort, owned earlier by Fred Morey, opened at Eagle River about 1898.

The actual turn of the century saw new resorts spreading hospitality to High Lake between Boulder and Land O' Lakes (then State Line), and to the future Phelps area (Hazen's, still active!) and to Star Lake. By then, too, Oneida County was seeing its share of lodges like the Northern at Minocqua and the even older Sanders House at Lake Tomahawk.

The standard resort format in early years was a lodge with cottages. The lodge served everyone with dining and socializing and some of the guests with sleeping rooms. Clapboards or even rough planks were hard to come by, especially in sites away from the railhead, so early resorts were mostly built of logs. Hewn square ones were the material for the Thomas resort's first lodge, which actually was the family home built in 1860. Bent's Camp used large horizontal logs with the bark still on for its first structures (one is still in use). The lodge at Orrin Sayner's was built of huge vertical logs in upright post fashion with only gable ends of boards and battens. The lodge at Coon's on Trout Lake, now in its ninth decade, is a rich, warm example of log lodge construction at its grandest.

Islands were sometimes popular as resort sites, partly because of the romance associated with them, partly out of the importance of fishing among early vacation interests, and partly as natural sites in regions where no resorts had early road access. Such an area was the Manitowish chain of lakes, all of whose visitors transferred from buckboards to launches at Rest Lake dam in order to reach resorts situated around the lakes. One of its island resorts was LaFave's. Island resorts had to expand upward, not outward, and LaFave's had a three-story lodge, with guest rooms on the second floor, guides' quarters on the third, and a ring of tiny cottages hugging the banks. Pig Island nearby served as its tiny farm and dumping ground.

At LaFave's as elsewhere, elegant gas-powered launches provided transport, but fishing was done from double-pointed clinker-built rowboats with legless captain's chairs affixed to the seats for the fishermen's comfort. Some resorts had huge fleets; the Thomas resort had 35 rowboats or birchbark canoes, not a surprising number in view of the resort's 21 cottages.

Indispensable to early sportsmen was the guide, for he not only pointed out choice fishing spots and fixed the shore lunch but also, with his strong arms, functioned all day as the predecessor of the outboard motor.

The style of early resorting was pretty uniform. It was room and board on the American plan. As Edmund Espeseth, himself a resort host, pointed out in a 1953 history of Vilas County hospitality, early guests "were in fact additions to the family home"—a home which, like its more elaborate lodge successors, was likely to be decorated with trophy fish and game. (What a sight the 45 deer heads must have been that graced the old Griswold Resort near Three Lakes and Eagle River!)

The lodge fireplace would be the focus of evening socializing and yarn spinning till its flames had turned to embers. The acme of the resort fireplace must have been the double fireplace in the 110-foot lodge of the De Haas Red Oaks Resort at St. Germain; it used four-foot logs!

Guests were usually prosperous and stays of a month, six weeks, even a full summer were the rule rather than the exception.

Supplies were a problem for early hosts, because of not only remoteness but also limitations in transport and refrigeration. (State Line, for example, received meat once a week, when the Friday train brought the meat car. The lumber company store in Phelps prided itself on its two-carload capacity coolers.) One answer was a farm on the resort, with garden, chickens, dairy cows (ten cows in the herd of Maple Grove Resort on Lac Vieux Desert). Ice for food preservation was cut on the lake in front (something still done at Woodruff). Though it is hard to envision now, even into the 1920s over forty resorts in the two counties had farms or small gardens and a cow or two.

Lodges grew ever larger and more elegant. One at Deer Park Lodge (since replaced) was 140 by 40 feet in extent, three stories in height. Sayner's was 126 by 40, Gauthier's at Flambeau 100 feet long.

In the 1920s, because more guests were arriving by car, resorts stressed garages among their features. The irony in being so accommodating was that the automobile's continued rise in popularity freed vacationists from the restrictions of vacationing only at lodges and from staying in one place for long periods. The housekeeping resort era would capitalize on the automobile and would build anew on the beginnings that the lodges had provided. The summer-home boom would build upon both of these in a third wave.

The housekeeping guest or the individual summer-home owner, though, never knew quite the drama that the lodge guest knew. For it was lodge guests who enjoyed traditions like the Sunday outdoor buffet at the St. Clair resort on Black Oak Lake at State Line. When the guests had finished eating, they would toss the wooden plates upon which they had just eaten into the bonfire to make it blaze the brighter. And at Musky Inn in St. Germain, when guests were ready to take their leave, the white-hatted chef who owned the resort would stand in the doorway, put his great French horn to his lips, and send an elegant farewell salute echoing across the lake and into the woods.

VILAS COUNTY
LAC DU FLAMBEAU

Lac du Flambeau is the cradle of western Vilas County history. It is both a civil town and a reservation of the Lac du Flambeau band of Lake Superior Chippewas. The boundaries of the two units are fairly similar, and the civil and tribal governments have an unusual intertwining of jurisdiction in their mutual area.

The Chippewas, one of the Algonquin-language eastern tribes, had made their way westward sometime within the past 700 to 500 years to take up a nomadic existence around Lake Superior. On foot or by canoe they moved with the seasons from inland maple sugar camps to spring planting grounds, on to summer fishing (often along Lake Superior), back to autumn harvest at wild rice beds and the planting grounds, and late fall hunting before settling in for the winter. Birchbark was the material for both their housing—wigwams—and their transport—canoes.

As the watery hub of a rich wild-ricing region and important canoe routes, the Lac du Flambeau site was a coveted one, upon which Chief Sharpened Stone settled his band around 1745. The Sioux contested their presence throughout the area, even after a U.S. government-sponsored truce in 1825 had theoretically ended the fighting, and battled with the Chippewas over the Flambeau site until the Battle of Strawberry Island around 1858 finally established local Chippewa dominance.

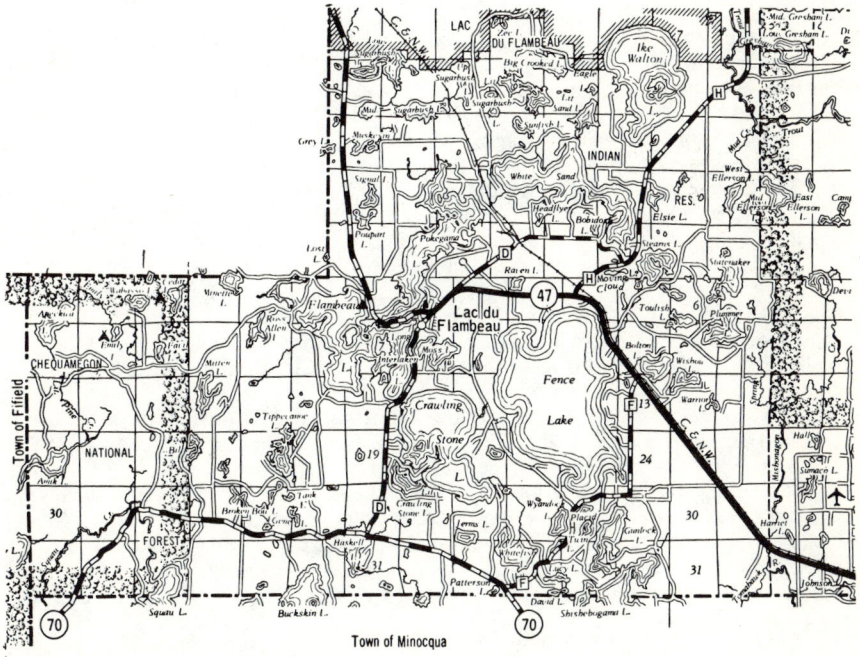

France had claimed sovereignty over this whole region in a dazzling ceremony attended by priests and warriors at the Sault in 1671. French traders, some free-lancing, ranged the northwoods. It was Frenchmen, seeing the Indians spearfishing by night, who named the site Lac du Flambeau, Lake of the Torch. Not until 1792, long after the French and Indian war, did a company dominated by Scotsmen finally establish a formal fur-trading post and district headquarters where the Flambeau chain empties into the Bear River. The canoe landing and little log fort enabled the North West Company to exchange cloth, pots, knives, and firearms for furs that the Indians had trapped. Another post or two may have engaged in the same sort of trading.

The War of 1812 upset traditional relationships in the fur woods. The fur trade was Canadian and British oriented, and most traders and Indians alike supported the British side, hopeful that the northwoods would end up under British control. The Chippewas, almost alone, were loyal to the United States; their chief even wore a medallion of George Washington!

John Jacob Astor's famous American Fur Company took control of the Lac du Flambeau trade around 1815. Between 1835 and 1844 as the fur trade gave out, the American Fur Company failed and Lac du Flambeau lost its post. The ties with LaPointe, the fur trade headquarters, however, also became spiritual ones as missionaries from there, Presbyterian Sherman Hall in 1832 and Catholic John Chebul in 1860, made the first religious contact with the Flambeau settlement.

An 1854 treaty established the Chippewas on reservations, including one at Flambeau, eventually 73,800 acres; some lands came to be sold, however, to non-Indian buyers, notably shoreline vacation frontage.

The greatest upheaval in Flambeau history was probably the opening of the reservation to logging in the mid 1880s. With this came an influx of additional Indians seeking employment, along with whites to direct logging, establish a community, and furnish such services as language interpretation. Two winters of cutting and spring log drives down the Bear River followed, but then the government suspended the logging, which had become an abuse. The arrival of a railroad in 1888, with a spur into town in 1893, made feasible the sawing of lumber right on the reservation, where at least it could provide jobs.

A village was thrown up and adjacent to it a huge lakeside mill. For 20 years rafts of logs floated through the chain, or cars of logs cut along the company's tracks fed the mill, which could saw logs up to 26 feet long. It delivered 12 to 15 cars of fragrant lumber to the Chicago & North Western every day. All fell silent the week of October 5, 1913, when the last log whined through the saws.

The drummers calling on the lumber company and the salesmen the company itself sent out had been housed, during their visits, at the hotel that Ben Gauthier ran to accommodate visitors of the Flambeau Lumber Company. They probably were the first to broadcast the area's fishing and vacation appeal. A trickle of pleasure travelers began, along with the resorts to accommodate them. Squaw Lake saw a resort as early as 1906, Sand Lake another in 1911; the mill hotel added cottages around 1913. The resorts increased over the years, with housekeeping cottages appearing later to compete with the costlier lodges. Perhaps 100 resorts were serving tourists by the 1940s; there still are over 40.

A few prosperous adventurers built private summer homes about the same time as the resort business began, and in the 1950s and 1960s their proliferation swept many resorts into subdivision for individual cottage ownership.

The strong white presence must have baffled and subdued the natives of the reservation; reports of the 1920s smack almost of their being regarded as curiosities whom non-Indian tourists would flock to see at their tourist park or popular Indian fairs. Those years still saw quiet respect for age-old traditions and values; there is record, for instance, of a medicine woman treating an illness in 1925 and of the activities of a venerated old medicine man, Bear Skin, in 1931.

Recent years have seen revivals of interest in native traditions. They have also seen a new face upon the central community (one of the county's largest villages, incidentally), as the tribal council with some outside help has worked to renew housing, add community service buildings, and, most recently, bring new construction to the business district.

SIGHTSEEING

HISTORIC SITES
• Old Indian Village location, Indian Village Road. No visible landmarks remain from the past in this historic area. The trading posts stood on the lakeshore near the Bear River outlet; the Bear was the Indians' and traders' travel route. The little dam is successor to the log-driving dam of the 1880s. The old village grew around the trading posts here.

• Flambeau Lake sites. Medicine Rock (water access) was an ancient ritual offering place. Strawberry Island saw the Sioux defeat in the mid 1800s. (Private; stay off.)

• Lac du Flambeau village grew up about the sawmill, replacing the old village. The mill stood along the Indian Bowl shore; the Flame Inn was once the old mill hotel. The old cemetery of 1895 is catercorner from the firehouse; few stones remain. The Indian Agency complex on Highway 47 was the 1895–1934 Indian boarding school; the agency office occupies the old dormitory for boys.

POINTS OF INTEREST
• Wa-Swa-Gon Indian Bowl and Pow Wows, in town; Pow Wows 8 p.m. Tuesday, Thursday, June–August. Past is recreated in authentic costumes, music, Chippewa-language chants. Dances range from universal to interpretive; authenticity embraces such details as distinctive toe-heel step employed in Chippewa routines in contrast to flat-foot step of other dances. Audience is invited to join one dance. Admission charge.

• Fish Hatchery, on 47 northwest; tribe operated. In its batteries of glass jars 30 million eggs hatch annually from black globules into busy little fishlets for eventual transplanting into reservation lakes. May–early June; public welcome.

• Community Center, in town on 47. Tribal offices and community services area.

• Flambeau Chain of Lakes. Ten lakes interconnected by navigable channels, headwaters that are spring fed. Good boating and canoeing.

• Lac du Flambeau Fire Tower, unmarked new hard road northwest from Highway D, 2.5 miles north of town. One of the north's rare, remaining stair-type towers, in unclimbable disrepair at time of my inspection, its site badly littered.

• Powell Marsh, Highway 47 northwest near Iron County line. One of northland's largest marshes, now a game area with dikes and canals in portion across railroad track. Pretty in fall when golden trees ring it. Nearly defunct hamlet of **Powell**, off 47 a couple miles farther (at campground turnoff), was once rail stop for Manitowish Waters visitors and boasted livery, hotel, store, post office, school, and homes.

• Memorial Grove (Caro Woods), Chequamegon National Forest, Highway 70

Lac du Flambeau/23

one mile west from Vilas County line. One of the most exceptional forest beauty spots in Wisconsin; 80-acre virgin hardwood tract memorializes fallen forest ranger servicemen. Mile-long nature trail (with short-cut loop), interpretive "birdhouse signs" among stunning forest giants, including aptly named hemlock cathedral. Picnic area.

TOURING

- Indian Village Road-Highway 47-Highway D loop, mixture of summer homes and village, varying woods and many lake views.

- Crawling Stone Drive off D south, short artery through luxury lake homes.

- Moss Lake Drive-Thoroughfare Road, pleasant wooded and interlake ride.

- East Boundary Trail between Stearns Lake Drive and Highway H, welcome sylvan solitude if you do not mind sand and a few bumps. Pretty.

- Highway 47 northwest has excellent fall coloring. For a longer loop, take 47, 182, Chequamegon National Forest Road 144, and come back via 70 and D.

- Bo-Di-Lac Drive. See Minocqua. Some superb lake views shortly south of 70.

RECREATION

BIKING
- Try the side roads listed above, partly chosen with cycling in mind. Most have lake access at more than one point for a rest or snack or a quick dip.

BOAT AND CANOE RENTAL
- Wa-Swa-Gon Marina, Highway 47 northwest, 588-3949.

CANOEING
- Bear River from dam at Indian Village Road; take out at West River Trail, East River Trail, or Highway 182. Probably more historic than scenic; streams in this country tend to run through wetlands.

FISHING
Talk of imposing special fishing fees for reservation waters comes up from time to time.

PARK, BEACH, RECREATION AREA
- Wayside on Highway 47, one mile northwest, picnic facilities and fine sand beach. Historical marker recalls the history of Lac du Flambeau.

SKIING: CROSS COUNTRY
- Dillman's Lodge, off Highway D north. Two trails, four miles.

SNOWMOBILING
- Orange-blazed trails lace Flambeau; sign maps at key points; map available.

TENNIS
- Lac du Flambeau school, one court.

SHOPPING AND BROWSING

- Gebic Shop, opposite Indian Bowl, May–September. Handy location for local bead- and craftwork; curios, small gifts; gebics (beaded rabbit's foot Indian charms).

- Mabel's Gift Shop, Peace Pipe Lane in town, May–Christmas. Tasteful, restful surroundings, home accessories like fur rugs, lamps; jewelry; local and distant Indian wares, gifts.

- Totem Trading Post, Peace Pipe Lane in town, May–mid October. Perhaps its greatest pride is its large Navajo rug selection, but Indian pottery, basketry, jewelry, and other craft work join non-Indian gifts and handcrafts here.

DINING

- Dillman's Sand Lake Lodge, Highway D north; nightly, most of year by reservation, 588-3143. Full menu, gracious dining with full linens in carpeted lake-view, American-plan dining room. Cocktails.

- Fence Lake Lodge, Highway 47 southeast; nightly, June–August, closed Wednesday, May and September, 588-3255. Intriguing, cupolaed old lodge; I'd choose from the German side of the menu. Cocktails.

- The Tower, Highway 70 at D; nightly in season, year round, 588-3400 (has not always taken reservations). An old standby now in new hands; long noted for salad bar. Cocktails.

LODGING

AMERICAN PLAN
- Dillman's Sand Lake Lodge, off Highway D north, most of year. Large variety of units, suites to full cottages with living room and fireplace; natural wood, carpeting throughout. Three beaches, water sports, tennis. Winter sports, trails (ski and snowmobile); rentals available. A progressive and respected resort.

FISHING RESORT
- D-Bar-D Resort, Highway D south (Route 1), from opening of fishing into fall. Structured, often competitive fishing program stretching over five-day weekends; no families, generally. Carpeted housekeeping cottages.

HOUSEKEEPING
- Hemlock Haven, Highway 47 northwest (Route 1, Box 833), May–October. Five cottages in the hemlocks; some carpeting and knotty pine inside; sand beach.

- Luetzow's on Crawling Stone, Silver Beach Drive between 70 east and D (Route 1, Box 381), May–October. Outstanding resort: four small homes, impeccably furnished, furnace heated; lovely grounds, sand beach.

- Schmuecking's Westview Resort, Pokegama Lake Trail off D north (Route 2, Box 38). Tidy complex of four sunset-view cottages; porches; nice beach. Excellent reputation; very clean.

- Silver Beach Resort, Silver Beach Drive at D (Route 1, Box 411), seasonal. Six cottages (rather modest) beneath sighing pines along fine sand beach. Bar.

- Watson's Holiday Beach, off Highway D north (P.O. Box 375), May–September. Eight cottages; happy-hearted resort with big repeat business; fine beach.

MOTEL
- Tower Motel, Highway 70 at D (Route 1, Box 430), all year, 588-3341. 13 units, five with kitchenette.

CAMPING

PRIVATE
- Wa-Swa-Gon Park, Highway 47 northwest (P.O. Box 61). 66 units.

CHEQUAMEGON NATIONAL FOREST
- Wabasso Lake Campground, Chequamegon Forest Trail, west four miles from Indian Village Road, 10 units.

- Emily Lake Campground, one mile west of Wabasso site above, 10 units, no beach.

EVENTS

- Colorama, fall color time, usually a dinner with Indian fare.

INFORMATION

- Lac du Flambeau Chamber of Commerce, P.O. Box 165, Lac du Flambeau 54538. Main information booth in Indian Bowl open daily, mid June–Labor Day, 588-3346; branch booth, Highway 70 at D, open Monday–Wednesday, 588-3080.

MANITOWISH WATERS

Manitowish Waters, now a prestigious summer and residential neighborhood and resort community, began life as a lumber camp. It was born as the 1880s gave way to what would be called the Gay Nineties, but its life was little but noise and sweat, not gaiety, for years, as lumberjacks sent its grand white pines down the Manitowish River in pieces and later floated its graceful Norway pines to railroad landings on Rest and Star lakes.

Hardy tourists rode all-night Pullmans on the North Western, switched to buckboards at the nearest depots at Manitowish or Powell, bumped overland to docks on the lake edge, then shifted to launches for the final lap to their rude cottages or primitive resorts. Or they took a rocking branch line train on the old St. Paul Road around the back side of the chain of lakes, to Rice Creek, hoping that the kids would not get sick as the coaches imitated the roll of a ship.

They were there early enough to mingle with berry-picking Indians or to watch them gather wild rice, but late enough to see second-growth timber begin to overgrow the slash of the rapacious loggers or the scars of sweeping fires. Vacation days were active ones as men fished, maybe with an old lumberjack as their colorful guide; women might play cards, go walking or canoeing, or even, as did one young woman whose diary I read, shoot frogs as a pastime!

In the second and third decades of the new century, the efforts of farmers who aspired to put down roots in the cutover sand collapsed in despondency and foreclosure; agriculture never returned to Manitowish Waters. Those years also saw two vacation revolutions: emergence of the auto as a vacation travel medium and development of housekeeping cottages to accommodate visitors. No longer need a family have a month or more of free time to make a vacation practical and a fat pocketbook to allow accommodation at a lodge

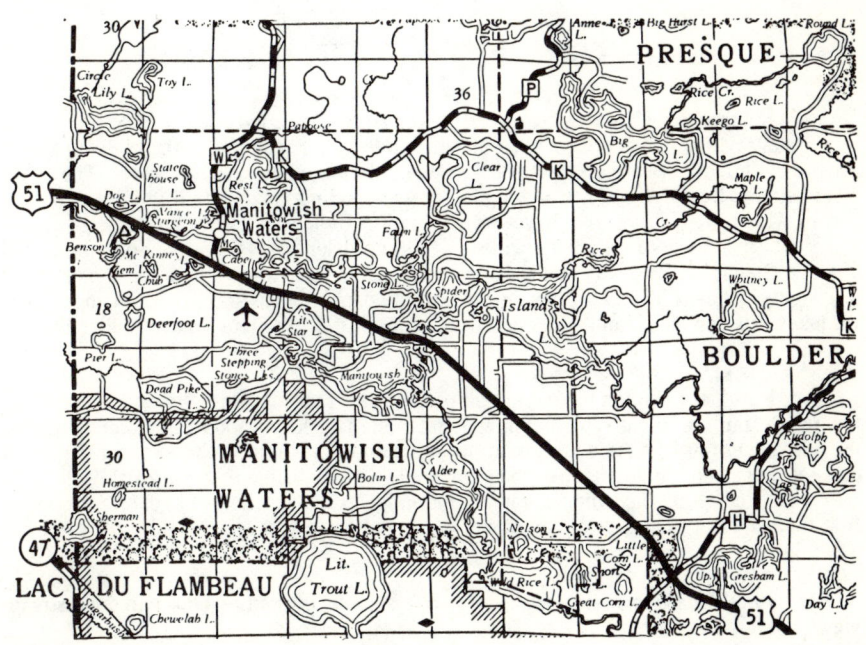

with luxurious meals. Northwoods sojourns became almost anyone's privilege. With those vacation revolutions came a civic revolution of sorts as Manitowish Waters folks formed a new town and separated from Lac du Flambeau in 1927; at that time they thought of themselves as the town of Spider Lake, though a short-lived post office on the chain was called Rest Lake.

The thirties saw the natives scraping along to meet their modest needs during a national depression, as boys from the tar paper CCC camp built fire lanes, planted trees, and trudged through the forests to eradicate currant bushes bearing blister rust—labors that are still paying dividends. This was also the era of the first paved side roads and fire towers. That decade and the forties saw most cottages get their first electric power and running water that did not require running to the pump.

The community as a whole did even better: it got its own airport and its very own post office, this time Manitowish Waters. The last big wave of new resort construction came in this first postwar decade, and when another wave followed it—a tidal wave of private summer-home construction—and resorters saw how valuable their lakefront cottages had become, many operators sold off some or all of their cottages. What you see listed below is the pick of the neap tide of Manitowish resorting, for now summer or permanent residents far outnumber tourists on the lakes.

Manitowish Waters doesn't have a central village broken down into tidy little blocks as many northern communities do; its homes are hidden on side roads or lakeshores. There is a central shopping area, where folks come to bank or to shop at LaPortes', to have coffee at Pat and Karen Murphy's, or to get a haircut from barber Dave Sorvald.

Its pioneers are gone now, most asleep under stones with inscriptions like "Emma Andrews, 1865–1965" or "William O. Strandberg, 1866–1936," or Peter Vance's claim that he had lived from 1844 to 1944 and was "Our First White Settler."

Manitowish Waters's terrain is not distinguished; it is mostly flat, second-growth popple, pine, or hardwood, with a great marsh on its southwest and a rare cedar swamp to its northwest, Powell Marsh and Circle Lily Swamp, respectively.

SIGHTSEEING AND TOURING

• Manitowish Chain of Lakes. 10 lakes above dam; two below. Loggers raised water levels perhaps a dozen feet to form a huge tide to flush logs down the rivers in spring drives, cutting off three lakes that "leaked" and diking other overflow spots. The chain offers almost limitless boating and sightseeing, including islands with interesting pasts: one in Manitowish Lake may have been sacred to Indians; the inhabited one in Island Lake held the chain's first resort, while its adjacent island was a hog wallow; the island near the channel in Rest was separated from the mainland to allow the loggers' steamboat a straighter haul with rafts of logs en route to the dam. Indians in birchbark canoes used the lakes between Island and Alder as a route between Lac du Flambeau and ricing areas.

• Rest Lake Dam in town on Highway W is the third or fourth on top of an original low rapids, built for log driving but now maintaining lake levels about eight feet higher for the joint benefit of lake residents and water users downstream (power and paper firms). A concrete enclosure on downstream side once held a novel fish lock to raise fish from river into lakes, and pilings are ruins of early dams and later fish hatchery. On the flat stood the first lumber camp; the old log structure, the town's oldest, was its smithy (private, not accessible).

• 30-30 Road (from hardware store) offers a mile of pretty woods and downstream views.

- Cranberry marshes, off loop of Powell, Alder Lake, and Cranberry roads. Cold-sensitive plants need spraying or flooding in bearing time and winter, hence the dikes, canals, and lake area locations; efforts here date from 1945–46. Harvest coincides with Colorama, when visitors are especially welcome.

- Powell Marsh is a huge natural marsh managed since 1957 for wildlife habitat with dikes, canals, plantings, controlled burning; viewing area on dirt portion of Powell Road; interior roads are gated but open to hiking. Actually there is little to see except during waterfowl migration, when 1,000–3,000 geese may be seen.

RECREATION

BOAT AND CANOE RENTAL

- Greer's Pier, Highway 51 at bridge, 543-8456.

- Little Star Garage, Highway 51, 543-8300. Fishing motors only.

- Rod n' Reel, Highway W at dam, 543-2326. Canoes.

CANOEING

- The chain is hub for many canoe streams, and the state DNR maintains many canoe campsites on both the streams and portions of the chain where canoeists can be expected to travel. Supplies are available at stores close to the dam. Day trips are popular and convenient. Consult DNR's Northern Highland Canoe Trails map.

- Manitowish River from Boulder Junction (popular put-in spot: Highway K), scenic on upper portion; easy day trip for families and a favorite of mine.

- Rice Creek from Round and Big lakes, prettiest between Round and Big where it is also slow enough to canoe upstream for a pleasant round trip from Big Lake access.

- Trout River from Trout Lake or Highway 51 bridge, prettier in its upper stretches before marshier backwaters of the chain; Highway H is a possible take out to avoid slow paddle to or through the chain.

- Manitowish River below the dam; take out at wayside on 51 four miles west, or at Highway 47 at Manitowish depot community, or along Flambeau Flowage. (Carry compass and detail map if you tackle the Flowage.)

PARKS, BEACHES, RECREATION AREAS
- Little Star Lake Picnic Area (DNR fee area). Picnicking, lovely beach.
- Community Center, airport on 51. Playground equipment; driving range, tennis.

SHOOTING
- Lions Club sponsors periodic shoots; there's also a practice range at airport.

SKIING / CROSS COUNTRY: RENTAL
- Musky Country Sport Shop, Highway 51, 543-8336.

SKIING / CROSS COUNTRY: TRAILS
- North Lakeland Community Services organization has begun developing trails in cooperation with other area agencies. See Winchester listings for one area. Another is proposed for the Lakeland school grounds, junction Highways K and P.

SNOWMOBILING
- Manitowish Waters Snow Skeeters groom local trails; maps available.

TENNIS
- Community Center, on 51 at airport.
- North Lakeland Elementary School, Highways K and P.

WATER SKI SHOWS
- Manitowish Waters Skiing Skeeters, near dam on W, 7 p.m. Sunday and Wednesday, late June to late August. Strong in barefoot skiing.

SHOPPING AND BROWSING

- Cricket Cove, in town. Tasteful shop for gifts, home items.

- The Ox Yoke, in town, seasonal. Gifts, home items; moccasins. Attractive.

- Yankee Studio, Gallery, Gift and Book Shop, in town, summer only. The same family has had a shop here for thirty years. Paintings, crafts of local artists; art supplies; unusual imports or gifts; books.

DINING

- Ehrich's Bavarian Inn, in town; all year, closed off-season Tuesdays, 543-2122. Popular for noon sandwiches and evening Continental fare, steaks, fish. Bar.

• Keep Schmil-Inn, in town at dam; closed Monday, all year. Noon sandwiches, nightly dinners, unusual finger foods. Small neighborhood tavern whose tables bear remarkable food knowledgeably prepared from scratch, like novel soups, tasty relishes, dumplings, Old World rouladen, chicken cordon bleu. Cocktails.

• Little Bohemia, on 51; nightly and from noon on Sunday (closed Monday in fall), May–November, 543-8433. Unrivaled combination of mellow Bohemian hunting lodge atmosphere and a half century of grand, hearty meals like superb kassler rippchen or famous duck; excellent soups served with a flourish. Cocktails. (The John Dillinger gang shot it out with the law here in 1934. Some relics of the event are on display in a little cottage; admission charged.)

• Voss' Birchwood Lodge, on 51; nightly, mid June–mid September, by reservation only, 543-8441. The genteel, quiet, unhurried atmosphere of a northwoods American-plan lodge, with flowers on the table, careful service, excellent meals from a menu that generally includes a roast, other homey items. Cocktails.

LODGING

AMERICAN PLAN
• Deer Park Lodge, off Highway 51 near the bridge, June–late August. Modified American plan. Large 250-guest resort with wide range of accommodations (bath, carpet in all; fireplaces in nine cottages); airy, pine-treed peninsula. Unusual on-premises activities like tennis, horses, heated pool, two bars, entertainment.

• Voss' Birchwood Lodge, on Highway 51 near bridge, mid June–mid September. Modified American plan. Graciously furnished cottages (22 units, carpet, bath, natural wood decor in all, fireplaces in 15, kitchens in several); comparable hotel suites. Thoughtful accents, antiques. Extensive shore; small sand beach.

HOUSEKEEPING
• Aschenbrenner's Manitowish Waters Resort, Spider Lake off 51, May–October. Six cottages, cozy rather than luxurious; well-kept grounds, fine beach.

• Bazso's Hillcrest Resort, leave 51 at Catholic church, May–October. Seven family cottages, very clean, on immaculate grounds; small beach on river.

• Coun-Tree Acres, Spider Lake, May into October. Five real log cottages, fireplaces; exceptional waterfront—even slides and volleyball in the water!

• Johnson's Millpoint Resort, Alder Lake, May–October. Five half-log, wood-paneled cottages; up-to-date, with porches; fine beach, airy, shady point of pines. One of the nicest housekeeping resorts on the chain.

• Sleight's Wildwood, Island Lake, May to mid fall. An excellent resort with 11 cottages ranging from rustic log cabins (completely modern, though) to lovely rental homes with touches like Heatilator fireplaces, cutting-board counter tops in kitchen. Remarkable spacing, privacy; sandy beach; extensive woods; trails.

● Voss' Breezy Point Cottages, Spider Lake Road, May–October. Excellent resort with nine log or knotty pine-finished cottages carefully appointed with lamps and other tasteful accents; floor furnace heat, considerable carpeting. Cottages scattered and all different; grounds and beaches vary with sites.

EVENTS

● Colorama, usually a musky dinner, self-guided drives to cranberry marshes and through Powell Marsh wildlife area (never otherwise open to public driving).

● Art fairs, notably Manito Art League's large show, late July–early August.

INFORMATION AND TRANSPORTATION

● Manitowish Waters Chamber of Commerce, Manitowish Waters 54545. Information booth, in Community Building, at airport, open weekends Memorial Day–mid June, then daily until Labor Day, and thereafter weekends until Colorama, 543-8488.

● Bus: Greyhound Lines, summer only; Wisconsin-Michigan Coaches, all year.

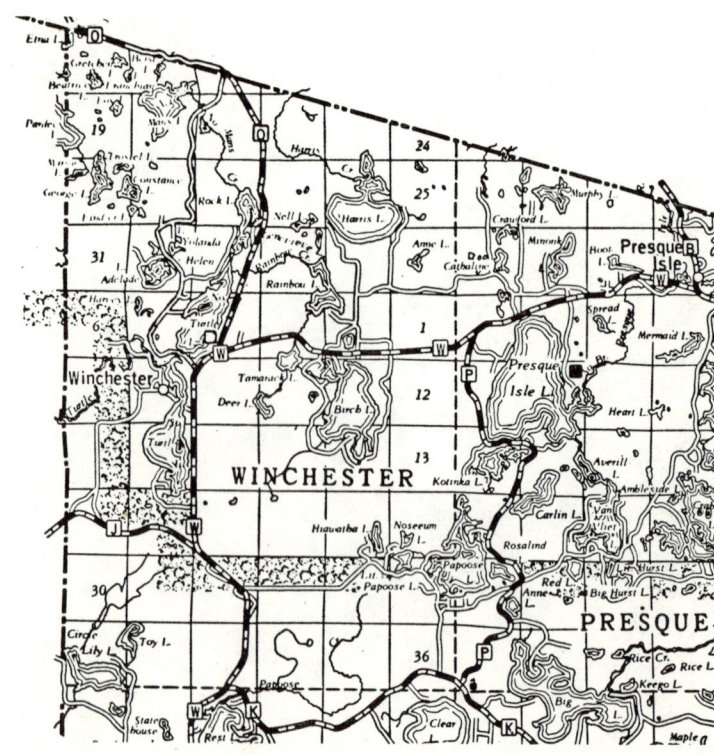

WINCHESTER AND PRESQUE ISLE

Winchester and Presque Isle share many similarities, especially those of history and landscape.

Both communities began as sawmill towns, and the companies that built them shared a number of common officers or owners. Both bore the names of mill figures (Walter Winchester and William Winegar till his namesake town changed its name in the 1950s to Presque Isle). They were both part of the same civil town—Presque Isle—till Winchester town was separated in 1921.

A great end moraine covers much of their area, except for a gentle, more level area that spills south from Harris Lake to Birch and Presque Isle lakes (where farming flourished to a remarkable degree and even today is commemorated by abandoned clearings). The moraine gave the area magnificent uplands that were a treasury of great hardwood trees that went unlogged in the flush of pine cutting and river driving. Railroads, however, made their exploitation possible, and in 1905 a branch line was pushed past Winchester and on to Presque Isle, then known (by the first of its three names) as Fosterville.

The Turtle Lake Lumber Company built a small mill where the railroad touched the lake, and a small cluster of tar paper houses sprouted around it. This mill cut the material to build a fine big mill down the lake a bit and then turned to cutting shingles for 20 years. Little Tar Town remained, but on a more pleasant hilltop overlooking the lake the company built a complete town of fifty-odd houses—precisely spaced in orderly rows behind boardwalks and white fencing—two inns, two community buildings, and a big store; this was **Winchester.**

From a little roundhouse behind the mill (where Car-Lee Campsite stands today) a network of private railway tracks began to range out in all directions, even up into Michigan, and little "sidewinder" Shay locomotives brought in log trains every day from the loggers in the woods. In winter teams and sleighs delivered logs from swamps impregna-

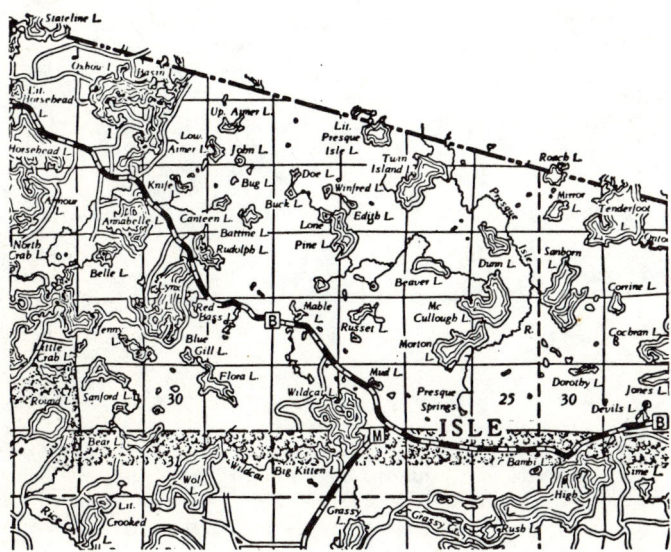

ble except when frozen, or tracts too small or remote to justify extension of tracks to them.

Rather abruptly, in early 1926, the company decided that it had done all the cutting that it cared to do, shut down the mill, shipped out its valuable machinery to a competitor at Hiles, Wisconsin, and sold the town and its remaining woodlands.

Fosterville got its mill and its village at the same time as Winchester, 1905–6. The operator there was Vilas County Lumber Company, and when the firm was on its knees a few years later, it was William Winegar who put it back on its feet and gave the town his name. This mill company logged with its own private log trains too, and even today abandoned rights-of-way can be traced around Presque Isle Lake, east as far as Lynx Lake, and north into Michigan.

The Winegar mill lasted much longer than Winchester's; for a new set of owners it sawed way into the 1930s, and the mill village had a less harsh transition to survival without the mill. Today's village, smaller than the 80 houses of its peak, reflects the newness of its 1956 name with the newness of most of the homes along its little net of streets.

The boom years brought a lot of colorful people into the moraine hills. Not surprisingly, many were Kentuckians to whom these hills were like the hills of home. Some Kentucks brought an unusual skill with them: moonshining. Many a still flourished in the hills, and growing grain for them accounted for more than a few of those farm fields mentioned above. One moonshine operation was interrupted in 1926 by a shootout that eventually cost two lives. That period saw Ku Klux Klan rumblings in these same hills.

The resort business in this vicinity had preceded even the timber cruisers. In 1895 George Washington Buck built his famous Divide Resort at the wasp-waisted narrows of Turtle Lake, so remote that the only way the first fishermen-guests could reach it was in a canoe towed up the Turtle River by men trudging along the bank all the way up from the train station at Mercer. The resort grew to a huge complex complete with its own pioneer electric plant and bowling alley, but withered and died in the 1930s. No comparable lodge ever followed it. **Presque Isle** resorting had begun about 1896 with a fishing camp similar to the early Buck camp; one sporting magazine of the period mentions a camp, just getting to which required a train trip, a stage ride, a boat trip, a mile and a quarter hike, another boat trip, and a canoe trip with two portages!

Lodges and housekeeping colonies followed a generation or so later, on Presque Isle Lake, notably, but the resort business never grew on the scale that it attained in southern parts of the county. Summer homes popped up here and there even before 1900, several by World War I. One of the lakes that was marked by early homes—impressive for their time—was Crab Lake, especially on its lovely islands.

Presque Isle bills itself as the last wilderness, but it is seeing a significant growth of activity, symbolized by the handsome summer homes lately built around its lakes and by new interest in winter hospitality and sports.

SIGHTSEEING AND TOURING

WINCHESTER AREA

- Winchester village, west shore of South Turtle Lake off old Highway O. Offers hints of what a mill village was like; townsite was sold a couple times before division as individual homes and lots, and homes were sold for materials in that time. Double or triple the number of uniform homes in your mind, for an accurate picture, and add a long narrow boarding house and inn on the northeast hillside and a big store below the hill. The quiet old barn in the town site was the lumber company's veterinary barn. An abstraction of standard home design can be drawn from common details and shapes among existing, remodeled homes.

- Highway W between Highway J and Highway O has early and bright fall colors.

- Papoose Lake Road has rugged landscape of small kettles and ridges; an entire little logging community, Buswell, with a large mill complex and rail network, once stood on Papoose Lake; it died after the mill burned in 1910.

- Lake Adelaide area, off old Highway O north; rugged landscape, pretty lake, site of opening scenes of film *Adventures of a Young Man*, based on early Ernest Hemingway short stories and still seen now and then on late-night television. Unmarked road, off north part of loop around lake, leads to Trostel Fire Tower, a ladder-type tower not for the faint of heart.

PRESQUE ISLE AREA
- Walleye Rearing Ponds of the DNR, in town; interpretive sign along road above them; 1949 renovation of early millpond area. Newly hatched walleye grow into fingerlings in a summer here. In laborious five-man seinings visible several mornings a week in August DNR employees net the fingerlings for planting in area lakes.

- Widowmaker Hill—if you can find it! Heavily overgrown, slight knob on ridge overlooking Highway B a few hundred feet north of village hall, marked by an apple tree and wildflowers in season, this was the potter's field for old loggers from 1905 to 1926; only a few stones stand or lie there, one ironically reading, "Gone but not forgotten."

- Highway B is extremely pretty all the way to Land O' Lakes. It offers two nice wayside picnic spots and views of rugged southern ridges, and passes many lakes and bogs on both sides. (See Land O'Lakes too.)

- Crab Lake Road south from B east. Lakes, deep woods, scenic homes; area near Crab Lake was logged for the first time only in 1942–43; the millpond still hides near Town Dock Road, artery to a good access to handsome Crab Lake.

- South Crab Lake Road, off Crab Lake Road near its south end, supplies, I think, the area's boldest ridge and kettle scenery, heavily shaded; follow 49ers Road to its end and a little monument to one Joseph Anicich, and the brief side run down Diamond Point Road.

- Lynx Lake Road, south from B, skirts north fringe of heavy ridge area.

RECREATION

CANOEING
- Horsehead to Crab lakes, including two intermediate lakes amid the finest of rugged northwoods scenery; four miles, landing to landing, but roam a bit en route!

CANOE TRIP SERVICE AND RENTAL
- Armour Lake Resort, Crab Lake Road, Presque Isle. Outfitting; pick-up service.

FISHING
- Moraine Springs Trout Farm, Palmer Road north from old Highway W. Fee

fishing for trout in pretty setting below the glacial moraine; 686-2461 for hours.

PARKS, BEACH, RECREATION AREA
- Presque Isle Lake County Park, south from Highway W. Public beach.

- Winchester Fishing Pier, off Highway W between two taverns in business district. Picnic tables, fishing pier, and (during my visit) aggressive dogs.

- Winchester Town Park, old O. Pretty river site; tables, play field, shelter.

SHOOTING
- Black Powder and Turkey Shoots, sponsored by Winchester Lions; check locally.

SKIING / CROSS COUNTRY
- Winchester Cross-Country Ski Trail, Highway W south near Highway J, 16 miles (novice to expert) in wrinkled moraine area opened 1977, with later extension possible. Joint effort of civic agencies and landowner, Consolidated Papers, Inc.

SNOWMOBILING
- The northwestern portion of Vilas County is closest to the snow belt that makes possible the ski hills of the Gogebic Range. Thus snowmobiling may linger later in this area or begin earlier than elsewhere in the county. Trails are groomed by individuals, businesses, or resorts, and by the Presque Isle Sno-Bunnies Club.

SHOPPING AND BROWSING

• Artisan Industries, downtown Presque Isle. Designers/manufacturers of quality custom furniture. Tables figure importantly in their line; the firm works only in northern hardwoods. Showroom closed Sunday.

• Steincraft, 4.5 miles east on Highway B, Monday–Friday in summer, by chance rest of year. In a workshop that has long been a tourist mecca, Cecil Stein fabricates or lathe-turns candlesticks and other wood items for home or gifting, plus a few pixyish novelties.

• The Wooden End, in town. An appealing little workroom and shop where a Stein protege makes turned-wood lamps and similar items.

DINING

• Skyview Supper Club, Highway W, two miles west of Presque Isle; closed Tuesday, all year, 686-2928. Carpeted dining rooms, small salad bar; family operated; very clean. Very good food and treatment of guests put the Skyview on my small list of personal favorites. Especially good fish fry. Cocktails.

• Zastrow's Lynx Lake Lodge, four miles east of Presque Isle on Highway B; nightly, all year, closed Wednesday, September–May, 686-2249. Small, low, rustic dining room; full menu, summer smorgasbord, fish buffet. Cocktails.

• During 1977 Winchester saw many changes in its dining places. The Bear burned, but is owner pledged the return of his "world record chicken." Two other dining places changed hands in mid season, and since its change, Turtle Lake Lodge showed real promise, with good and reasonably priced meals, including steaks; Highway W, business area; evenings, all year, 686-2343.

• The Retreat Bar, Highway P about two miles south of W; all year. A neighborhood tavern that I like for its companionable owners and clientele, its sandwiches or Tombstone pizza, and its stressing Leinenkugel's beer. Raccoons often feed outside the picture window.

LODGING

• The Bear, Winchester business district. Dormitory or private room accommodations (central toilets, showers) for Art LaHa's Bow Hunters Camp in fall and for skiers in winter. Colorful north country atmosphere (new in 1977). Bar, dining.

• Brown's Point Resort, Presque Isle, east side Presque Isle Lake off P, all year. Housekeeping, seven paneled cottages, mostly carpeted, on a scenic point with sandy cul-de-sac beach in its lee; very nice lake; hospitable young hosts.

- Shorewood Resort, Highway P near W (Route 1, Manitowish Waters), mid May–mid October. Housekeeping, four charmingly remodeled little cottages with carpet, paneling, little decks facing lake; sand beach, nice lake. Pleasant owners. Bar.

- Simon's Sunrise Resort, Highway P at Presque Isle Lake (Route 1, Manitowish Waters), seasonal. Housekeeping. Fine physical plant of lawns, uniform cottages (six) side by side, well equipped and appointed. Sand swimming area.

- Sportsman's Resort Motel, Highway W south, Winchester, all year, 686-2232. Six motel units, kitchenettes in all. Scenic lake, beach, dock.

- Zastrow's Lynx Lake Lodge, four miles east of Presque Isle on B. American plan all year or housekeeping September–June. 10 comfortable cottages or new duplexes; sand beach. Winter sports. Dedicated and energetic owners never stop upgrading. Bar.

CAMPING

- Car-Lee Campsite, west shore of Turtle Lake at Winchester townsite (Route 1, Box 20), May–October. 20 units.

- The Pondorosa, Presque Isle, on W, May–December. 24 sites.

EVENTS

- Independence Day, Winchester.

- Walleye Fry, Presque Isle, a Friday in July. Features the walleye capital's specialty. Since 1965.

- Firemen's Picnic, Presque Isle, a Sunday in early August. Contests, water fights between fire departments, refreshments.

- Colorama, both towns, with different dinners or festivities.

- Ice Fishing Jamboree, January, Winchester fishing pier; also Presque Isle.

INFORMATION

- Write Winchester Township Chamber of Commerce, Winchester 54567 or Presque Isle Information Center, Presque Isle 54557.

- Public library, in town, Presque Isle town hall. Hours posted.

ARBOR VITAE AND WOODRUFF

Arbor Vitae and Woodruff have always presented a few contrasts. Today's contrast is between rural Arbor Vitae and concentrated Woodruff, but the Town of Woodruff is

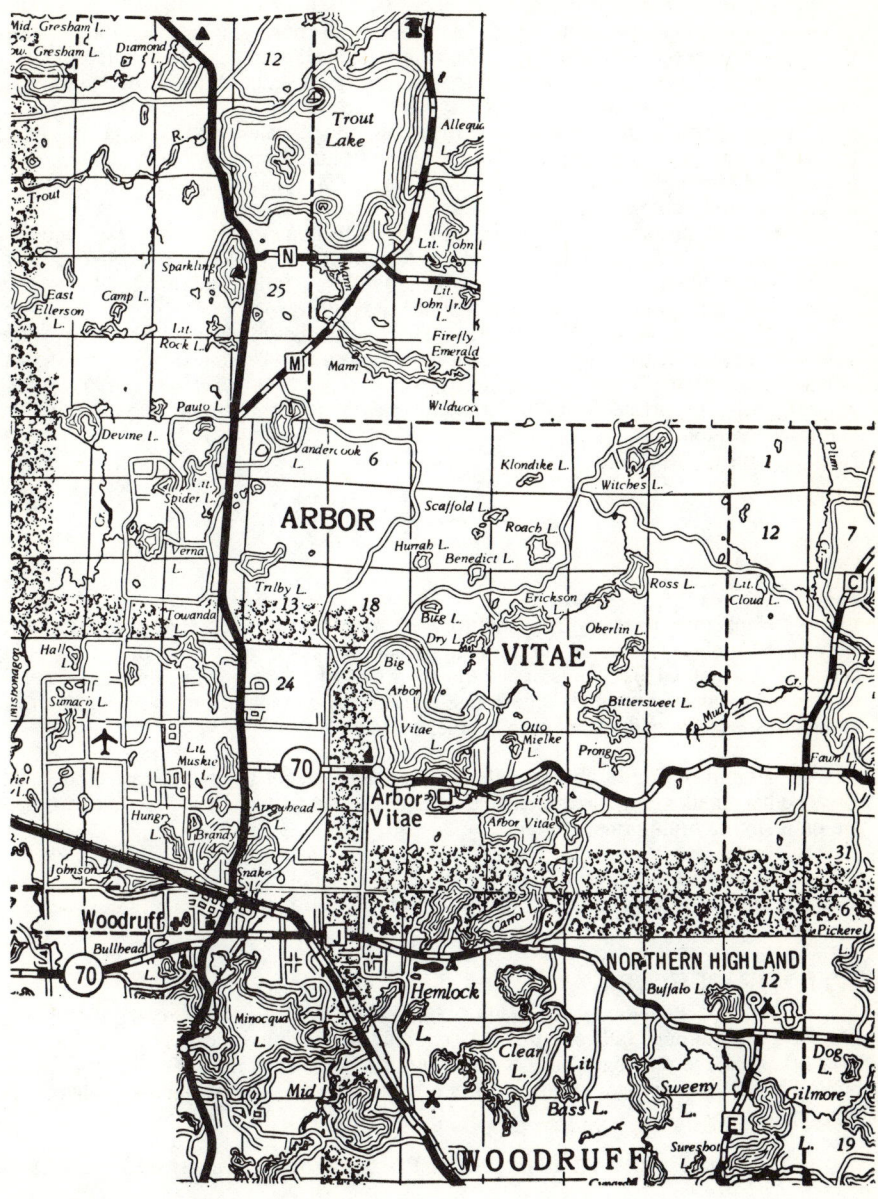

itself a contrast between the commercial center and residential area at its west and a vast expanse of state land that occupies most of its eastern area.

Arbor Vitae, named for the cedar tree found there, grew as a lumber settlement in the 1890s when John Ross moved his lumbering operation up from Lincoln County and built a sawmill and sizable village of uniform, dowdy little cottages, most with only one window in each wall. He sold out eventually to Yawkey-Bissell, which built logging railroads to feed logs to this mill and another at Hazelhurst.

The mill made its last cut in November 1912. Rather than let the village rot, the company brought in a wrecking firm, which sold off the houses or salvaged their materials. Barely a trace remained, by 1914, of a village that had been home to hundreds; maybe a dozen families stayed on. (Traces still visible today are an old brick vault and the mill boiler house, which is now the Blue Crest bar and restaurant.)

Yawkey-Bissell sold much of its cutover land to the state for $1.25 an acre, giving the state a nucleus for today's Northern Highland State Forest. Arbor Vitae turned to tourism and farming. Its tourism is still viable, but the farming, much of it concentrated in a belt west from town to the area of the present airport, has died out.

Woodruff, histories report, began from an 1890s homestead but very early took on the crossroads role astride two railroads and between Arbor Vitae and Minocqua. It served as a lumbermen's headquarters town and, with something like fifteen saloons, as a lumberjacks' playground, but was not a major sawmill town.

Trout Lake funneled some of the first resort guests through Woodruff as early as the 1890s; by 1912 there were at least three lodge resorts on the lake, one of which boasted an oddity for the northwoods: stucco buildings.

Maturing, the greater Woodruff area saw growth in commerce, industry, hospitality, and transportation.

SIGHTSEEING

ARBOR VITAE AREA

- Henkelmann's Museum, Highway 70, one mile east of Highway 51, daily, May–mid October. Visitors wind through animal displays, mostly the work of traveler-taxidermist Reinhold Henkelmann and mostly arranged by regions to combine an area's birds, small and large animals together. Some displays animated, and some historic or antique displays as well. Admission charge; souvenir-gift shop.

- Drumlins: Trout Lake area; one large one just west of Highway 51 north of Trout River; other smaller egg- or cigar-shaped hills in the swarm lie across 51, a bit north; all are on a slight north-northeast angle.

- State scientific areas: The Bittersweet lakes (shorelines) and bird nesting areas near Sweeny and Trilby lakes; all are unmarked, hard to pinpoint.

WOODRUFF AREA

- Antique Phonograph Museum, 617 Second Ave. (enter in rear), afternoons, Memorial Day through fall color time. A very unusual, tasteful little museum showcasing over 60 venerable phonographs from morning glory horns to the sunset of the 78s. If not too busy, the proprietor usually plays a few for visitors. Modest admission charge. A fun idea!

- Historical marker: Million Penny Parade; World's Largest Penny. School-grounds, one block west of 51, in town. Schoolchildren's fund-raising efforts, inspired by desire to see a million of something, helped fund this area's first hospital; drive in 1953 raised far more than a million pennies, is commemorated here.

• Medical complex, in town, west of 51 via Town Line Road, grew out of the Penny Parade and other efforts, including the television appearance of Woodruff's "Dr. Kate" Newcomb (the Angel on Snowshoes) on *This Is Your Life*. First just the tiny Lakeland Memorial Hospital, it burgeoned into a regional complex. A bequest by summer resident Howard Young made possible a new hospital bearing his name. The Monticello entry wing was a stipulation of the gift.

• Woodruff Fish Hatchery, Highway J, east of 47. Largest warm-water hatchery in the world. Interesting activities include net making and mending in winter; netting mature fish in area lakes in April and milking them of spawn and milt; hatching of eggs in glass jars and tanks; movement of fry to ponds till later planting. Visitors welcome. Show ponds; guided tours, small aquarium in summer.

TOURING

• American Legion State Forest is one of the area's major recreation resources, with beaches, picnic areas, campgrounds, boat landings, trails, and a wealth of lake and forest beauty. Also a hard-working forest, it is managed for timber, and sections are harvested from time to time.

• Woodruff Road between Highways J and 47 passes deep moody woods, pristine lakes.

• Highway J east from 47 blends deep young forests, Carroll Lake vista area, and a photogenic canal about eight miles east. (Less pretty east from there.)

• Blue Island Road between J and Highway 70; stunning woods, wrinkled terrain.

• Little Bass Lake boat-landing road, south from J, one-lane dirt track, occasionally a tree tunnel, other times in cuts or fills, maybe an old rail grade; one mile.

• Witches Lake Road, unpaved, off Buckhorn Road (leaves 70 near Henkelmann's), is one of the best showcases of moraine scenery: ridges, kettles, kettle lakes in the Muskellunge end moraine. Exit either via Ross Road at mile 4.4 (east to St. Germain past burn openings, sandy regions, and logging) or via Plum Vitae Road north at mile 5 to N (3.1 miles). Look in on the lakes with landings, too.

RECREATION

BIKING
• Try loops involving 47, J, and Woodruff Road; or J, Blue Island, 70, and Rudolph Road, with side trip to Clear Lake Picnic Area.

• Buckhorn Road from 70 to dead end, 3.5 miles; picnic beach along the way!

BOAT AND CANOE RENTAL
- Joe Kelly's Landing, Woodruff Road.

- Thrall's Boat and Canoe Shop, Highway 70 just east of 51, 356-5367. A business with a 30-year reputation and unique skills: Arnold and Bob Thrall also build boats now and then in the grand old tradition of hand steaming, bending, and fitting the oak ribs and cedar planking. (Rentals: canoes, ski and fishing rigs.)

CANOEING
- Creek between Sweeny and Cunard lakes, roads to both lakes off Highways J and E.

- Trout River. See Manitowish Waters.

GOLF
- Trout Lake Golf Course, Highway 51. 18 holes, 6,142 yards; daily fee, carts.

HIKING AND NATURE TRAILS
- Buck Lake Trail, Woodruff Road at Raven Trail parking lot; 3.9 miles.

- Raven Nature Trail, same location. 1.5-mile interpretive trail designed to be taken with explanatory booklet available in area. Glacial bog, pond; lake; rolling terrain, representative forests, grand hemlocks, and solitude.

- DNR snowmobile trails are sometimes hiked (q.v.).

PARKS, BEACHES, RECREATION AREAS
- Big Arbor Vitae Lake Picnic Area (DNR), Buckhorn Road. Sand beach.

- Brandy Lake Park, west from 51 in Woodruff. Sand beach, lifeguard; changing house; tables, playground, tennis, hockey.

- Carroll Lake Boat Landing, on J. Tables; note tree growing around rock!

- Clear Lake Picnic Area, off J. DNR fee area; excellent beach, changing booths.

SHOOTING
- Trilby Lake practice area, Highway 51 north. 25-, 50-, 100-yard stands. Free.

SKIING / CROSS COUNTRY: RENTAL AND CENTERS
- Bennett's Sport Shop, Highway 51 South, 356-3900.

- Easy Slider Ski Touring Academy. See Minocqua.

SKIING / CROSS COUNTRY: TRAILS
- Escanaba Lake Trail. See Boulder Junction.

- Indian Shores camping resort, Highway 47 east.

- Madeline Lake Trail, north from J. 9.5 miles; novice, intermediate.

SNOWMOBILE RENTAL
- Roberts Sports Center, Highway 70 west, 356-5824.

- Shamrock Sales, Highway 51 north, 356-9451.

SNOWMOBILING
- Highland Trail (State), access on Highway 70 east of Arbor Vitae. Main trail to Sayner and Boulder Junction.

- Lakeland Trail (State), access from 47 and Woodruff Road or at Lake Tomahawk. 18.2-mile main loop.

TENNIS
- Brandy Lake Park, Lemma Creek Road west from 51, two courts.

SHOPPING AND BROWSING

- Art Long, wildlife artist and taxidermist, Highway 51 near Highway M (Route 1), daily in summer and fall (closed Wednesday and Sunday), by chance rest of year, 356-6717. Self-taught, Long developed his art out of close wildlife observation as taxidermist. Paintings have a unique, subtle, almost clairvoyant air that I think makes them both beautiful and distinctive.

- Elf Hut, 1620 Mattke Road, 1.5 miles north of 47 west, June–September. Tiny shop in elfin setting; handwrought jewelry, especially featuring stones.

- The Mill, on 47 east, in town, all year. If it's old or collectible, The Mill has it somewhere in its antiques trove. (See *WISCONSIN trails*, Spring 1976.)

- The Old Swimming Hole, on 51 north, in town, seasonal. What you buy here will not last, but the memory will. Leo Schlezewske cuts lake ice and puts it up in the age-old manner; here he sells it. (See *WISCONSIN trails*, Winter 1976.)

- Ye Olde Workshop, on 51 north, in town, all year. General antiques line.

DINING

- Captain's Galleon, on 51 north, in town; lunchtime to closing, all year, 356-5636. Cozy little bar and dining area, outstanding charcoaled sandwiches, hearty and creative, definitely among the very best in the north country!

- Kelly's Supper Club, on 51 north in town; all year, 356-9925. Evenings with salad bar, full menu, and specials; some luncheons. Dependably good food.

• Pine Cone Inn, on 70 just east of 51; lunchtime till closing, all year, 356-2110. Bar with spartan dining room but big menu of Mexican items (tasty, generous, and authentic); also Italian fare. Cocktails.

• The Plantation, Highways 51 and 70; evenings, all year, 356-9000. Spacious, airy dining room done in soft blue, white, and dark wood—a welcome deviation from northwoods rustic! Attentive service, very fine entrees, interesting appetizers (perhaps a little too precisely meted out). Cocktails. A rare adventure in gentility!

• Thunderbird Supper Club, on 51 near Highway M; evenings except Tuesday and off-season Mondays, all year, 356-5433. Big log dining room, full menu. Cocktails.

LODGING

AMERICAN PLAN

• Cardinal's Manitowish Lodge, on 51 at Trout Lake (Route 1), June–Labor Day. Full American plan. Maintains its heritage with strong northwoods atmosphere. Begun in 1888 by John Mann in some cottages still used today, it was sold to the Cardinals in 1910; they have improved it ever since. This was Jack Vilas's lodging in summer 1915 when he made his pioneering patrol flights from the lake. 19 lakeside log cabins, 17 with fireplace; rustic appointments include *real ice boxes* serviced daily. Complete waterfront, beach; tennis, shooting.

• Coon's Franklin Lodge, on 51 at Trout Lake (Route 1, Box 72), mid June–Labor Day week. Substantial resort with pride and a past. The huge, mellow log lodge dates from 1892; Mr. Coon had found the site with a camper friend, Franklin Jennings, hence the name. Over a mile of shore, 26 cottages, all with fireplace, refrigerator, some with multiple bath. Full American plan. Fine waterfront, tennis (four courts), walking paths, game room.

HOUSEKEEPING

• Butler's Blue Island Resort, Blue Island Road off 70 east (Route 1, Arbor Vitae), all year. Eight units, famous fishing lake, up-to-date and comfortable. Conscientious hosts. Popular with snow visitors; bar.

• Helminski's Woodland Beach Resort, Big Arbor Vitae Lake, Arbor Vitae, June–October. Arc of nine lakeside cottages; safe beach; very popular.

• Holzinger's Pine Arbor, just off 70 on Big Arbor Vitae Lake, Arbor Vitae, May–October. Fragrant pines shelter five modest cottages; beach.

• Kangle's Timberlane, follow 51, Farming and Thiedeman roads to 11397 (P.O. Box 622, Woodruff). Secluded mini resort of three nice modern units, good beach.

• Saunoris' Retreat, Big Arbor Vitae Lake, Arbor Vitae, seasonal. Good mini resort of three well-equipped cottages on beautifully landscaped tract; beach.

MOTELS

Mailing address unless specified is Route 1, Woodruff, for these motels.

• Arbor Vitae Motel, Highways 51 at 70, all year, 356-3393. 20 units; beach.

- Buckhorn Lodge, Buckhorn Road, Arbor Vitae (P.O. Box 289, Woodruff), seasonal, 356-5090. Six units; beach.

- Country Lane Motel, on 47 west in Woodruff, all year, 356-5421. 11 units, seven with kitchenette; on lake.

- Edgewater Motel, on 51, six miles north, all year, 356-3820. 12 units.

- Northern Motel, on 51, five miles north, all year, 356-3605. 14 units.

CAMPING

PRIVATE
- Arbor Vitae Trailer Resort, on 70 east, seasonal. 37 trailer, 26 tent sites.

- Fox Fire KOA, on 51 north (Route 1), Woodruff, seasonal.

- Hiawatha Travel Trailer Resort (P.O. Box 529, Woodruff), seasonal. 200 sites.

- Indian Shores, on 47 east (P.O. Box 12, Woodruff), all year. 200 units.

STATE FOREST CAMPGROUNDS
- Buffalo Lake, Highways J and E. 52 units.

- Carroll Lake, on J. 20 units.

- Clear Lake, Woodruff Road near 47, all year. 107 units.

EVENTS

- Arbor Vitae Firemen's Picnic, August.

- Woodruff Summer Fun Days and Summerfest, August.

- Colorama Fly-In and Breakfast, during fall color season, at airport.

INFORMATION AND TRANSPORTATION

- Arbor Vitae-Woodruff Chamber of Commerce, P.O. Box 226, Woodruff 54568. Information booth on Highway 47 in town is open daily June through August, daily except Sunday in May and September. All-year phone: 356-6171.

- Bus: Greyhound Lines, summer only; Wisconsin-Michigan Coaches, all year.

- Car rental: Lakeland Rent-a-Car, airport, 356-3891.

- Charter air service: airport, 356-3891.

BOULDER JUNCTION

Boulder Junction has led many lives, none more interesting than the one it leads now as vacation center and musky capital of the world (a title it holds with the official endorsement of the U.S. Patent Office).

Twice it led the life of a logging center. First pine loggers worked their way up the Manitowish River for white pine to be floated down to big mills around Eau Claire or even down the Mississippi. Ruined dams like the one just below Highway K are relics of the log drives. The second logging career came when Boulder was literally a junction of four railroad lines, one in each direction, and all four had logging spurs branching off from them. Logs were even rafted across Trout Lake to trackside loading ramps. For the loggers, Boulder Junction was a headquarters town and a play town, and they often filled the little 1890s hotel. They logged the east, south, and west sides first and finished up on the north and into nearby Michigan about 1920. When the loggers had finished, a person could stand on a slight height near Trout Lake or near Manitowish Waters and see the buildings of Boulder Junction eight or ten miles away, without a tree to block the view.

As early as 1900 summer vacationers were joining lumberjacks in the coach or caboose of the informal train. The first estates were built about that time, even with the improbable combination of wood-floored tents for sleeping, yet a library for leisure! Turn

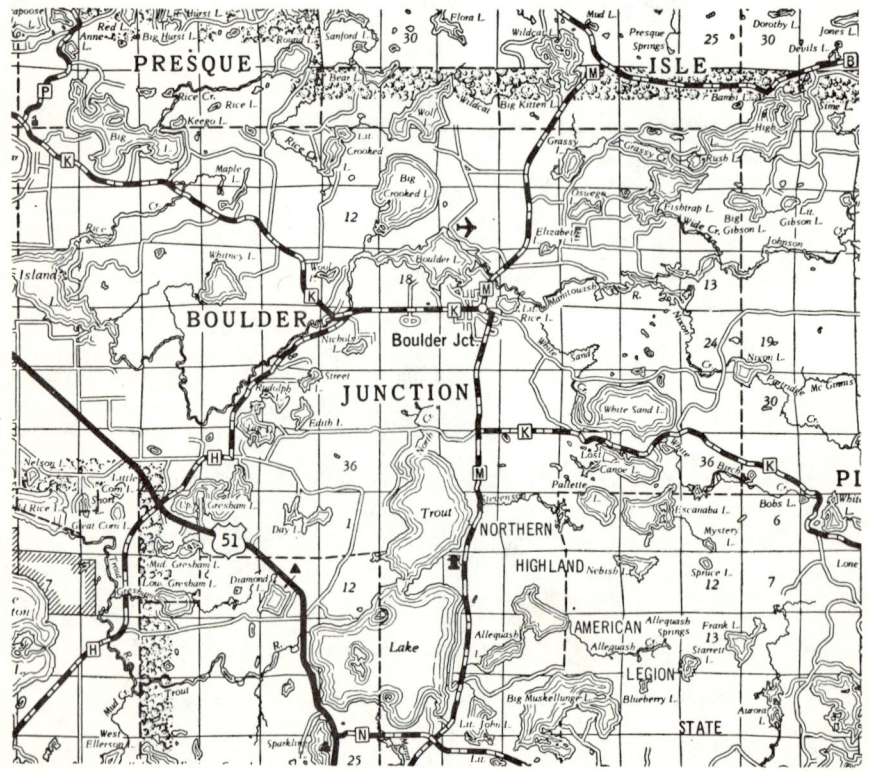

46/Vilas County

of the century visitors had a choice of the hotel or lodges on Trout, High, or Clear Crooked lakes and soon on Boulder and Wolf lakes besides. One wealthy Chicago meat-packing family eschewed either resorts or estates. They had the railroad put in a side track near Wildcat Lake, I am told, and spent the summer there in the urbane elegance of their private palace car.

A unique, slightly pathetic breed of characters developed in the lonely woods north of Boulder and Star Lake after the logging had ended. Lumberjacks who declined to move on westward when the logging moved from here to Idaho and Washington shacked all alone in huts or abandoned camps, hunting, trapping, maybe doing a little guiding or making a little moonshine. A few were involved in dramatic murders but most died quietly and alone, just as they had lived.

An entirely different sort of character who lived in Boulder was the revered Angel on Snowshoes, Dr. Kate Newcomb, whose gravestone in the local cemetery on Highway K bears her photographic likeness.

An important role for the state in the Boulder area began sixteen years before Boulder Junction even became a separate township. In 1911 the state set up a forestry headquarters and pioneer tree nursery along Trout Lake. State landholding is important in the township; most of this land is part of the Northern Highland State Forest.

Boulder Junction enjoyed dramatic growth in the 1945–78 era. The profusion of private homes (retirement and residential, as well as vacation) is mostly hidden along side roads and lakeshores, but the accompanying growth in stores or shops is evident along the streets of the village.

SIGHTSEEING

POINTS OF INTEREST

● Historic markers along Trout Lake honor the beginnings of the state forestry program (at Trout Lake DNR headquarters, q.v.) and first use of airplanes for forest fire surveillance (at boat landing along Highway M).

● Manitowish River dam, at Highways K and H (below highway), now in ruins, shows timber crib and earthwork construction of old log-driving dams; they penned up heads of water to flush logs downriver in spring drives; this one, circa 1890–99, is probably the oldest structure in its vicinity.

● Glacial landmarks. An esker or its glacial double carries Ridge Road high above Grassy Creek for half a mile (access off Highway M via High Lake Road; drive a scenic mile beyond the ridge before turning back). Drumlins, near Boulder fire tower (about one mile south from K via unmarked dirt fire lane running due south from K—which means an acute angle turn if you come from the east—about one mile west of H and the river). Geologist F. T. Thwaites noted classic form of the drumlin where the fire tower stands, and clear-cutting in 1975–76 will allow several years of tree-free viewing of its contour or those of other hills nearby. Ladder-type tower, 84 feet.

● Northern Wisconsin National Canoe Base, Boy Scouts of America, Highway K east, is hub of summer canoeing, ecology study, and winter camping activity.

● Wild ricing on Little Rice Lake, in town, by chance around early September.

FEE ATTRACTIONS

● Aqualand, Highway K east, from about May 20 to October 1. Four chief features: indoor aquarium, outdoor fishponds; zoo with representative wild animal species; Uncle Pat's Farm with special appeal to all ages: pettable fawns, lambs, and goat kids who nuzzle up to visitors for treats. Plenty of slots for your nickels or quarters: soda for the bears, corn for the goats, a bribe to make a caged chicken perform. A few cents more will buy a live frog if you lust to see a pond musky lunge. Gift shop. Admission charge. Trout fishing; fee.

• Shrimp's Wildlife Displays, Highway M north, afternoons, May–October. Uncountable glass-cased northern animals and birds, including uncommon specimens like albino deer, black beaver. Carpeted area also includes nonnative species, like sharks, and various mementos of the owners. Worth the modest fee.

• Seaplane rides offer a sightseeing high; Boulder Junction airport, 385-2293.

NORTHERN HIGHLAND STATE FOREST

• The Northern Highland State Forest, while being managed for timber, game, and other resources, as well as recreation, is in effect one of the biggest state parks in the United States; state land here totals over 140,000 acres.

• Trout Lake DNR Headquarters has both historic and sightseeing interest. Here Wisconsin state forestry began with a nursery in 1911, and here on October 20, 1977, another landmark was reached when the *one billionth* tree grown under the program was planted by the very same forester who began the nursery 66 years before, Fred Wilson, 90 years old! It was the same site as in 1911, though the nursery here was closed in 1952. A historic marker on the spot tells more. Cathedral Point, west end of paved drive just north of main office, is a beautiful beach and picnic area with lovely shore, mammoth pines.

• Five Lakes fish experiment area, Five Lakes Road, due east from Trout Lake Headquarters; year-round unrestricted fishing with permit from office at Escanaba Lake. A picnic site, the drive through leafy tunnels, and the scenic lakes of the project make Five Lakes Road a recommended side road.

• Wild areas: A new state wild area between Highway M, Frank Lake, and Razorback Road near Sayner has been proposed. Existing access routes will remain, notably to lovely Allequash Lake landing, but development in area will be curbed.

• State scientific areas: Trout Lake Conifer Swamp, Highway M south of DNR offices; Escanaba Lake Hemlocks, a hemlock island in a swamp east of the lake; Johnson Lake Barrens, a classic pine stump-bracken fern area east of the lake.

TOURING

• Highway K is scenic eastward to Star Lake, notably in heavy woods in Lost Canoe-White Sand lakes area; walk down to the lakes at accesses provided, for both lakes are especially attractive; beach at White Sand wayside.

• Highway B. See Presque Isle and Land O' Lakes.

• High-Fishtrap lakes roads, northeast of town off Highway M, scenic in their own right; also connecting Fishtrap Dam Road (the dam site may be the loveliest little spot in the area: ruins of dam, pretty creek, footbridge, lake views; campsite) and Ridge Road (esker and good forest and wetland views).

- Trout Lake shore drive, between a Highway M turnoff and South Trout campground; a thin margin of trees separates road and lake; superb sunset vistas. (This view was on the cover of *WISCONSIN trails,* Summer 1976.)

- Concora Road along north side of White Sand Lake between old K and Nixon Lake Road, exceptional birch stands along White Sand; interesting drive on lip between highland and swamp east of there; 2.6 miles, old rail grade. If it looks unnervingly sandy as you enter, park and hike it, or bike it if you can handle biking in sand.

RECREATION

BIKING
- Try town roads, listed above, especially High-Fishtrap and Ridge.

BOAT AND CANOE RENTAL, TRIP SERVICE
- Reuben Schauss, in town next to the Catholic church, 385-2434. Canoes and camping equipment; pickup service. Also sailboats, pedal-boats.

CANOEING
- Boulder is hub of many canoe adventures; get a copy of DNR's Northern Highland Canoe Trails map, which indicates 100-plus canoe campsites (free camping, one-night limit) and suggested canoe routes. (Don't expect much white water.)

- High-Fishtrap-Boulder lakes to Highway K, 12 miles; can be lengthened by:

- Manitowish River, Highway K to Island Lake, Manitowish Waters (q.v.), eight miles, an ideal family trip one way with landings at both ends.

- Gresham lakes and Jag Lake to Manitowish River, 6.7 miles, two portages.

- White Sand-Lost Canoe-Pallette-Escanaba-Trout lakes via Stevenson Creek, several portages. Mileage varies according to route; trip may be lengthened by about 18 miles by following Trout River to the Manitowish chain.

- Round-Big-Island lakes via Rice Creek, 12 miles. See Manitowish Waters.

- Big Crooked Lake, all by itself, has two island campsites for canoeists.

HIKING AND NATURE TRAILS
- North Trout Lake Nature Trail, off Highway M. From sandy hillsides to wetlands via boardwalk is its range; interpretive signs for natural, historical items.

- DNR Highland snowmobile trail is open to hikers, Boulder-Sayner-Arbor Vitae.

PARKS, BEACHES, RECREATION AREAS
- Cathedral Point, beach and picnic area, DNR facility. See Sightseeing.

- North Trout Lake Beach, Highway M, a DNR facility, at the boat landing.

- Nichols Lake Picnic Area, off Highway H at junction with K. Beach, play area, picnic sites, and facilities. This is a DNR fee (sticker) area.

- Highways H and K wayside, picnicking, pump, toilets; river, old dam, rapids.

- Highway K wayside on White Sand Lake, informal beach; pump, toilets, tables.

- Chamber of commerce grounds, in town along M south; sports and play area.

SHOOTING
- Boulder Junction Gun Club, Five Lakes Road east of Highway M, trap.

SKATING
- A rink is usually provided in town. Local parents take turns as chaperones.

SKIING / CROSS COUNTRY: RENTAL
- Northern Highland Sports Shop, in town, 385-2134. Also a good shop for any sporting need; gifts and moccasins; pleasant service.

SKIING / CROSS COUNTRY: TRAILS
- Escanaba Lake Trails, Five Lakes Road, east of M. Three loops, 11.6 miles.

- Wildcat Lodge Trails, north on M at resort that provides them. 12.5 miles.

SNOWMOBILE RENTAL
- Jolin's Marine Center, Highway K, in town, 385-2295.

SNOWMOBILING
- The DNR grooms the Highland Trail, main street of western Vilas County snowmobiling; it goes to Sayner and Arbor Vitae.

- Locally the Boulder Junction Snowmobile Club does the area grooming. Maps.

TENNIS
- Chamber of commerce grounds, in town on Highway M south, two lighted courts.

- North Lakeland Elementary School grounds, Highway K at P.

SHOPPING AND BROWSING
- Arvilla's Antiques, in town, seasonal.

50/Vilas County

● The Bookworm, in town, May–October. Concentrated stock of regional, best-selling, gift, or children's books; gifts with northwoods themes; paperware.

● Cousin Willy, in town, all year (by chance in quiet months), sculpts wooden birds and small animals in his glassed-in workroom. Pieces are natural wood, stained, so shape and grain must collaborate to create their identity; priced from $5.

● In Stitches, in town, includes hand painted canvases among needle wares.

● Junction Country Store, in town, May–Christmas. Handcrafts and Christmas items in cute, old-time country store milieu.

● Ronbach Shop, in town, May–October. Charming smells and sights (rough-board decor, rugged floor); handcrafted home and gift items; decorations for Christmas.

● Uncle Dick's Workshop, in town, all year, by chance after busy season. Wildlife subjects in natural unpainted wood, sculpted to highlight the grain; a specialty is lamps.

DINING

● George's Steak House, in town; noons and evenings, closed Monday, all year, 385-2350. Very attractive dining room: knotty pine, plaid carpet. Full menu, a good salad bar, attentive preparation; roller-skating bartender!

● Headwaters Resort and Bar, north on M; nightly, closed off-season Tuesdays and Wednesdays, 385-2416. Tiny star lights once twinkled down on ballroom dancers from its dome; today diners enjoy tasty fish, other full meals, nice treatment.

LODGING

AMERICAN PLAN
- Forest Lodge, Highway B (Star Route, Land O' Lakes 54540), May–October. Large resort with cottages spread along lakeshore drives, hill crests; beach.

- Motel in the Woods, on K east near Star Lake, seasonal. Modified American plan; cottages in extremely attractive wooded lakeshore and brookside setting; neat beachfront; separate dock area; also lodge rooms with bath. A very nice lodge-cottage resort, not at all a motel in the roadside sense of the term. Beer.

- Resort of the Woods, on M north, May–October. Varied cottages hug lake bank or lie inland; many activities, beach. Modified American or housekeeping plans.

- Wildcat Lodge, on M north. Really two complexes, one American plan (May–October; 10 comfortable cottages in lake- or beach-view row) and the other housekeeping (all-year homes set nicely apart, two storied with circular stairs, carpet, fireplace, lots of glass). Many summer or winter activities. An admirable resort!

HOUSEKEEPING
- Birchwood Cove Resort, on B east (Star Route, Land O' Lakes 54540), May–October. Seven natural wood-finished cottages, carpeted; pretty site, beach.

- Copp's Cabins, Wild Rice Lake west of Highway 51 on Manitowish chain (Route 1, Woodruff 54568), May to freeze-up. Five carpeted cottages, natural wooded grounds, fine sand beach. This resort is a standout for professionalism: appliances and mattresses replaced on rigid schedule, a beach raked each daybreak, a standby electric generator, and *five* man-hours of cleaning at each turnover.

- Gasper's Cabins, on K west of river, all year. Six small homes with carpet, fireplace, TV, pine interiors, floor furnaces; two waterfronts, beach.

- Jung's Modern Cabins, on B east (Star Route, Land O' Lakes 54540), seasonal. Seven beachside cabins in rustic woods; new rec building; interested hosts.

- Resort of the Woods. See Lodging: American Plan.

- Shelter Bay Resort, Fishtrap Lake, May–October. 11 cottages varying in size and style, sand beach, hiking trails; delightful hosts who are grand to guests.

- Wildcat Lodge. See Lodging: American Plan.

- Wittig's Point Resort, on point of Fishtrap Lake and Manitowish River, May through hunting season. Eight cottages, always filled; beach, teen den, bar.

- Woody's Resort, Wild Rice Lake on Manitowish chain (Route 1, Woodruff 54568), May–October. Unusual value; seven cottages, partial carpeting; sandy beach.

MOTELS
- Jolin's Motel, Highway 51 south of Highway H (Route 1, Woodruff 54568), 385-2123. 12 units, beach.

- Northern Highland Motor Lodge, in town, 385-2150. 12 units, large and beautifully appointed and kept; fireplace lobby, air conditioning, sauna. Outstanding!

CAMPING

PRIVATE
- Birchwood Campground, off K west at river. 20 units.
- Camp Holiday, Highway H. Over 100 units.

STATE FOREST CAMPGROUNDS
- Big Lake, off K on P north. 73 units.
- North Trout Lake, on M south. 66 units.
- South Trout Lake, on M south. 24 units, no beach.
- Upper Gresham Lake, off H. 27 units.
- Primitive camping, Allequash, Day, Nebish, Wildcat lakes.

EVENTS

- Musky Jamboree, mid August, is one of the major events of a northwoods summer—in 1977 it drew between 5,000 and 6,000 people! Parade, outdoor musky bake, queen coronation, special sales, other festivities.
- Colorama, September, often with a game barbecue at noon, dinner at night.
- Winter Fun Day, late February. Sports; kids' contests, lunch.

INFORMATION AND TRANSPORTATION

- Boulder Junction Chamber of Commerce, P.O. Box 51, Boulder Junction 54512. Information booth at south edge of town on Highway M open daily Memorial–Labor days; Friday and Saturday to early October; all year telephone, 385-2400.
- Car rental: Boulder Junction Airport, 385-2293, May 1–October 1.
- Charter air service: Airport, 385-2293; seaplane service also available.

ST. GERMAIN

The story of St. Germain contains the usual northwoods elements of logging, farming, and hospitality, but here they have taken a couple of unusual turns.

The loggers, to be sure, came here just as they did everywhere else. The river-driving pine loggers had camps where the river from Big St. Germain Lake meets the Wisconsin, as early as 1883–85, using the lake and rivers to float away the pine; 25 years later an enterprising settler did very well salvaging the sunken logs out of the lake and sawing them on a portable mill. No common carrier railroad ever entered the township, but log spurs off the trunk line near Sayner reached into the woods at least around Lost Lake for timber.

The land that the loggers had denuded promised a golden age of farming, everyone thought, and pride in that prospect caused them to establish a separate town in 1907 and call it Farmington. The unusual twist: farming never amounted to much, and the town ended up changing its name (not with unanimous enthusiasm) around 1930 to that of its famous lakes.

Pioneer resorts like Red Oaks and Musky Inn (both circa 1904) were joined by others, all following the tried and true lodge-and-cottages format. The era right after

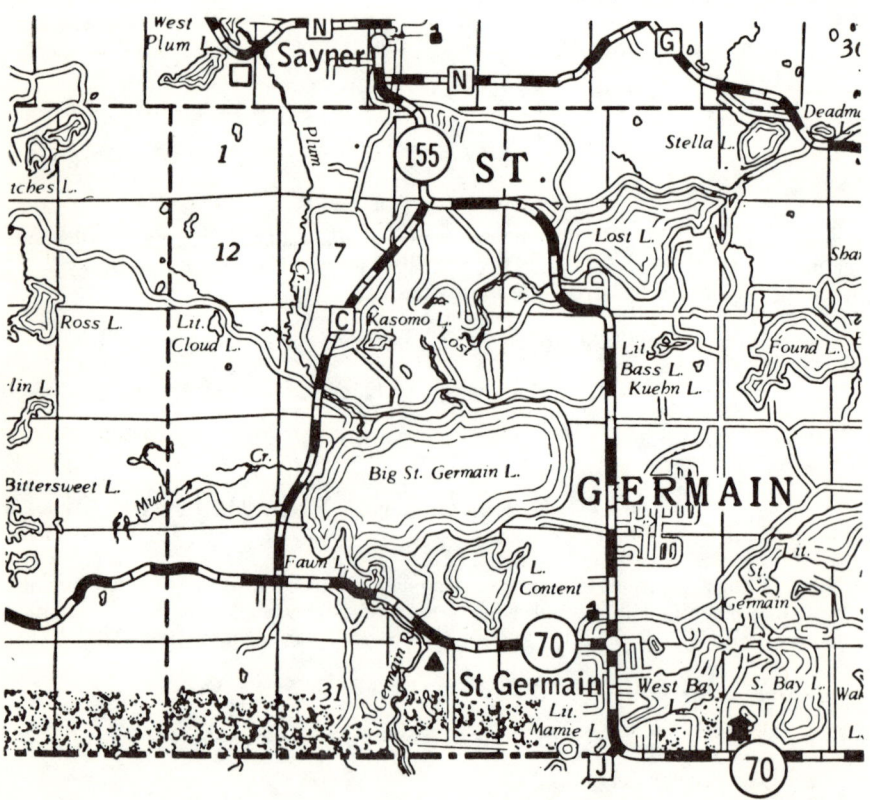

54/Vilas County

World War I realized a surge in resort building: more than one a year; housekeeping resorts first made an important impression at that time. Related businesses appeared too, like a machine shop and boat factory. In winters, because no one had yet found ways to plow roads, resorts went into hibernation.

St. Germain's second unusual twist is that when resorts and cottage colonies elsewhere began selling off into subdivided summer-home parcels, its resort business did not follow the trend. It now has the highest concentration of housekeeping resorts in either Vilas or Oneida county. Moreover, the fascination of winter sports has made St. Germain, even in that season, a vacation capital, for many of its best resorts stay open then.

Man's presence may line its lakes and roads, but the natural wonder of St. Germain's landscape still remains. You can find a fantastic belt of ridges and glacial kettles stretching from north of Big St. Germain Lake across Highway 155 and on toward Found Lake.

St. Germain has no concentrated village except for its main shopping area along Highway 70 between its junctions with Highway 155 and Highway J.

SIGHTSEEING AND TOURING

● The information booth grounds, in town at the 70-155 intersection, contain an all-year picnic shelter and facilities, a statue of the mythic Chief St. Germain, and a monument to an airport that never was! Weber Field was planned for this corner and the dedicatory plaque ordered. The field was never built but the marker that would have dedicated it is on the grounds.

● Highway 155 is more scenic than most state routes: rugged, with deep forests.

● Juve Road is a near tunnel of pine and hardwood green—or gold in autumn.

● Four Corner Lane, Juve Road to Highway G, is pretty with kettle hollows, gentle landscapes, a few old farm clearings, and varied woods.

● A circle using Found Lake Road, Four Corner Lane, and the North Lost Lake Road blends the attractive woods of the first, the variety of the second road, the upland views and forests of the Lost Lake drive; note the quaint stone house and grounds of the pioneer Forest Primeval resort.

● Big St. Germain Drive has the beauty of hardwoods, scenic Lost Creek, lake on one side, a ridge hugging the other.

● The Plum Creek Fishing Grounds road, west from Highway C, signed as Plum Creek Avenue, splits. Left is a fork to Plum Creek, an unsung beauty spot. Drive no farther than the creek culvert and park carefully in the sand, but be sure to hike a few hundred feet on down the road to sense the scene—not just see the firclad river bottom or little creek but smell its fragrance, feel its coolness, touch its moss, dip into its waters. The other fork of the road skirts the top of the creek valley.

RECREATION

BIKING
● Shields Road north from 70, dead end, gentle hills, lake views.

● Lost Lake circle, above.

- Big St. Germain Lake circle of Highways C, 70, 155, and Big St. Germain Drive.

- Little St. Germain loop of 70, 155, and rolling, lake-touching Birchwood Drive.

CANOEING
- Lost Creek.

- St. Germain River, between Big St. Germain and Pickerel lakes; easy round trip.

- Wisconsin River between Otter Rapids near Eagle River or similar accesses on Highway 70, and landings near St. Germain.

- Trips out of Dave's Landing on Highway J; see below.

CANOE RENTAL AND TRIP SERVICE
- Dave's Landing, Highway J, 479-8350, rentals; pick-up service can be arranged for an eight-mile, three-hour trip down to the Wisconsin.

- Hawk's Nest Bait and Tackle Shop, Highway C, 542-3421. Drop-off, pick-up and shuttle service; guided shore lunch trips (including Wisconsin River).

HIKING
- Four trails, color marked, near Lost Creek, Stella, Found, and Bass lakes. Attractive, helpful map-folder available. Some use these as cross-country ski trails.

SKIING: CROSS COUNTRY
- Hiking trails, above.

- Resorts with trails are Musky Inn, Pride o-th' North, Eagle Crest, Lofty Pines.

SNOWMOBILING
- Bo-Boen Tribe groomers keep 100 miles of trail in shape with huge, costly groomer tractors, run nightly if necessary. Its trails are among the north's best.

STABLES
- Elmer's Saddle Horses, on 70 east.

- Ride-A-Long Ranch, Birchwood Drive.

- Tepee Trails, on 70 east.

TENNIS
- School grounds, in town.

SHOPPING AND BROWSING

- Red Apple, on 70 east, seasonal, closed weekends. Antiques, gifts.

- Stonehouse Antiques, northeast end of Lost Lake, seasonal or by chance. Primitives, general items in grand old stone house on charming rail-fenced grounds.

DINING

- Blink Bonnie Supper Club, on 70 west; nightly, all year, 542-3678. Pleasant ambience (tartan carpet, Franklin fireplace, knotty pine), fine attention, delicious sirloin tip meal made my visit a delight. Cocktails. Woods animals can be seen coming for handouts.

- Eliason's Someplace Else, in town; evenings, closed Monday after Labor Day, all year, no reservations. Very popular for constant quality; full menu, specials, cocktails.

- Molgaard's Indian Lodge, on 70 east; nightly but Monday, May–late October, no reservations. Two log dining rooms (the smaller is nicer); spotless kitchen; full menu; cocktails. My dining here spans 25 years; I've always been pleased.

- Musky Inn, just west of 155; nightly in summer, variably rest of year, 542-3768. Mellow dining room of time-patinaed wood dates from 1904–6; here, despite a quiet fall evening, I found warm service; full, fresh salad bar; a hearty serving of tasty veal. Cocktails. Also American plan lodging in 11 carpeted units, some with fireplace, mini refrigerator, year round; also some housekeeping. Lake sports, beach. Cross-country ski trails.

- Spang's Italian Restaurant, on 70 east; nightly in summer, Thursday–Sunday in early fall, then weekends only, no reservations. Novel milieu: old church pews form booths around central fireplace; very good pizza. Cocktails. Lots of fun!

LODGING

AMERICAN PLAN
- Musky Inn. See Dining.

HOUSEKEEPING
- Connors Lingering Pines Resort, Found Lake Road, all year. Six newly remodeled cottages beneath big pines along clear sand beach. Very nice. Bar.

- Cox's Estrold Resort, off Halberstadt Road, all year. 10 northwoodsy-appointed cottages, fireplaces, varying lake orientation, style; beach, tennis.

- Hiller's Pine Haven, off 70 in town, all year. 11 homey log cottages in a lakeshore row; carpeted, nicely updated, paneled. Sandy beach; personable hosts.

- Lehor's Twin Cabins, Found Lake Road, all year. Eight uniform, clean cabins in a row facing beach. Making this special is its thoughtful host couple. Bar.

- Lofty Pines Resort, Big St. Germain Drive, all year. Something different: 11 units—single cottages, duplexes, main building with complete, private-entry apartments, all appealing and tastefully appointed; several fireplaces. Good beach.

- Perveiler's Dor-Way Resort, Lost Lake Road north, all year. 11 half-log cottages and a duplex; unusually picturesque hillside, long sandy shore. Decor and appointments vary but nice details occur, like upper galleries and catwalks in some units! A resort with character. Cozy bar.

- Pride o-th' North Resort, Birchwood Drive, all year. A leading resort exhibiting professionalism, foresight, careful maintenance in the form of 11 nicely appointed cottages and probably the area's fullest all-season activities program, from a seesaw in the lake to ski trails in the woods; sandy beach.

- Smith's Birch Lane Resort, off 70 in town, May–October. Six cottages, most facing the sandy shore, varied in style and appointments; neatly groomed complex.

- Twin Waters Resort, Big St. Germain Drive at the creek (which is the second water of the title), all year. Six cottages, lovely setting (ducks were on the lake just in front as I stood on the sand beach); some units in pine, with fireplace.

- Worthen's Murmuring Waters, Lost Lake Road south, all year. 13 cottages in tall pines facing clear, sandy shore of Lost Lake; nicely carpeted and appointed. Bar.

MOTELS

- Holiday Court Motel, on 70 in town at the curve, 479-8770, all year. 10 units.

- Rustic Manor Motor Lodge, on 70 east, 479-9776, all year. 20 fine units.

CAMPING

- Eagle Crest Campground, Juve Road, all year. 70 units.

- Lofty Pines RV Park, Big St. Germain Drive, all year. 35 units.

- Lynn Ann's Campground, Normandy Court Road, May–October. 90 units.

EVENTS

- Independence Day, sometimes a week or more in advance of July 4.

- Colorama, late September.

- Snow Skoal, usually in late February, snowmobile events.

INFORMATION

- St. Germain Chamber of Commerce, St. Germain 54558. Information booth at Highways 70 and 155 open weekends all year, daily in peak periods, 542-3423.

• Marked logging-camp sites, another Star Lakers Club courtesy, dot the roads of the area like K and Camp 2 Road.

• Ballard-Partridge lakes portage, recleared in 1977, follows the original Indian portage. Tourists of the preroad resort years from 1895 left their train at the Ballard end of the portage and boarded boats for the resorts on Ballard Lake's other shores.

• Star Lake Forestry Plantation, off K in town (along Nature Trail). In 1913 the first 68,000 pine seedlings from the state's new nursery were ready for planting and the trees were divided between cutover land here and a site near Trout Lake. Experiments here were Wisconsin's first ventures in scientific silviculture, and some studies being conducted here (such as investigations of the results of thinning) will not be concluded till the year 2013! Signs along the Nature Trail explain some of the experiments.

• The Nature Trail, same site, is one of the state DNR's outstanding contributions to its public. The trail is beautiful, winding through deep pine groves, dense hardwoods, and bogs so soft they demand boardwalks, and skirting the lakeshore on an ice ridge. Thirty educational signs interpret the vegetation and even the glacial history. If you have not taken this trail, you really don't know what you could about your northwoods!

• Star Lake Hemlocks and DNR Rearing Pond. Follow either White Birch or North Star Lake roads from K, and then take Rearing Pond Road southward. At a T where unfortunately all signs read Rearing Pond Road, take the *southeasterly* leg. Your reward will be a drive through the most sublime, deep forest grove I have discovered in Vilas County; continue through these hemlock ridges, past the rearing pond (temporary home to nurseling fish in early summer), to the lake; walk to the hemlock grove on the point, whose dense canopy has starved out all undergrowth. The lake here is Star Lake, and part of the forest here is a state scientific preserve.

• Partridge Lake Wilderness. See Lost Region.

• Highway K is the scenic backbone of the Star Lake area, richest in beauty just east of its junction with Highway N; hardwoods here are among heaviest in the county, and fall color among the most glowing in the region.

• Camp 2 Road reaches a remarkably scenic boat landing complex at Ballard and Irving lakes; both the road and a lily-padded stream tie the lakes together.

• White Birch Road links with North Star Lake Road; leaving K it meets, in order, Razorback, Rearing Pond, and North Star Lake roads; varied but scenic hardwoods, conifers, lowlands, and a lake or two.

• Lake Laura Road is rugged, rolling, wooded, and little developed.

• East Lake Laura (Deerfoot) Road leads to unusually scenic boat landing.

• Old Star Lake Road cuts southeast from Highway K east, connecting with Dad's Lake Road (pretty chiefly near Dad's Lake and exiting on Highway G) or finally emerging at Boot Lake; on its way it plays tag with log railroad grades and pretty wetlands and less pretty burn areas with seventy-year-old stumps.

• The Star Lake area is so scenic that if one were able to spend time in only one sightseeing effort, I would probably point him to that remarkable region!

SAYNER AREA
• Sayner village. A good point to begin, even on foot or on a bike, is the town dock, passing from an active waterfront and some interesting little businesses (would you believe, a pool hall with a name in German?) to the post office. The post office bulletin board is a little landmark in itself, bearing everything from an Avon Lady's ad to a paper plate with a scribbled plug for the next Sayner Saynts baseball game.
   You can see those Saynts (they're girls) at the next corner, of a Wednesday evening, perhaps, or go on past the unfenced, carefully mowed cemetery whose names are a roll of local giants like Gabe, Froelich, or Rismon. What looks to be a mausoleum across the street isn't one at all; it's the town hall, and the Plum Lake township library is downstairs. The main street, left at the corner, has all the typical village businesses and a brown building with an old boat. The boat? It's the old 1890s launch used from 1904 onward, by the first boys' camp on Plum Lake. The building? It's the...

   • Vilas County Historical Museum, open daily in summer, free (donation). It began with the lifetime collection of the late Mable Sayner DeWitt but has grown to include home antiques, fashions, rarities like a complete carriage, a small post office, and its treasure: the small sled with the track, radiator, and outboard motor that is the world's first practical snowmobile! (It was built in Sayner.)

   • Historical marker on museum grounds commemorates Carl Eliason and the first snowmobile.

   • Muskellunge Hill, 1,860 feet, highest point in Vilas County; fire tower (ladder type); limited views from tower base. Gravelly hill may be a glacial kame and served as a ski hill in the 1950s–60s. About two miles west of town on N, then south at unmarked, unpaved crossroad to gate; driving is poor within; walk in. (The unmarked road to the gate road is Plum Vitae Road, connection to Witches Lake Road; see Arbor Vitae.)

- Fallison Lake Nature Trail, on N west, near Crystal-Muskellunge camping area. Two-mile trail, keyed to interpretive booklet available nearby; common things like tree types and rarities like bog evolution, formation of hummocks.

- Razorback Road, scenic road north from N west of Plum Lake.

- Aurora Lake Scientific Area, a rice lake-marsh at end of lovely sand lane off Razorback Road; lane is a leafy tunnel, marsh vista is sweeping and novel.

- Frank Lake boat landing road, off Muskellunge Lake Road, condenses more uncommon terrain into a half mile than any other road I know: sandy flat scrub woods, bogs, a low ridge, a high esker-type rise with deep kettles, and finally Frank Lake itself, an undeveloped, very northerly looking lake. A new DNR wild area will include this lake and all the area between Razorback Road and Highway M, to be called the Frank Lake Wild Area. This little road will be retained; it deserves a visit.

- East from Sayner, Highway N to Star Lake crosses high ridge-deep kettle area and twists between wet or dry marshes.

- Weber's Wildlife Farm, Highway 155 at C, May–October. Pettable and caged animals, wild or domestic, in a little compound; modest admission charge.

RECREATION

BOAT AND CANOE RENTAL

- Ellerman's, on K west, Star Lake, 542-3700, boats at landings on area lakes. Laurence Ellerman is a fishing guide, and if there is any gentleman in guiding whose company is a privilege for a day outdoors, it is Mr. Ellerman. Bait.

- Fredricksons' Minnow Stand, Star Lake townsite, 542-3788. The Fredricksons are Star Lake natives and pioneers—as Mr. Ellerman is (above)—charming sisters worth meeting even if you don't buy minnows or rent a boat. People like these are part of the magic of Star Lake.

- Jim's Shell Service, Sayner, in town, 542-3465.

- W Sport Shop, on N west, Sayner, 542-3800.

CANOEING

- Small lakes galore, like Frank, Starrett, the Five Lakes, Firefly, and its neighbors. No canoe streams in the area.

GOLF

- Plum Lake Golf Course, Sayner, east from town hall; nine holes, daily fee.

HIKING
- East Star Lake Campground Trail to Star Lake village, one mile.
- Fallison Lake Nature Trail. See Sightseeing and Touring, Sayner, above.
- Highland Trail, DNR snowmobile trail just west of downtown Sayner.
- Star Lake Hiking Trail, adjacent to Star Lake Nature Trail, extends to point.
- Star Lake Nature Trail. See Sightseeing and Touring, Star Lake.
- Trampers Trails, extensive series of walking trails lacing the Star Lake area and frequently updated and extended; three trails were added or rebuilt in 1977, for instance. Get detailed map in Star Lake or at chamber of commerce.

PARKS, BEACHES, RECREATION AREAS
- Crystal Lake Picnic Area (DNR fee area, sticker required); magnificent beach.
- Plum Lake County Park on lake at Highway N, small picnic park only.

SCUBA
- Crystal Lake is uniquely clear for diving.

SHOOTING
- Target range west toward snowmobile trail, Sayner.

SKIING / CROSS COUNTRY
- Escanaba Lake Trail. See Boulder Junction.

SNOWMOBILING
- Highland Trail (DNR) to Boulder and Arbor Vitae, access from downtown Sayner.
- Sayner Barnstormers, local organization, even has a snowmobile ambulance!

WATER SKI SHOWS
- Plum Ski-Ters, 7 p.m. Sunday, Tuesday, Thursday, Sayner dock, on Plum Lake.

SHOPPING AND BROWSING

- Hartshorne Sport and Gift Shop, in town, Sayner, May–October. Woolens (Pendletons), moccasins, some local Indian crafts, gifts.

• Pop and Ole Dean's Gift Shop, on 155 south, May–October. Tiny shop with the fruits of a busy couple! The Deans handcraft a host of things from deerskin apparel and mythical "shilldillies" to soap and preserves and jewelry, but half the fun of dropping in here is just making friends with the charming, lighthearted Deans. Pop also smokes fish and game for fishermen and hunters. MMMMmmmmmm!

DINING

• Bill and Holly's, on K west in Star Lake; evenings, all seasons, phone for days and times: 542-3652. If Hansel and Gretel had an inn, this would be it! Tiny, slightly Tyrolean dining room, dim bar. Salad bar, full menu. The two of us had a divided verdict on the meal and service; I enjoyed my whitefish amandine.

• Froelich's Sayner Lodge, just northeast of Sayner business district; May–October, reservations are vital: 542-3261 or 542-3993. Gracious dining in the gentility of crystal and full linen, in carpeted, lofty dining room; sophisticated menu with some surprises like sweetbreads and ham. Cocktails. Not inexpensive.

• Idle Forest Inn, in town, Sayner; closed Monday, all year, 542-3939. Unusually decorated small dining room with individually lamplit oil paintings or carved wood panels (depicting holidays), tables and benches, carpet, air conditioning. Home-cooked food like tasty liver and onions or creole haddock; cocktails. Idle Forest may be Vilas County's best-kept dining secret—and was mine, till now!

• Lost Lake Resort, Highway 155 south of Sayner; nightly, seasonal, 542-3221. Full menu; unusual, colorful dining room built around live pines! Cocktails.

LODGING

• Char Rose Motel, on N west, Sayner, all year, 542-3614. Seven very nice units.

• Froelich's Sayner Lodge, Sayner, in town, late April–October. Full American plan. Deserves its many laurels. Lovely grounds, gardens; cottages carefully appointed with lamps, accents; many activities like tennis, sun deck, beach. Guest dining is apart from, less lavish than, public dining. Bar, entertainment.

• Lost Lake Resort (Gabe's), on 155 south of Sayner, seasonal. Modified American plan. 31 units, motel type to cottages. Tall pine-shaded grounds, tennis; bar.

• Silver Muskie Resort, North Star Lake Road, May–October. Housekeeping. Very accommodating hosts with eight clean cottages. Beaches vary.

• Tall Timbers Resort, on N east of Sayner, May toward October. Housekeeping. Seven hilltop or lower-level cottages in knotty pine finish; sun deck, good beach, lift on hill. A good resort reflecting nice owner attitudes.

• Wah-Wah-Taysee Resort, in town, Sayner, into September. Housekeeping. Nine cottages, nicely appointed, attractive, in a tight, very well-planned and maintained grounds-and-beach complex; good beach; location near lots of activity.

CAMPING: STATE FOREST CAMPGROUNDS

- Crystal-Muskellunge, on N west. Almost 200 units.
- East Star Lake, on N east. 43 units.
- Firefly Lake, on N west, all year. 70 units.
- Plum Lake, on N west. 18 units.
- Razorback Lake, Razorback Road off N west. 56 sites.
- Starrett Lake, off Muskellunge Lake Road via Razorback. 43 units.
- West Star Lake, off K at townsite. 18 units.

EVENTS

- Fire Department Carnival, July, Sayner; games, chicken cookout, dance.
- Colorama, early fall, Sayner.
- Chicken cooking is a specialty in Sayner; the park has a big barbecue pit and tables. So if an event comes up with chicken involved, you can be sure it's good!

INFORMATION

- Sayner-Star Lake Chamber of Commerce, Sayner 54560. Information booth, in the historical museum, open June into September, daily in summer, 542-3789.
- ZIP code of Starlake (the postal service spells it as one word, the public as two): 54561.
- Library: Plum Lake Woman's Club Library (public), town hall basement, Sayner.

THE LOST REGION

Occupying a vary large area in the towns of Boulder Junction, Plum Lake, Conover, and Land O' Lakes in the rectangle bounded by Highways K, S, B, and M is a region with remarkably little development. It is as many as twelve miles wide and nine miles north to south (equal almost to three townships). Here a person can drive half an hour or more and see not a utility pole or more than a tiny, isolated house or two.

The area was logged, much of it, remarkably early, during the 1894–1906 activities of the Williams and Salsich (later Salsich and Wilson) lumber firm, which had the mill at Star Lake and had logging tracks almost up to the site of present-day Highway B. Evidence of logging grades is still visible on the landscape and in names such as Siphon Creek and Springs, where logging engines must have stopped to suck up water for their boilers; old plat books before 1910 also map the rail lines. Other firms logged fringes of the area, too, such as Brooks and Ross around Boulder.

In the 1920s the A. H. Stange lumber firm of Merrill moved into the area with its new network of logging railroads, some probably relaid on the old pre-1906 rights-of-way; till the mid 1930s it stayed busy as far north as Palmer Lake; at its behest the mighty Milwaukee Road ran its big engines all the way up to Indian Lake to pick up trains of logs that Stange's little engines put together for movement over the Milwaukee to Merrill. Indian Lake, incidentally, was the brief setting for the Potawatomi settlement that had moved north from the Star Lake area and eventually returned thither.

In 1937 the county built a new Highway B, relegating the old B to use as a gravel town road, and the region saw even less traffic along its northern edge, only sportsmen, pulp haulers, and a rare sightseer now and then.

In the mid 1970s the state, which owns much of this land, proposed a program to ensure preservation of part of it in a wild state, using a set of designations for different degrees of strictness in preservation, like "natural areas," "wild areas," and "wilderness areas." Many streams and spring ponds here may fall under the first two categories, and no new management or development is likely among them. The "wilderness" designation

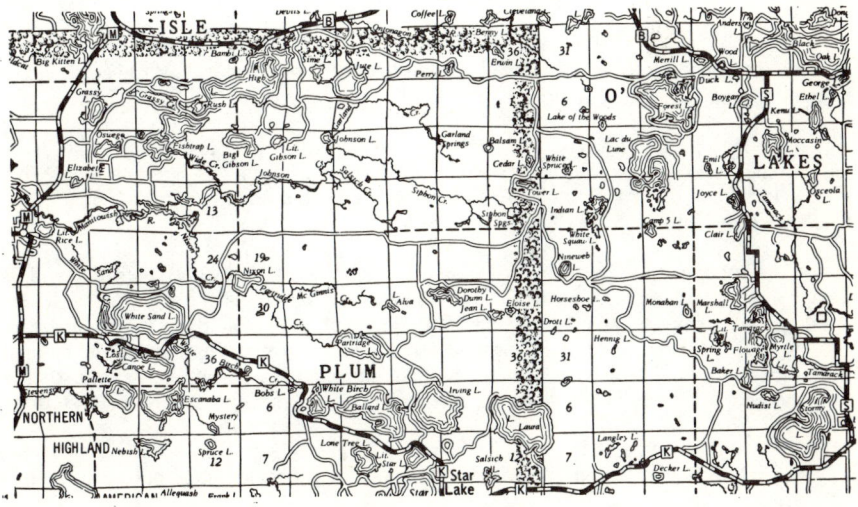

Lost Region/67

is proposed for a large area focusing upon Partridge Lake; under this plan even existing development would be abandoned to allow the land to follow its own course in freely reverting to the wild.

Not only did loggers scar the region; huge burns did too. As a result, much of it is not just in second-growth timber but is second rate from a scenic point of view. And yet because it's there, and so vast, this lost region has a certain appeal to some visitors, as it has to me. For want of a formal name for it, that is just what I dubbed it—the Lost Region—for purposes of this chapter.

SIGHTSEEING AND TOURING

• Nixon Lake Road is the main artery through this central wilderness, beginning at Highway K and White Sand Lake. Its first intersection is that with Concora Road, which is mile zero for this chapter; Concora is a former rail grade, and within 500 feet of the intersection are three spurs that once ran off the Concora grade. Next come a major creek and marsh—Nixon Creek, used as a canoe route out from Nixon Lake to the Manitowish River system. Then come a rolling jackpine area, rolling scrub woods, clear-cuts around mile 2 or mile 3, and a big burn area revealing very clearly the terrain and—to the south—a rail grade. Cuts and fills are one guarantee of a rail grade; another is "swede holes," hand-shoveled pits in lieu of ditches along the track, dug for fill but easier to dig than continuous ditches.

At mile 4.1 the road drops into a phenomenon that I have not seen duplicated anywhere else on my northwoods travels. It resembles a deep dry river valley, except that it lacks a stream or evidence of any past stream that could have worn such a channel. My guess: a glacial spillway, for it meets all the textbook characteristics. At once the road remounts the high ridge on the other side.

At mile 5 Nixon intersects Camp 2 Road; forests here are poor second-growth popple with openings and clear-cuts, with a short stretch of beauty at mile 7.3. Nixon Road ends at mile 8, the main intersection of the central no-man's-land. The land from here east and north becomes much prettier; it is higher, covered more with hardwoods, and is more uneven with ridges and hollows, for this is the beginning of end moraine that stretches east to the Wisconsin River or Highway 45. There are four possible exits from this intersection.

• Tower Lake Road goes directly north to old B (which exits east toward Land O' Lakes), through gradually improving forest scenery and past pretty Tower Lake.

• Nineweb Road loops southeast amid rolling scrub popples, and at mile 2.7 to mile 3 meets two successive roads from the left (north) within a few hundred feet, White Squaw Road and Clair Fire Lane. At this point Nineweb takes a new name, Baker Lake Road, at Fire Number 5173.

• Abandoned logging-camp site, on the north side of Nineweb/Baker road and the west corner of its intersection with Clair Fire Lane. Visible is the banking of several buildings; old camps had banking of earth around the buildings (held in place by boards or logs at a level that made the banking into a handy bench for sitting outside the camps). When the log camps rotted or burned, the banking remained to outline the ghost structures; several are here. The land survey marker gives the elevation as 1,806 feet, remarkably high.

• White Squaw Road is not pretty because of much logging, but somewhere it

to the shores of Lake Laura. They moved on to what is now known as Indian Lake, preferring a degree of isolation there to the encroachments of the loggers' culture nearer town. Accounts report that disease hit them hard at the new site, and the survivors moved closer to town in the early 1900s.

One of the remarkable things that characterizes modern Star Lake is the spirit in the community, far larger than its permanent population of 60 or its hundred summer families. The spirit is not new; in 1933, for instance, an outing club gathered to cut hiking trails throughout the area for everyone to enjoy. Today's symbol of that spirit is the Star Lakers Club, and nearly anything that a modern tourist enjoys has the brand of the club on it, for it has created historic sites, marked others, and restored and expanded the hiking trails of the 1930s.

Sayner, in contrast, did not undergo a boom-bust mill town cycle, though it never reached the 500 or 600 population figures that Star Lake might have claimed, either. Instead it has had a slow, steady growth as residential village, marketing community, and hospitality center. It served as a logging center but the logs within reach of Sayner were hauled to their distant mills by Merrill and Tomah lumber companies, which pushed tracks into woods on both sides of town. Their rights-of-way can still be seen on both sides of Lost Lake, and even the bridge piers of a log track are still visible in orderly rows across Plum Lake near Highway N... a ghost track for over sixty years.

Sayner's resort era has had considerable glamour, to which resorts like Sayner Lodge (now Froelich's) and Lost Lake Resort (Gabe's) contributed. It was Orrin W. Sayner who started it all by laying the groundwork for Sayner Lodge even before the railroad came through in 1894 and took his name for its nearby station stop.

A little hotel accommodated drummers or humble travelers, but the elegant guests went to the lodges, another of which was Warner's; it was Warner's donation of land that helped get Sayner its golf course by the mid 'teens.

The state paved the way for far-reaching effects in Town of Plum Lake in 1911 when it began its forestry program nearby. In 1913 it transplanted its first trees near Star Lake. These efforts helped spawn today's Northern Highland State Forest and the recreational facilities and programs that bring many of Star Lake's and Sayner's visitors.

So did a Sayner resident named Eliason, when in 1924 he perfected the snowmobile, which has now turned his northwoods from snowy prison to winter playground.

SIGHTSEEING AND TOURING

STAR LAKE AREA

• Star Lake townsite. Begin at the big, carved wood signboard on Highway K, opposite the store. It shows all lakes and original camps and settlements. Where the sign is now stood the original cruisers' camp. All around it, on the land still clear, stood the 80-odd houses of the 1895 village; only one survives, across the road and a couple hundred feet eastward. (The hotel is hidden by woods over the hill.)

The mill stood on the low shore, and right on the shore was the railroad yard. That yard till 1944 was the terminus of the northwoods edition of the Milwaukee Road's famous Hiawathas.

• The old cemetery, east on K, is one of the loveliest anywhere, a carefully mowed, rounded, and pine-shaded hillside that in a less peaceful time was potter's field to many nameless loggers. The Star Lakers have marked all detectable graves with new cedar or pine crosses and carved the names of all persons definitely buried there on a marker-sign. One of those was Harry Starr, a pile driver for the mill company who died on the job; it is the name of Harry Starr, and that of his surveyor-brother, Bob, that Star Lake bears.

60/Vilas County

STAR LAKE AND SAYNER

The Town of Plum Lake is the only jurisdiction in Vilas County to have two separate communities and post offices, two countrysides that are surprisingly dissimilar. The Star Lake area, with a tiny town center and light sprinkling of residents, occupies a rugged area dressed mostly in hardwood forests.

The Sayner area has a little village cut into city blocks with named streets, and its countryside, typified by Highway N a bit east or quite a distance west, is more gentle and wears more popple.

If their appearances differ, so do their histories.

Star Lake grew in one burst, as a major sawmilling center in 1895. In 1894 a vanguard of timber cruisers and builders had put up a log-cabin camp and the first train had threaded its way gingerly up a brand new railway that December 6.

The mill company rushed to complete about 85 houses for the employees who rode a special train to the town in August 1895. The houses, laid out in rows along the hill of the townsite, aged paintlessly for the company knew it would not need them long—and the end came after July 20, 1906, the day the sawmill cut the last logs that the Salsich and Wilson lands and logging train network would give up. What houses the remnant population did not need were torn down by 1911, leaving the open field seen today along Highway K.

The Waldheim Hotel, which had boarded mill company folks from owners down to clerk, also accommodated tourists. Their growing number inspired new lodges, like Ferncroft in 1899 and Rismon's in 1924, and later came the cottage colonies.

Star Lake has had a tiny Indian satellite at times, some Potawatomis who had come

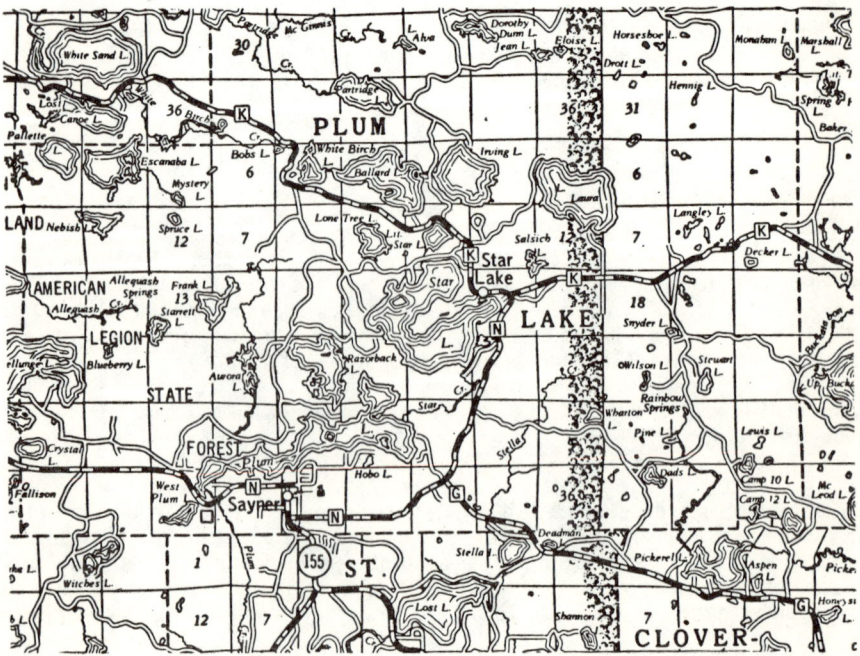

quietly adopts a new name, Indian Lake Road, and a new nature: great beauty! Hugging the hills above the lake, the road uses the old rail grade, and the wide curve at the boat landing was the yard where the logging trains turned over their logs to the Milwaukee Road; in the best of woods, north a bit, the grade takes off northeastward. The road follows an independent but scenic course to join Tower Lake Road in a set of openings that still betray old grades.

• Clair Fire Lane is one long leafy tunnel; the fills on which it rides betray its first life as a rail grade too. Note a cabin built of ties along it. Exit on County Highway S; the lake here was used by the lumber company as a log pond. The ride is especially pretty; it may include patches of sand; just roll steadily through.

• Baker Lake Road is lonely and tortuous but the reward is forest variety and a natural spectacular at mile 2.5; here the road rides a very high ridge with precipitous drops to low kettles or hollows on each side, an esker or its glacial ice-born twin. The road exits onto paved Stormy Lake Road at mile 6.3.

• Old County Highway B is the north edge of this large central area. It was replaced by a new route in 1937 that passed closer to population centers like the Cisco chain of lakes. Both its forests and its terrain make old B very pretty—often a leafy tunnel with the sky completely shaded out—between High Lake at its west end and Forest Lake at its east, but the segment west of Tower Lake Road sees neither heavy use nor frequent maintenance, and its surface makes it tedious to drive.

• State protective designations are proposed for Garland, Salsich, and Siphon springs and creeks. There is no easy access to them.

• The proposed Partridge Lake Wilderness would embrace 11,690 acres bounded by Nixon and Nineweb roads and Highway K, except for the south sides of White Birch, Ballard, Irving, and Laura lakes. Even if all its roads are closed, visitors will still be welcome to hike its woods and walk the old roadways as they grow over!

• Camp 2 Road may be closed to enhance wilderness reversion processes in the Partridge Lake Wilderness if plans become fact. As long as it remains open it links Nixon Lake Road with development on Partridge, Irving, and Ballard lakes (beyond which it is needed for home access and less subject to closure). Between Nixon Lake Road and Partridge Lake are a marked logging-campsite and some fir woods so deep that one might expect to see elves peeking between the trees. Walk or drive east one-third mile on the Jean Lake Road to see a remarkable forest-type line, where firs gave way to popples in the space of ten feet! (Jean and Dorothy Dunn lakes roads will close if the wilderness materializes.)

RECREATION

CANOEING
• Ballard, Partridge, and Nixon lakes have one canoe campsite each and can be linked in a route with a portage between Ballard and Partridge and partial portaging along the creek between Partridge and Nixon if the water is too low.

EAGLE RIVER

The Eagle River area is a center not just of county government or of population but of vacation and recreational activity. Greater Eagle River consists of the city and the three civil towns that encircle it: Cloverland, Lincoln, and Washington. The city proper has been the county seat ever since Vilas County was created in 1893. Earlier the area had been part of the counties of Marathon, till 1874, Lincoln, to 1885, and Oneida or Forest. At its formation the county took the name of William Freeman Vilas, longtime University of Wisconsin luminary and cabinet member in Grover Cleveland's two administrations.

Traders like Dan Gagen and farmer-loggers like Joshua Fox were the first settlers in the area, in the mid 1850s and 1860s. Here they found a potential for trading, but more than that, a treasure in pine timber and the streams down which to drive it to midstate mills. The first logging is consistently reported to have been done in 1856, but the long time needed for driving logs down to mills—two seasons—eventually resulted in moving much of the sawmilling upriver to Rhinelander.

The loggers of a century ago put in a log-driving dam on the Wisconsin at Otter Rapids; organized logging and logging camps were common by then. In 1883 a village was born as eager settlers hiked up the raw, unfinished right-of-way of the Milwaukee, Lake Shore & Western railroad, ahead of track-laying crews. A tent city at the Eagle River popped up overnight, followed by shanties and within one year more solid homes, stores, and hotels.

Early Eagle River was a bustling town of loggers, settlers, and merchants. Streets were alternately muddy or dusty, and few trees shaded them or the bare yards, whose little fences kept children in and wandering pigs and chickens out.

The glow faded after the river-driven logs were gone, though modest revivals came in the 'teens and twenties. Vacationists who had begun coming to crude resorts in the

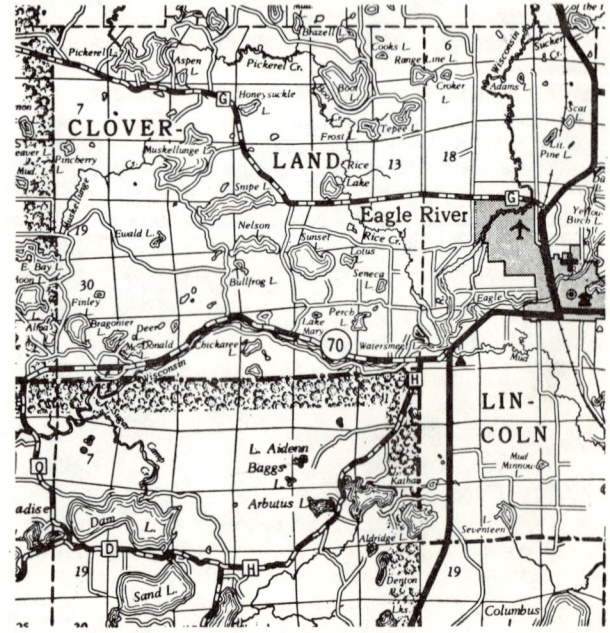

being, and recreation, but the big dividend for most visitors is its beauty and its fun.

• Franklin Lake Interpretive Trail, end of Forest Road 2181, stands out even among all the other magic of the Nicolet. One-mile trail; suggested hour's walking time could be doubled to savor the creek, little bridges, Avenue of Giants (unbelievably tall white pines), Hemlock Cathedral, and Butternut Lake shore. Interpretive signs cover topics like meander corners; little glass boxes identify soil types, cone types; tree identification wheel. Exceptional attraction, delighting 10,000 visitors a year.

• Adjacent Franklin Lake campground has more than passing interest, too. CCC workers between 1934 and 1937 built the buildings, many out of prize logs cut for a display at the Century of Progress in Chicago but not shipped in time.

• Programs have been held at Franklin Lake and Anvil Lake campgrounds, but year-to-year continuation depends on funding. In the past these have included guided nature walks, bog tours, and "critter hunts" for kids.

• Black Jack Springs area, between roads 2178 and 2199 south of their intersection. Access only on foot, preferably with a guide; no trails, and likely to remain that way. Four spring ponds, little bubbling wells, small streams, all surrounded by deep bosky forest. Proposed for wilderness area status (5,975 acres).

• Road 2178 south from here gradually waxes scenic between the Deerskin River and 70; northwest it is less pretty, and 2199 toward Eagle River is duller still.

• Scenic loop of Highway 70 and 2176, 2179, 2425, 2181, and 2178. Road 2176 was engineered for scenery, like forests, not homes, lakes like Quartz with its mini park, the seeded trails of Kimball Creek's hunting area, and logging grades and openings. Road 2179 ties together a leafy tunnel and Butternut Lake; 2181 (east to Franklin Lake, west to 2178) waxes more scenic and densely shaded as it works west. Road 2178 bumps south to Three Lakes or north to 70 in shady grandeur. 16-mile loop.

• There is no end of pretty roads in the forest; these are just a few highlights.

RECREATION

BIKING
• Nicolet Bikeway links Phelps, eastern Eagle River area, and Three Lakes in a 70-mile, mostly paved loop planned by experienced bikers. Map is necessary since signing is limited (by law) to nontrunk roads; get one locally. Many opportunities to relax in scenic spots, picnic, even sneak an impromptu dip.

BOAT AND CANOE RENTAL
• Boat S'Port, on 70 east at Thoroughfare, 479-8000.

• Holiday Harbor, Chain O'Lakes Road, 479-4250.

• Tomlinson Auto and Marine, on the Eagle River in town, west of 45, 479-4471.

• Warner Marine, on 70 east at Thoroughfare, 479-4834.

BOAT TRIPS
- Crystal Springs Boat Rides, River Street east of 45 north, in town. Scheduled two-hour pontoon boat cruises; morning, afternoon, summer; afternoon only, September.

CANOEING
- Deerskin River, putting in at Highway A, or in the Nicolet. Clear, cold, sometimes deep and quick wilderness stream, now managed for trout; no rapids.

- Wisconsin River, downstream from Conover or Land O' Lakes (qq.v.), or toward St. Germain and Rainbow areas, from Otter Rapids or Highway 70.

FEE ATTRACTIONS
- Buck and Doe Forest, on 45 south, summer. Walk-in animal area; zoo. Mini golf.

- Pleasure Island theme park, on 45 north, about June 20–August 30. Western frontier area with cute saloon, simulated town, shootouts, gold panning, museum, lookout tower. Train, miniature car, stagecoach rides (extra cost)—the train holdup is fun even for jaded adults. Fantasy area includes small, unusually clean zoo, tot rides, and amusements. Lots of action in a park that is clean and neat and whose young workers show a good spirit!

GOLF
- Eagle River Country Club, east from 45 north of the bridge. Nine holes.

- Lake Forest Golf and Country Club, north of 70 east. Nine holes.

HIKING
- Anvil Trails, mostly ski trails, q.v.

- Franklin Lake Hiking Trails, near beach and into Big Tree area.

- Franklin Lake Nature Trail. See Sightseeing.

- Sevenmile Campground Trail, pretty little trail circling swamp.

- Spectacle Lake-Kentuck Lake Campgrounds Trail. See Phelps.

PARKS, BEACHES, RECREATION AREAS
- Eagle River Municipal Beach, Silver Lake Park. Interesting complex of piers, confined toddler area, raft, changing areas; concessions; picnicking. Very nice.

- Riverview Park, along Eagle River west of 45 in town. Band shell, tennis, play area.

- Eagle Lake County Park, off Chain O' Lakes Road. Lovely, semirustic pinewood park; sand beach, greensward, picnicking.

- Russell Oldfield County Park, Highway G at Wisconsin River. Tables, toilets, canoe landing, good take-out spot on trips from Conover area.

- Anvil Lake Picnic Area, on 70 east in the Nicolet. Beach, picnic facilities.

- Butternut Lake Picnic Area, Nicolet Forest Road 2179. Tables, toilets; nice.

- Franklin Lake Picnic Area, Nicolet Forest Road 2181. 23 picnic units, slightly pebbly but very fine beach. Beautiful spot for picnicking, hiking.

SAUNA
- Leo's Sauna, end of Loon Lake Road off 45 south, 479-4010. Old World authenticity.

SHOOTING
- Eagle River Trap and Skeet Range, five miles west on Highway G, 479-4974.

SKATING
- Indoor ice skating in season at ERRA sports complex; outdoors at park on river.

SKIING / CROSS COUNTRY: RENTAL AND CENTERS
- Chanticleer Inn, off 70 east, 479-4486.

- Crossroads Sports/Nordic World, Wall Street, 479-9544. Rentals, instruction. Also rentals for camping.

- Eagle River Nordic Ski Center, Wall Street, 479-7122 or 479-7285. Rentals, instruction, tours using outlying facilities. New operation.

- Thunder Lake Ski Touring Center, on 70 west (P.O. Box 164), 479-7008. Rentals, instruction (including videotaping), excursion service. New operation, 1977.

- Trees for Tomorrow, in town. Live-in workshops; rentals available.

SKIING / CROSS COUNTRY: TRAILS
- Anvil Trails (Nicolet Forest), 8.5 miles east on 70. Three trails, all classes, over 12 miles, rest facilities. Scenic.

- Chanticleer Inn, off 70 east. Four to six miles of trails; rentals, instruction.

- Eagle River Country Club grounds and the snowmobile park are used for skiing.

- Various Nicolet Forest hiking trails (q.v.) are sometimes used for skiing.

- Trees for Tomorrow. Trails in two locations; check on public-use policy.

SKIING: DOWNHILL
- Chanticleer Inn, off 70 east, small hill, rope tows, rentals.

SNOWMOBILE RENTAL
- Dyna Manufacturing Company, on 70 east (P.O. Box 286), 479-9811. Clothing too.

- R & M Sales and Service. See Three Lakes.

SNOWMOBILING
- Funded trails and Nicolet Forest trails; map sign at information bureau.

STABLES
- HiPines Stables, on 45, one mile north of G.

TENNIS
- Riverview Park, west of 45 near fairgrounds, four lighted courts.

EAGLE RIVER RECREATION ASSOCIATION

ERRA is a civic group that owns the sports arena on Highway 70 east and sponsors many programs. These include winter hockey and figure-skating programs and summer clinics in both (three one-week sessions), Silver Blades Ice Show (March, repeated in July) presented by its figure students, and Baroque Music Festival (August). Its arena houses the Wisconsin Hockey Hall of Fame.

ENTERTAINMENT

AUTO RACING
- K-G Raceway, Cloverland Drive off 70 west, Tuesday, June to September, stock or midget cars.

MUSIC
- Baroque Music Festival, ERRA arena, in August, chamber music concert and main festival concert with soloists, chorus, and orchestra.

WATER SKI SHOWS
- Eagle River Chain Skimmers, Sunday, Tuesday, Thursday evenings, late May through August on riverfront off Silver Lake Road at end of Bond Boulevard.

SHOPPING AND BROWSING

ARTISTS, ARTISANS, GALLERIES
• Eagle River Pottery, west edge of town on 70, May–October or by chance. Tony Staroska hand turns and fashions stoneware, functional pottery, sculpture at his rustic, rough-wood studio-gallery. The mysteries of pottery are a little less unfathomable if you get a glimpse through the studio door as he prepares his captivating creations. Much concerned about the world of art, he showcases alongside his own work the work of fellow artists, from photography to furniture.

• The Hangup, on 70 west in town, all year. Bob Schwartz painstakingly recreates wildlife (especially fish, birds) and northern scenes in paintings and sketches that form the heart of his gallery, along with prints, even notepaper of his art. He also offers work of other artists (including his wife Donna's ceramics), supplies that make these possible, and the framing that gives the final touch. Tasteful gifts too.

• Wons String Instrument Shop, Highway G (Fire Number 6036). John Wons has transplanted the violin, guitar, and lute maker's art from Madison to a little log shop rich with the smells of finishes, warm with the heat of a barrel stove. His career grew out of his violin playing and desire to make his own violin. Violins are still his most challenging product, the hardest to endow with perfect sound, but his lutes demand the most talent-teasing craftsmanship. He usually has an instrument or two there to typify his work, but most are shipped away on special order.

SHOPS
• The Christmas House, 519 E. Wall, May–December. Christmas and seasonal gifts and items in an appealing, very pleasantly managed shop.

• Cranberry Gift House, in town on 70 west, May–Christmas. Cranberry food items, cranberry glass, candle-making demonstrations, and their end product.

• Cranberry Winery, McKeever complex, east on Wall Street, is the transplanted Three Lakes winery. Wine manufacture, testing, sales; 365 days a year.

• Lehner's Jewelry and Gifts, downtown. Restful shop, tastefully uncluttered and showcasing glass, china, lamps, even Kaiser porcelains up to $1,095.

• Meadow Ruh Gift Shop, on Highway X near Burnt Rollways (follow signs from 45 at Evergreen Road), May–October. Jewelry, small gifts, many on northwoods and bird themes. Visitors are encouraged to roam the grounds, which include a creek, small bridge, plantings, landscaping, and busy bird feeders.

• Strawberry Patch, downtown. Country furniture, home decorative accessories, china in unusually effective, creatively lighted area—an old theater!

• In addition to the varied shops above, Eagle River has a range of shops where you may want to look for certain specialties or gifts: House of Antiques, Highway 70 east (seasonal) or The Village Shop in Mrs. Edna Fisher's home at 118 N. Main (seasonal; antiques, primitives, wood items, backed by 22 years of integrity); Bluebird Doll House in Mrs. Billie Liesegang's home at 121 N. Main (toy and collector dolls, custom clothes, furniture); The Camera Shop, downtown (where I buy film but am always afraid to take a deep breath for fear its universe of small breakable gifts will come tumbling down on me); or Crossroads Sports and Gifts, downtown (perhaps the largest gift assortment downtown, personal and home); Moccasin Shop, downtown; Arrow Gift Shop, downtown; Red Wing Trading Post, downtown; Big Barn Shops at Pleasure Island; Spiess Sporting Goods, downtown (carpeted, tasteful store with sportswear as well).

DINING

• Ar-Ber Supper Club, 70 west at edge of town; nightly except for a month or so around March, closed Thursday, September–May, 479-4300. Three things bespeak excellence: log interior gleaming with care; totally attentive service; superb food such as delicious breaded pork chops or precisely done filet. Cocktails.

• Czecho Supper Club, four miles east on 70; nightly except Monday, all year, has not taken reservations. Good reputation, restful decor, salad bar; food nicely presented, attentively served. Duck is popular. Cocktails.

• Darton's Char' Lou Supper Club, Chain O' Lakes Road; nightly except Monday, closed Tuesday in winter, all year, 479-4975. Cathedral ceilinged, picture-windowed pine dining room; hearty soup preceded my interesting flaming shishkebab, a specialty. Nice treatment of customers. Cocktails.

• Golden Eagle Supper Club, Wall Street east of downtown; noons and evenings, closed day has varied, all year. Very large dining area, rough wood, carpeted, with brawny furniture; new management: I noted an improvement just in a few months, from a lunch with brown lettuce to a dinner with excellent steak. Cocktails.

• Mint Bar, downtown; noons and evenings, closed off-season Sundays, all year. Excellent huge sandwiches. Tables, booths as well as bar.

• Napoli Supper Club, on 45, east edge of town; nightly except Tuesday, all year, 479-4141. Full menu includes many Italian items; salad bar. I felt that I received good value with the salad bar and tasty homemade ravioli. Cocktails.

• Persian Paradise, two miles south on 45; nightly, Sunday brunch, closed off-season Mondays, all year, 479-9779. Great red-carpeted, balconied log dining hall. Full menu, some ethnic items; excellent food. Sunday brunch here is a memorable epicurean experience, with a groaning table of delicious entrees and extras. Cocktails.

• Pine Gables Supper Club, on 70 at west edge of town; nightly except Tuesday, May–December, 479-8080. Small log club; some entrees like ravioli and details like dressings, rolls, kolacky are homemade. Restful. Cocktails.

• White Spruce Inn, 45 north at the bridge; nightly except Sunday, late May–September, 479-9090. Ancient log cabin (or lake-view dining room); the advertised smoked ribs are delicious, the thin homemade pizza superlative. Cocktails.

LODGING

AMERICAN PLAN
• Chanticleer Inn, off 70 east, all year. Large resort, leader in many activities: lake

swimming, tennis, water skiing with excellent instruction; snowmobiling, downhill and cross-country skiing, with rentals. Variety both of accommodations (motel units, older cottages, excellent condominiums) and plans (from lodging only to modified or full American plan); so be sure to have clear understanding of rate, plan, and accommodation when reserving. Public tennis club, cocktails, dining.

• Eagle Waters Resort, off 70 east, mid May–mid September. Full American plan with special attention to dining, which is excellent. Over 100 units in a wooded lakeshore compound, all with bath; some are in suites or self-contained cottages. Swimming pool, tennis, kids' program. Cocktails, entertainment; public dining.

HOUSEBOAT

• Holiday Harbor, Chain O' Lakes Road (Route 3), seasonal. Five outboard-powered boats combine mobile home and pontoon boat elements and have the freedom of nine lakes; usually return in mid week for service and dumping. Rentals for three, four, seven days. A really novel vacation possibility!

HOUSEKEEPING

• Knotty Pine Resort, Catfish Lake off 45 south (Route 2), seasonal. Six cottages, three with fireplace; pine interiors; sand beach, rec room. A good, tidy resort.

• Lake Aidenn Cottages, off Highway H (Route 2). Mini Walden of three unusual, rustic, seasonal cottages (designed by a bridge builder years back); touches like mini loft, fireplaces; one lovely all-year home; picturesque woods, private lake, beach.

• Maplewood Resort, Dam Lake, on Oneida Highway D (Fire Number 5214), seasonal. Six well-appointed, carpeted cottages on slope toward beach; good resort.

• The Meander Post, East Carpenter Lake Road. Quality mini resort, three remodeled log cottages, in shade; sand beach, tennis court. Seasonal.

• Schrock's Resort, Cranberry Lake off 45 south (Route 2), May–October. Seven uniform, well-kept cottages in shady, orderly compound; gradual sand beach.

• 7-mile Pinecrest Resort, Forest Road 2179 at Sevenmile Lake, off Military Road (P.O. Box A), all year. 16 cottages from carpeted and luxurious to plain; fine beach, tennis; ski trails, rec room; very farsighted, professional operation.

• Timberlands Resort, Chain O' Lakes Road (Route 3). Five seasonal, one all-year cottage, all with fireplace; natural wood decor, pleasant furnishings; four are on the shore, well spaced for privacy; nice beach area. Excellent little resort!

MOTELS

• Braywood Motel, Catfish Lake Road off 45 south (Route 2), 479-6494. Beach.

• Chic-A-Dee Motel, on 45 south (Route 2), 479-8671. Six units.

• Gira Motel, 45 north, in town, 479-4481. 12 units.

• Hiawatha Motor Inn, on 45 north (Route 2), 479-6431. 28 impressive, big units, well appointed, air conditioned; lake setting. Heated indoor pool!

- Meadow Lark Motel, on 45 north at 17 east (Route 3), 479-4150. 10 rooms.
- Persian Paradise Motel, on 45 south (Route 2), 479-9779. 24 units; beach.
- Riverdale Motel, on 70 west (Route 2), 479-4373. Eight units.
- Shoreline Motel, 45 north, 479-9988. 17 units.
- Traveler's Inn Motel-Hotel, downtown, 479-4403. 14 units in hotel, 10 in new building (with kitchenettes).
- White Eagle Motel, on 70 west, 479-4426. 22 units, heated pool, dock, boats.

CAMPING

PRIVATE
- Coe's Deerskin Campground, Chain O' Lakes Road, May–September. 60 sites.
- Kairis Campground, Forest Road 2178 north off 70 (Fire Number 1816), seasonal. 20 sites.
- Otter Lake Trailer Bowl, Chain O' Lakes Road (Route 3), seasonal. 30 sites.
- Pine-Aire Resort and Campground, Chain O' Lakes Road (Route 3), all year. 115 sites.

NICOLET NATIONAL FOREST CAMPGROUNDS
- Anvil Lake, 10 miles east on 70, May–November. 18 wooded units.
- Franklin Lake, end Forest Road 2181, May–October. 81 units.
- Kentuck Lake, 16 miles east on 70 to Road 2194 (some maps show 2176), May–September. 22 sites.
- Luna-White Deer, Road 2176 south from 70, May–October. 41 units.
- Sevenmile Lake. See Three Lakes.
- Spectacle Lake. See Phelps.

EVENTS

- Silver Spur Horse Show, late June.
- Independence Day Celebration.
- Artarama, mid July, outdoor arts and crafts show.

- Antique Show and Sale, late July or early August.

- Vilas County Free Fair, mid August at the fairgrounds. Animal, farm produce, flower and craft judging and displays. Carnival midway, refreshments, horse show, evening program. Admission free to grounds. Lots of fun in an unusual grass-roots close-up of Vilas County "at home."

- Snow Skoal, winter long, countywide program of events beginning with December kickoff banquet.

- World Championship Snowmobile Derby, mid January. Largest event in the northwoods. Races, qualifying trials, and special events, with the feature race Sunday afternoon. Up to 400 entrants compete for purses exceeding $30,000.

INFORMATION AND TRANSPORTATION

- Eagle River Municipal Information Bureau, Eagle River 54521. Office, Railroad and Wall streets, open all year, daily in summer, 479-8575.

- Public library facilities in Eagle River received a boost with a large bequest in 1977, and a new library was the result, between the courthouse and Wall Street.

- Car rental: Northwinds Aviation, Eagle River Union Airport, 479-4929.

- Charter air service: Northwinds Aviation, Eagle River Union Airport, 479-4929.

- Taxi: City Cab, 479-8911.

CONOVER

The Town of Conover is a large one, and its long east-west distance bridges the county's widest variety of topography. At the west it begins in rugged, forested end moraine, sliced by few roads. It levels out at its center into pine flats, some almost impoverished looking, and in the east rises into pretty, gently rolling ground moraine where in the early 1900s a number of farmers labored to establish not only their own toehold upon the land but also to plant upon it a visible token of their faith. The first farmers were the brothers Reed about 1892, but most of the rest were Swedes who had been born in an expatriate Swedish colony in Finland. Many bought their land about 1902 in a cheap land promotion but continued to work in iron mines in Michigan for a few years before hiking in to their lands with their chattels on their backs. One sign of their success is the clearings they left, though many are just residential sites, not active farms now. Another is their beloved Pioneer Lake Lutheran Church, set carefully to overlook the lake of its name.

Later many Germans joined the early settlers, along with others like the French-surnamed Dussaults as early as 1912. Five little schools served the scattered settlers; the fact that only one school, Tamarack School, was west of the Wisconsin River shows how settlement patterns developed.

Lumbermen worked the area, of course, long before the farmers, maybe even before 1883 brought the railroad. Modern loggers still work in Conover forests, for considerable pulp harvesting is done on extensive county acreage in Conover.

It was a tourist whose early fishing customs gave Conover its name. Plymouth cheeseman Seth Conover had a favorite spot to get off or on the train during his fishing expeditions to the Twin Lakes. His routine led to references to Conover's Stop and this

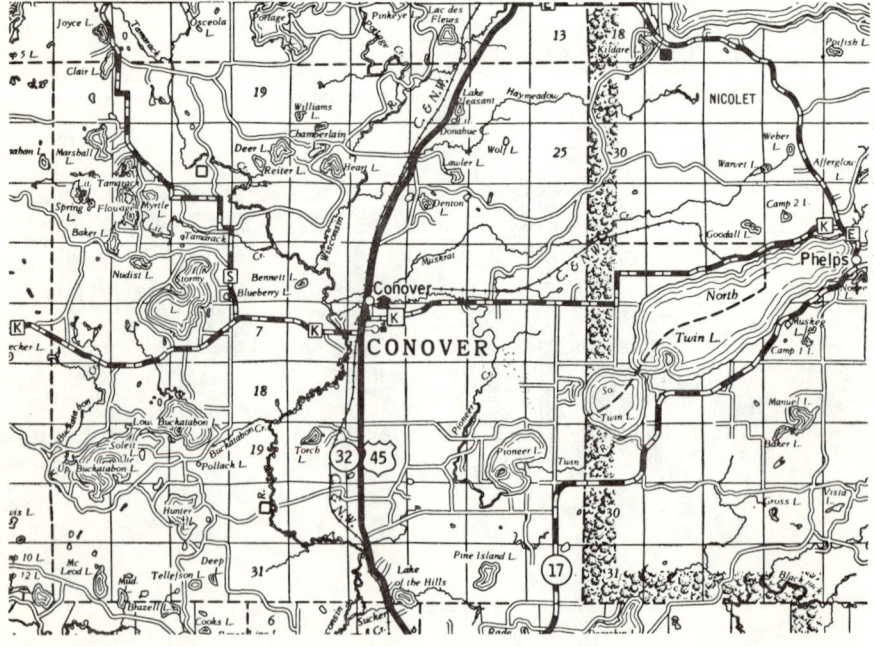

82/Vilas County

came to be formalized simply as Conover.

Tourists followed in fisherman Conover's bootsteps and a great resort, begun by 1893, grew up on Big Twin, important enough to have its name on its own post office: Lakota. Many other resorts followed it along the Twins' shores and west of town in the Stormy Lake and Buckatabon areas. Lakota was the landing for tote roads overland from the tracks at Conover, and there launches took the travelers and barges the freight for points near what would later become Phelps.

Meanwhile early Conover could boast its unusual industry, the brickyard. Clay from a local pit was fired in ovens that stood in ruins till some enterprising individuals cut them up for the scrap iron in World War II, long after the lack of local markets and the costly need to ship brick to outside markets had killed the business.

If Conover's trains did not carry bricks, they certainly carried blueberries. Storekeeper George Dobbs brokered and shipped locally picked berries, 17,139 quarts of them in 1922 alone, and the train even came to be referred to as the Blueberry Train. (Its real name was the Wisconsin Lakes Special or the Ashland Limited, if it had one, but it was only a branch train from the main line at Monico. Still on Labor Day weekend it would be so long with Pullmans that two engines could hardly ease it over mile-long Conover grade, and when the last steam engine passed through town around 1960 the schoolkids were let out to watch it steam into history.)

New generations of residents keep discovering Conover. Today's include many retirees drawn by its good life and many commuters who live there but drive to work outside the township.

SIGHTSEEING AND TOURING

• Lakes. Interesting Conover lakes include very large and scenic North Twin, deep and large Stormy Lake, which boasts a trout population, and the Buckatabon lakes. Hard roads encircle all these.

• Highway K is scenic west of Highway S and very pretty farther east as it rises near North Twin and rollicks among rugged lakeside hardwood ridges; especially beautiful in fall because of the very thick hardwood cover.

• Rummles Road, between 45 north and Highway S, typical scenic cross-section.

• Razorback Road, from Rummles north, just west of Wisconsin River, crosses pretty Portage Creek, flies above woods and Lac des Fleurs on apparent esker.

• Baker Lake Road, wild, ridgy. See chapter on the Lost Region.

• Monheim, Church, McPeak roads exhibit farmsites, the Pioneer Lake church, and gentle scenery; note the tiny jewel of a chapel across the road (private). Notice too how the farm terrain rolls gently; some of the region is ground moraine.

RECREATION

BIKING
• Try town roads around the lakes and in the Pioneer church area.

- The Nicolet Bikeway uses some town road mileage and Highway K west and north of North Twin Lake, in its loop between Three Lakes and Phelps.

CANOEING
- Wisconsin River. Busy and popular. Put in or take out at Highway 45, north near Land O' Lakes, at Rummles Road, Highway K, River Road, or Highway G. I think the best stretch lies between 45 and Rummles Road, where the river runs between solid banks and high, well-drained woods. Here it is narrow and swift. Tributary Portage Creek widens it considerably and tames it.

PARKS
- Conover Town Park, on K east. Tables, toilets, play, skating, small ski area.
- Tamarack Creek County Park, Tamarack Road between Rummles Road and Highway S. Pretty site, creek impoundment, and remains of old dam.

SHOOTING
- Unnamed range on 45, south about three miles. Three stands; pretty road in.

SNOWMOBILING
- Area trails include connections to Land O' Lakes and Eagle River. The local club is the Sno-Buddies. Rest area on Wisconsin River Trail.

SHOPPING AND BROWSING

- Aman's Gallery and Gifts, in town, seasonal, features Fred Aman's sculptures with paintings, pottery, and crafts by others, generally on northwoods themes.
    Aman is undoubtedly Wisconsin's only wildlife sculpture working principally in lost wax bronze as his medium. His works, from four to 24 inches in height, are a unique achievement in capturing detail, action, or movement, a hint of the surroundings and a touch of drama, as in a bass rolling beneath a lily pad, an Indian stalking with his bow, a pheasant rising in the clutches of a fox, or a canoe-borne Indian about to spear a fish by night.

- Denton's Sports and Gifts, in town, May–December. Wide range of gifts and curios from jewelry and home decorative items to moccasins and shirts.

PICTURESQUE PUB
- Burnt Bridge Tavern, four miles west on K. Rustic log tavern, picturesque pine grove. Outside the picture window raccoons in summer and deer in winter feed on treats put out by owner Ed Evert; so do flying squirrels. Pizza.

LODGING

- Deerpath Resort, Jacoby Road off West Buckatabon Road, seasonal. Housekeeping, five exceptional cottages and chalet, carpeted, some with fireplaces, dishwashers, antiques. A very unusual woman, Mrs. Sophie Gonzalez stinted not one bit in putting the finest of everything into these lovely cottages. Beach. *Outstanding.*

- Four Seasons Resort, west leg of Stormy Lake loop, all year. Housekeeping; appealing, very comfortable cottages, nice beach and setting.

- Heulla Lodge, on K east along North Twin Lake, May–October. Impeccable use of hilly site gives this housekeeping complex a Black Forest air. Deep woods, stone walls, landscaping. Six well-equipped cottages (two are boathouses), some with porch, fireplace. Clear lake, sand-pebble beach where DNR men net and milk spawning walleyes in spring for eggs. Unusually nice resort.

- Northland Motel, on 45 in town, 479-9333. Eight units.

- North Shore Resort, West Buckatabon Road, seasonal. Housekeeping, five cottages; big repeat business from hosts' interest in their guests; beach; pleasant.

- Thomson's Resort, off K via Monheim and Twin Lakes roads, all year. Housekeeping, six cottages, paneled and carpeted, five in a beachside row (sandy beach). Enjoys a fine reputation and loyal following.

EVENTS

- Conover Horse Show and Conover Country Music Night, weekend in early July.
- Colorama, around the end of September.
- Winter Frolic, February.

INFORMATION

Conover Chamber of Commerce, Conover 54519. Information booth on Highway 45 in town, weekends from Memorial Day to Colorama, daily late June to Labor Day, 479-4928.

LAND O' LAKES

Land O' Lakes and Vilas County's northern tier of woodlands and lakes are historic and scenic. It is likely that this was the first place in the two counties where the red man ever beheld his paler counterpart, perhaps in the person of Jesuit Father Rene Menard, who according to traditional accounts said mass on the shore of Lac Vieux Desert on his way from Lake Superior down the Wisconsin around August 1661 and disappeared shortly afterward. Frenchmen were showing the lake on their maps by 1718 and one, we know, wintered here in 1791.

Civilization in the Land O' Lakes area grew around three early axes. . .

One was Lac Vieux Desert, a natural location since it was the source of the Wisconsin River and already had an Indian settlement. When the river downstream near Stevens Point drowned his homestead and his wife, G. L. Draper packed his six little children and his belongings in two birchbark canoes and paddled to the river's source, vowing that the river would never work such harm upon his family again. He settled at the lake in 1852 and began to work a bit of land and deal a little in furs. His daughter married a visitor and the couple founded the resort industry in the deep north when they offered room and board to fishermen and visitors around 1882 (probably before the railroad, since the first guest arrived by canoe from the east via a six-mile portage to Lac Vieux Desert).

The Military Road between Green Bay and Fort Wilkins, Michigan, had brought interesting traffic by the old Draper post over the years, even before it was completed as a wagon road in 1872. Stories are told, for instance, of a herd of cattle being driven up the road, with extra feed on their backs or tied to their horns. But it was arrival of the railroads in 1883 that made fishing and vacation resorts like Drapers' practical. Another resort joined theirs by 1902 and then several others followed in quicker succession, along with

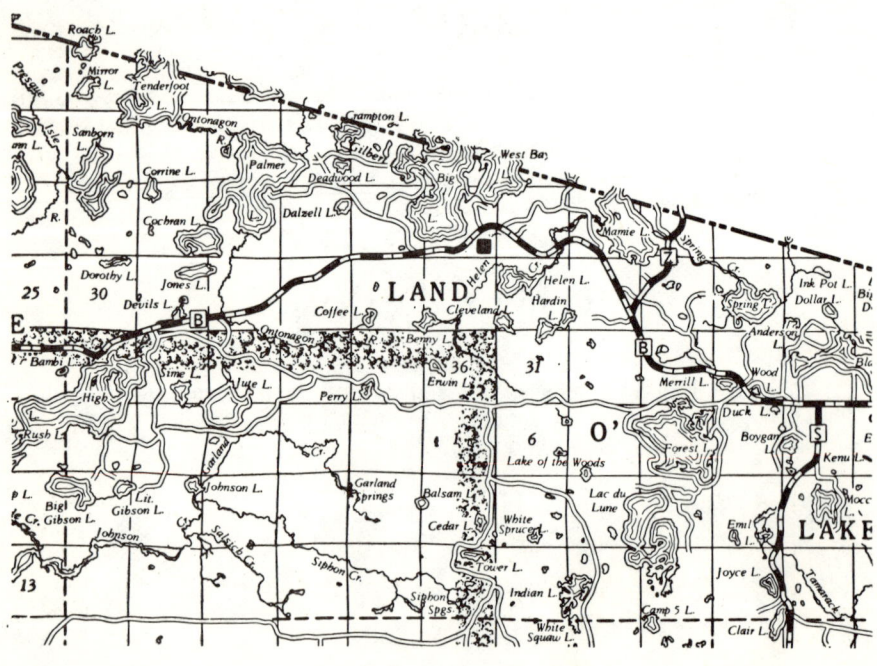

luxury homes. One resort was so large that in 1923 it had its own sawmill and a herd of 10 cows.

The second axis, present-day Land O' Lakes, was two early settlements. Today's townsite was called State Line when the railroad reached it in 1883. Somewhere nearby a mill was reportedly operating by 1878, giving the community a history now in its second century. But the biggest boost was construction of a mill and housing area on Mill Lake, a mile or two west; the village was eventually called Donaldson after one of the partners in the Mason and Donaldson lumber firm from Rhinelander, its owners. The railroad was pushed to Donaldson in 1887 and not removed till 1917. The mill had burned in 1908, and shipment of lumber left on the yard ended two years later. This left State Line as the focus of commerce and employment. Erection of the Gateway complex·in the late 1930s established the community more than ever as a tourist center; by then it had shed the name State Line in favor of the more sparkling title, Land O' Lakes.

The third axis, and for a long time a very distinct one, was the Cisco Chain of Lakes, on the state line west of present Land O' Lakes. Charles Bent built his resort, Bent's Camp, in 1896, at first lugging guests and supplies in from State Line in a lumber wagon. (A resort still operates there under that name, even using one of the original log cabins!) One Johnny Franks began a tavern and cottage compound on nearby West Bay lake a decade or more after Bent. Most Cisco Chain visitors chose to arrive or depart via the Chicago & North Western Railway at Gogebic Station or its spur right down to the chain when service was available there. Service even included Pullmans to Chicago all summer long. Helping more than a little to keep up service might have been the fact that the Hughitt family had a home on the chain and the fact that two Marvin Hughitts, father and son, served as president and vice president of the railway. Logs from the area also took the train from here. Travelers rode between resorts and train in launches, their freight in scows. The logs just were herded to their doom in rafts.

Development of roads drew all three axes closer together and made possible the growth of hospitality. That development has been long, and has taken the form of both resorts and summer homes, and the businesses that service the visitors.

Farming played no great role at Land O' Lakes but it did play one interesting small one. Resorter-farmer George St. Clair raised Triumph potatoes on his lonely property, to feed his guests, and when it was discovered that 13 generations of isolation had made his potatoes immune to mosaic disease, the strain that he had unwittingly developed was given his name and used for planting in mosaic-prone areas as far afield as Texas!

Sawmilling is still important at Land O' Lakes in the second century of that activity there. The ultramodern Nagel mill and yard sprawls along a half mile of Highway B, west of the village (no plant visitors).

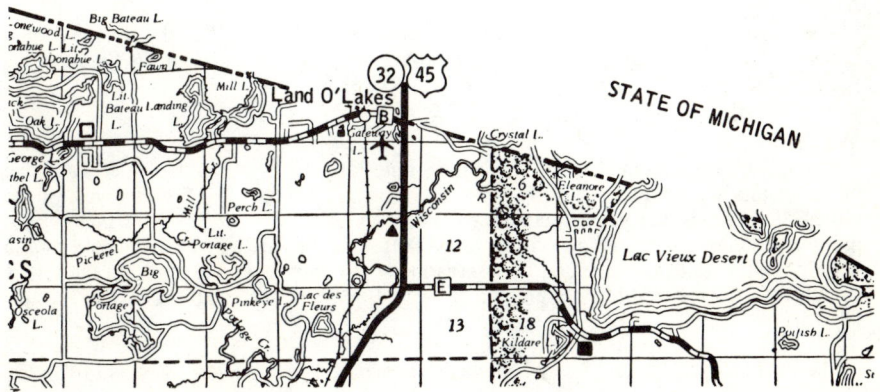

SIGHTSEEING AND TOURING

The varied points of interest and drives in the vicinity can best be grouped into the directions one travels from town to visit them.

EAST
- Lac Vieux Desert. Large, historic, and scenic lake, the northern part of which is in Michigan. Nomadic Indians used its islands as planting grounds, putting in seed as they passed in spring and returning in fall to reap, hence the name given by the French, meaning old or deserted planting grounds. There is no longer anything accessible at the Indian site.

- A dam marks the outlet of the Wisconsin River, at a charming little park on the shore reached by a fir-cooled path; also tables, pump, lake wading.

- Historical marker at the park honors the lake's historical role.

- The Wisconsin is only a creek as it slips under its first bridge.

- The Military Road followed this western shore of the lake, and a marker at the Nicolet Forest picnic area recalls its story. (Road 2205; tables, beach.)

- The Wisconsin-Michigan state line makes an interesting if invisible bend in the lake east of the islands, going between the south big island (Duck Island) and its northern sisters. Early planners drew the line from the east to the lake and thought that the Montreal River ran westward from the lake and would form the entire western part of the state line. When they discovered that there was no Montreal River at all for a big part of the border distance, they drew a straight line between the Montreal's headwaters and Lac Vieux Desert, remedying their 50-mile dilemma but creating the little bend.

- A monument next to the chamber of commerce building on Highway 45 marks the state line and commemorates its surveyors. The rest of the line is marked with 160 small concrete monuments.

SOUTH
- Historical markers along Highways 32-45 south honor 32 as the Thirty-second Division Memorial Highway and explain the importance of the Wisconsin River.

WEST
- Highway B is the backbone of the 18-mile-long Town of Land O' Lakes and one of the county's most magnificently set roads, from a point about 6.5 miles west of the village. Dim roadside forests alternate with deep-set lakes, swamps, and rare openings to provide excellent scenery and vistas, especially colorful in fall. Merrill Lake has a wayside with dedicatory plaque to conservationist William Ruth. At night on the lonely stretch west from there I have often seen coyotes. B remains scenic all the way to Presque Isle (q.v.).

- The Cisco Chain of Lakes lies in both states; 15 connected lakes and over 200

88/Vilas County

miles of shore, much of it almost Canadian-looking in its wooded grandeur.

- Devil's Lake and the Subcontinental Divide. A marker on B explains that the attractive little glacial kettle lake below the road drains, via a creek on its north side, into the Atlantic watershed and, via a creek to its south, into the Mississippi and Caribbean as well.

- Highway Z north from B crosses a photogenic interlake thoroughfare before ducking into woods on the Michigan side that end at Sylvania, 8.5 miles from B.

- Forest Lake Road, encircling the lake in its name, off B at Archdale's. This is the prettiest lake and woods circle I know in Vilas County: deep woods of maple, yellow birch, clumped ferns. This is the access road to old Highway B, which leads into the Lost Region part of the county.

- Old State Line Cemetery, closer to town on B, contains earlier burials, many unmarked, but one homemade stone is lettered with marbles.

NORTH
- Sylvania, west of Watersmeet, Michigan (north on 45, west on U.S 2), 21,000-acre, mostly virgin wilderness. It came under federal ownership in one piece in 1966 after serving as a private preserve and estates. Main attractions are its forests, unspoiled lakes, opportunities for extended wilderness hiking or canoeing, and a large beach and picnic area for auto-borne tourists. A handsome Visitors Center at Watersmeet offers information, an excellent interpretive film, and a summer program of weekly films and guided walks. A quarter-mile interpretive trail begins beside the center.

- Ottawa National Forest adjoins Wisconsin, providing campgrounds, recreation, and education. Points of interest near Land O' Lakes are the Toumey Forest Nursery at Watersmeet (public welcome; no interpretive services) and the Imp Lake interpretive tour area along Highway 2 east from Watersmeet.

RECREATION

BIKE RENTAL
- The Gateway, in town, 547-3321.

- Morrison's Sports North, 45 south, 547-3205.

BIKING
- Circle tours on public roads, like Forest Lake Road, a larger circle around Little Portage Lake, or an even longer loop from the state line monument to Lac Vieux Desert via Michigan Highway 210, Forest Road 2205 and Highways E and 45.

BOAT AND CANOE RENTAL
- Cisco Chain Marina, on B at the chain, 547-3761. Fishing, ski, pontoon, sailboats.

- Dickman's Land O' Lakes Motors, in town, 547-3717. Fishing, ski boats, motors.

- Headwaters Marine, in town, 547-3555. Fishing and pleasure boats, canoes, motors.

- Morrison's Sports North, 45 south, 547-3205. Canoes, windsurfers.

- Sylvania Outfitters, Highway 2 west, Watersmeet, 906-358-4766. Canoes.

CANOEING

- Northern Highland Canoe Trails. Big, Palmer, and Tenderfoot lakes are the outermost lakes with DNR canoe campsites; portages or channels link them to Cochran, Jones, Devil's, and High lakes and the Manitowish River system.

- Sylvania. Extensive wilderness lake canoeing; portaging required. Eighty-four wilderness campsites in 29 clusters serve either canoeists or hikers.

- Wisconsin River. My local advisers suggest putting in at Highway 45 wayside, not at Lac Vieux Desert; the bottom is muddy in places upstream from 45. See Conover for details.

CANOE TRIP SERVICE AND OUTFITTING

- Morrison's Sports North, 45 south, 547-3205. Also outfits bike, hiking trips.

- Sylvania Outfitters, Highway 2 west, Watersmeet (Michigan 49969), 906-358-4766. River trips and Sylvania wilderness trips, with lighter canoes and sailing rigging if desired for the wilderness canoeing. This is a remarkable little enterprise run by a very knowledgeable and committed young Watersmeet native, Bob Zelinski.

GOLF

- The Gateway, in town. Nine holes.

HIKING

- Sylvania has a large trail network.

PARKS, BEACHES, RECREATION AREAS

- Land O' Lakes Town Park. Under development; tables, shelter, play areas.

- Black Oak Lake County Park, on B west. Excellent beach; picnicking.

- Lac Vieux Desert. Two picnic areas, see Sightseeing; the Nicolet Forest site has a formal beach on a rather reedy shore; the park at the dam has impromptu beach.

- Clark Lake Picnic Area, Sylvania. Large complex with beach, tables, rest rooms.

- Wayside on 45 south at Wisconsin River. Unusually attractive picnic site.

SHOOTING
- Gateway Gun Club, 45 north, in Michigan. Trap; also special meets.

SKIING / CROSS COUNTRY: RENTAL
- The Gateway, at the ski hill on 45 south, 547-3321.
- Morrison's Sports North, 45 south, 547-3205.
- Sylvania Outfitters, 2 west, Watersmeet, 906-358-4766.

SKIING / CROSS COUNTRY: TRAILS
- The Gateway. Over 18 miles of trails, all classes; membership arrangement or resort guest use; check locally on use by general public.

- Sylvania Trails. Six-, seven-, eight-mile trails; Sylvania Outfitters has spearheaded development of these trails and links to its shop and to Land O' Lakes from the wilderness area. Pineaire Resort Motel has also cooperated in this.

SKIING: DOWNHILL
- The Gateway, ski area on 45 south. Nine runs; rentals, instruction; chalet.

SNOWMOBILE RENTAL
- Dickman's Land O' Lakes Motors, in town, 547-3717.

SNOWMOBILING
- Frosty Snowmobile Club grooms area trails.
- Ottawa National Forest trails.

TENNIS
- The Gateway, in town, by reservation only, 547-3321. Reservation charge.

SHOPPING AND BROWSING

- Bernadette's, in town, May through October, closed Sunday. Appealing rough-wood and antique-decorated shop made all the more so by a gracious hostess and her choices of handcrafted and collector items: dishes, glass, basketry, pottery, other gifts.

- Gateway Gift Shop, in The Gateway, all year. Wide variety from selected men's, women's clothing (like sweaters from Scandinavia) through jewelry, gifts, some toys, stitchery; eskimo carvings.

- Trading Post Internationale, in town, all year. Clothing, gifts, and imports; a few primitives; but most important, real Indian jewelry and rugs. Two fellow merchants, one across town, one across the county, stressed the owner's reputation in antiques, rugs, jewelry: "What he has, he knows; and it's good."

- Treasure Chest, in town on B. One of the county's best antique shops; the owner personally does much of her searching; also some gifts or handcrafts.

DINING

- Archdale's North, seven miles west on B; evenings (closed Monday; Tuesday, Wednesday, December–March; all April), 547-3662. Pine decor; attentive service—my waitress asked if she might bone my rainbow trout. Full menu, cocktails, salad bar.

- The Gateway, in town; all meals (may close one early weekday in off season), all year, 547-3321. Big lodge-type dining room, high ceilinged and rustic. Full menu, specials (like a generous fish buffet, even with broiled fish). Cocktails. A new spirit is afoot here; look for big things.

LODGING

RESORTS
- BranAnn's Colonial, on B at Cisco chain, all seasons. Housekeeping, five cottages, as attractive inside as out, with picture windows, natural wood decor, rustic exteriors, neatly planned grounds of natural birch and fir, nice waterfront.

- Dittman's Resort, on B at Cisco chain, May–October. Housekeeping, nine cottages, with carpeting, tasteful color-keyed decoration; unusual ones like a polygon show Mr. Dittman's engineering flair. Swimming pool in addition to lake setting.

- The Gateway, in town, all year. A grand old northwoods tradition is receiving new life and spirit. Large lodge-type inn, 105 rooms with bath; indoor pool, dining room, many resort services like tennis, golf, winter sports. Bar.

- McPartlin's Cottages, east end of Lac Vieux Desert off Highway E, May–October. Housekeeping, 16 units almost resemble a little white village on spotless grounds along lake. Sand beach, raft, unique, lovingly preserved fleet of real wood boats with old-fashioned golden wood interiors! Friendly, beautifully kept resort.

- Sunrise Lodge, west end of Lac Vieux Desert on Forest Road 2205, May–October. Full American plan, some housekeeping units. Green-shuttered cottages of sitting, bed, bath rooms vary in orientation to beach; golf driving net, tennis, trails.

- West Bay Resort, on B at Cisco chain, May–October. Housekeeping, 10 barn-red units scattered around sandy, piney point. Guests keep coming back—one who chatted with me was in her twenty-fifth summer there! Nice shore and beach.

MOTELS
- Bel Air Motel, in town, 547-3343. 11 units.

- Lakeside Motel, Michigan 210 east (P.O. Box 251), 906-544-3457. Six units, beach.

- Pineaire Resort Motel, 45 north (P.O. Box 437), 906-544-3800. Outstanding complex of 11 lovely units nestling separately in the pines; wood interiors. Charming breakfast shop with fireplace fire each morning. Beach, boats; also winter sports.

CAMPING

PRIVATE

- Benedict's Mobile Home and Trailer Park, on B at Cisco chain, May–October. About 20 of 50 units available.

- North Shore Campground, Highway 210 or Forest Road 2205 on Michigan side of Lac Vieux Desert (P.O. Box 264), May–October. 20 pads.

NATIONAL FOREST AND OUTFITTING

- Lac Vieux Desert Campground, Forest Road 2205 along west shore, end of April–mid October. 31 units.

- Sylvania. 84 wilderness units in 29 clusters.

- Outfitting available from Morrison's Sports North or Sylvania Outfitters. See Recreation: Canoe Trip Service, above.

EVENTS

- Fun Day, mid July, games, booths, food.

- Canoe Race and Corn Roast, late August, Black Oak Park.

- Colorama, end of September.

INFORMATION AND TRANSPORTATION

- Land O' Lakes Chamber of Commerce, Land O' Lakes 54540. Information booth, Highway 45 at B, open weekends, May–September, daily June–August, 547-3432.

- Public library in town hall.

- Car rental: Dickman's Land O' Lakes Motors, in town, with advance notice, 547-3717; Land O' Lakes Flying Service, at Kings-Land O' Lakes Municipal Airport, 547-3336.

- Charter air service or scenic flights: Land O' Lakes Flying Service, airport, 547-3336, all year.

PHELPS

Phelps is the jewel of Vilas County, a little village in a setting of leafy hillside and sparkling lake. As if that were not enough, every access to it is scenic, and the roads to its east promise the longest vistas that the county can offer.

It is heavy forests that help make its approaches so scenic, and it was the early predecessors of those forests that account for Phelps's presence. Early loggers took only pine, which could be floated away, ignoring the abundant hardwoods, which they were not equipped to move. This gave the forests of future Phelps a reprieve of twenty years before the loggers turned in their direction, armed with sleds, big wheels, tugboats, and the most formidable weapon of all, the logging railroad. Logging by rail lasted here till 1935, when truck logging, which had been making inroads since its introduction in 1929, replaced it altogether. (Near Spectacle Lake the Thunder Lake narrow gauge logged for a Rhinelander mill till about 1938, closing the rail-logging era in Vilas County.)

The big company at Phelps was the Hackley Phelps Bonnell Company, which gave the town two names, first Hackley and then Phelps (because Hackley was confused with Hatley, near Wausau; now, town biographer Joseph Albrecht wryly observes, it is confused with Phillips). The company had its first machinery laboriously tote-hauled over-

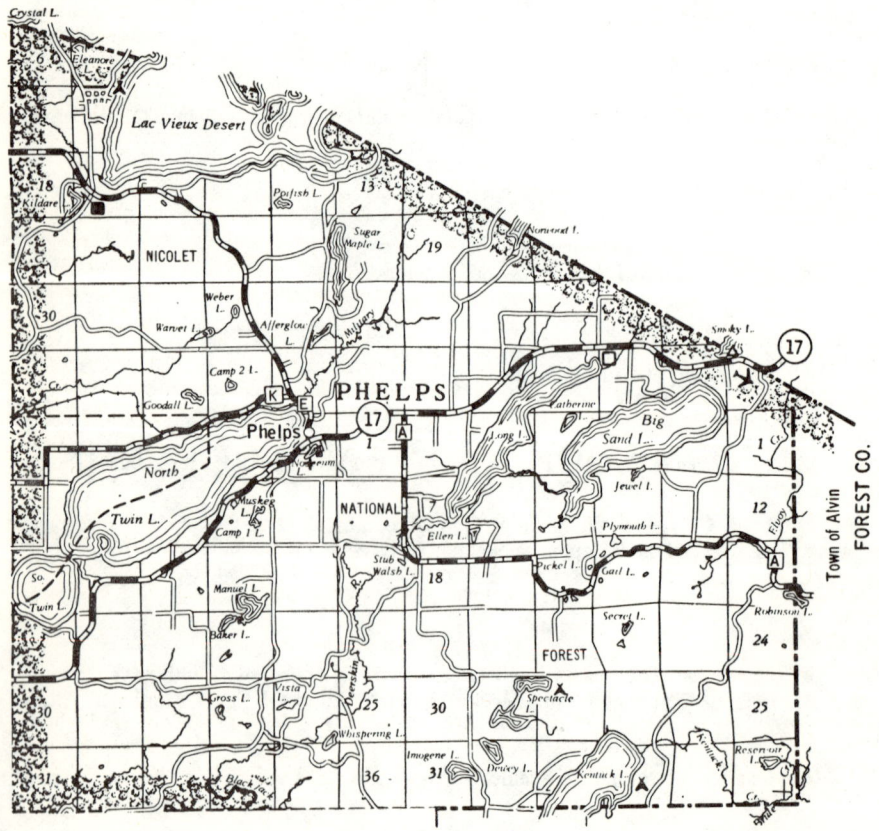

land to Lakota and barged to the shoreside mill site in 1902 and began sawing a year or two later; it had lots of lumber ready on the yard when the railroad was completed from Conover in 1905 to take the lumber out.

The lumber industry at Phelps wasted very little, and one result was a tidy industrial complex. Slabs were burned in mill boilers; "sixteen-inch wood" was sold for firewood, and other cordwood was used in a chemical factory that burned it and distilled the gases to produce both charcoal and alcohols. Even the charcoal found a local use, for a brief period, in an iron smelter that was built next to the other plant in 1914; it never reopened after a 1916 fire.

The C. M. Christiansen Lumber Company succeeded the Hackley organization in 1928 and kept the mill going almost another 30 years; it is still in business as a supplier of utility poles. Part of the old mill and grounds see use now for pallet manufacture and building materials distribution. Phelps also has a modular-home manufacturer, Amwood Homes, so it still has a more varied industrial base than any other northwoods town of its size.

Traces of its mill village ancestry are faintly visible in a few places in Phelps, such as the row arrangement of a few homes and their uniform silhouettes, but most of the original mill houses (up to 80 in all) have been remodeled or replaced. The town is unusual among northwoods settlements in having a network of cross streets, even if only a few, along with a compact little downtown area with pleasant surprises like a Chevy-Buick dealership in business since 1922.

Also unique among county villages of comparable population are its large hospital-nursing home complex, its fine public library, and its own K-12 school system. (Years ago kids from as far away as Conover used to take the train over to Phelps each day to go to high school!)

Gone are some of the landmarks of the last century, like the Wausau-Ontonagon Road that was built in 1860 to connect with the projected Military Road up into Michigan (they met at North Twin Lake). Gone too is the Military Road, and some of the earliest resorts like the pioneer northwoods hostelry, the Thomas resort of 1882. In town the old boarding house-hotel burned in 1934, and the opera house and movie theater serve different uses.

Still active are some of the farms on the rolling hills where the glaciers laid down their gentle ground moraine of arable soil. Hearty Finns cleared many of these in between their mill or woodcutting duties, and these farms south and east of town are one of the county's most satisfying sights.

The large, scenic lakes naturally drew vacationists. The first establishment was the old Twin Lakes Hunting and Fishing Club around 1885; this was the predecessor of the Lakota Resort, which was completed in time for the summer guests of 1893, burned that very autumn, was later rebuilt, and ran for forty years. (The site was the west end of North Twin, actually in the Town of Conover; all of the north shore of the lake is in Conover, the south shore in the Town of Phelps.)

A former steward from the hunting and fishing club, C. E. Hazen, bought land on Long Lake, even before Hackley was built, and toted his building materials from Conover to his property, with an intermediate barge trip on Big Twin. His resort, founded in 1901, is still delightfully active and inspired many summer homes on adjacent lots on Long Lake.

The next long, narrow, hill-set lake to the east is Big Sand, on which a big private club began before 1900; it is still there too, along with many private summer places.

Phelps's lakes are unchanging, but their surfaces reflect new uses, like the resorts and clubs, the smaller housekeeping cottage clusters and private summer or permanent homes, and new fun, like water skiing or sailing—Phelps is the sailing center of the northwoods. Perhaps the area that sees the least change is the Smoky Lake Reserve, a 13,000-acre private hunting and fishing preserve six miles east (not open to the public).

SIGHTSEEING AND TOURING

• Phelps townsite embraces past and present. Note the unusual business center, with the lakeshore occupying one side of the main street and giving the town much of its pleasant character—a bit like the Finger Lakes communities of New York State. For a pretty look at the lake, circle the hilltop behind the library-community building. One of the most pastoral instants in my Phelps visits was spotting the weekly freight train in a September twilight; the caboose lights twinkled as the big diesel moved about in ankle-deep grass to assemble its little train of three cars. The North Western keeps trying to abandon this, its tiniest but most picturesque branch line, but Phelps keeps fighting just as hard to keep it.

• Military Road, built in the 1860s and 1870s, followed much the same route as present Forest Roads 2178 and 2199, County E, and Road 2205. Marker in 2205 picnic area.

• Phelps lakes are scenic and unusually large. Note too how most are long and narrow, lying on a north-northeast axis in between high ridges in parallel rows. They follow the direction of the glacial lobe. Notable lakes are North Twin, Long, Big Sand, Smoky.

• Black Jack Springs, proposed wilderness area. See Eagle River: Nicolet Forest.

• Lac Vieux Desert is covered in Land O' Lakes chapter.

• Highway 17 east, while generally scenic all the way to Michigan, with its lakes and woods, offers two unique treats: long-distance vistas from ridge top to ridge top (the only true vistas in the county, over farm-forest valleys); and a wooded stretch with tall hemlocks, a tree species rarely seen except in secluded spots.

• Highway A toward Forest County. Its first miles pass working farms, many rather pretty. Particularly scenic approaching the eastward turn around mile 2. Woods dominate the road eastward in an area noted for spring trillium displays. Access off A, also, to small dam at outlet of Long Lake, rather scenic.

• Forest Road 2199 south from the supper club traverses farms; nice northward prospect at mile 1.5. Side roads here are pretty with farms as well.

• Highway 17 west skirts lake, then hides in young hardwoods, bright in fall.

• Highway E west passes little development in subclimax hardwoods, nice in fall.

• Highway K west. See Conover. Rugged and very, very pretty.

RECREATION

BIKING
• Nicolet Bikeway. A good part of this mapped and tested 70-mile loop to Three Lakes is in the Phelps area; get a map since trunk routes are not allowed signs.

CANOEING
- Military Creek is canoeable for perhaps a mile through wetlands from access on Highways K and E in town; very quiet; no place, however, to leave the canoe.

- Deerskin River from Highway A toward Eagle River chain. See Eagle River.

GOLF
- Big Sand Lake Golf Course, seven miles east on 17. Nine holes, scenic.

HAYRIDES AND SLEIGHRIDES
- John Volkmann, Pine Valley Farm, south of town. One of the northland's exceptional treats is a sleighride in deep snow-muted forests, among heavy evergreens and past forgotten log cabins; this is John Volkmann's specialty; also summer hayrides. Minimum group is 15; John will help combine groups to meet that figure. Reservation only, 545-2510.

PARKS, BEACHES, RECREATION AREAS
- North Twin Lake, downtown. Tables and dock, nice for a snack.

- North Twin Lake Park, opposite hospital on 17 west. Sand-pebble beach in a nice setting; tables and grill.

- Spectacle Lake Picnic Area, off Highway A. Four picnic units, beautiful beach.

- Wayside on Highway 17 east at Smoky Lake. Beautiful long lake with high wooded hills on both sides. Tables, impromptu water fun area at boat ramp.

SAILING
- Regattas and races are frequent in this hotbed of sailing activity and headquarters town for the Northwoods Sailing Association; check locally for dates. Sailing on the Phelps lakes is excellent.

SNOWMOBILING
- Phelps Twin Lakes Snowmobile Club; about 16 miles of funded trails.

SHOPPING AND BROWSING

- Hackley House, in town, May–fall or by chance, closed Sunday. Antiques. The home that the mill company provided for its superintendent has been beautifully reworked to become an exceptional antiques shop, unique in the quality and variety of its stock, in its warm hospitality, and in its approach: each room in the home contains only the antiques, furniture, and primitives appropriate to that room's role in family living! Only discreetly marked prices remind you that your walk through history is taking place in a shop and not in a museum. Excellent reputation.

• Art Holt's minnow stand is a Phelps institution, at Highways E and K's crossing of Military Creek. He is open 24 hours a day, catches his own bait, is a delightful source of interesting information. In winter he goes fur trapping.

DINING

• Hazen's Long Lake Lodge, off 17 east; June–October, evenings by reservation only, 545-2554. This is the warm, mellow, spotless log dining room of an American-plan resort rather than a supper club, so only two entree choices are offered, one usually a roast. Everything possible is genuine and homemade (by three generations of the family working side by side), from the muffins to the relishes. The vegetables, the table flowers, many of the fruits come from the family garden, a tradition here. Excellent food—with a warm welcome. Beer. My repeated visits make me bold enough to place Hazen's at the top of all this book's dining recommendations.

• Holiday Lodge, on 17 west. Rustic decor, mounted game. Full menu, many items homemade, like soups, dressings, memorable cheesecake. Daily noon and evening summer hours taper off to winter weekend evenings only; closed March–April. Bar.

• North Twin Supper Club, on 17 west, in town; closed Tuesday, all year, 545-2775. Appealing meals, tastily prepared, with touches like creative appetizers (even tiny fried shrimp on my visit) and wild rice with their duck; good soups. Big-city steak-house decor offers a switch from constant northwoods rustic. Cocktails.

LODGING

• Afterglow Lake Resort, Sugar Maple Lane off E, all year. Housekeeping, 12 units with carpet, fireplace, wood decor on private lake; sand beach. Remarkable activities spectrum: all winter sports; water sports, vigorous summer sports and team activities (handball, racquetball, tennis, volleyball, softball). Appeal is to those inclined toward socializing and exertion rather than solitary privacy.

• Hazen's Long Lake Lodge, off 17 east, June into October. Full American plan. Carpeted, fireplace-equipped cottages on brow of lakeshore hill, also lodge rooms with bath. Sand beach, raft, sailing. Noon meal often takes form of cookout or picnic in Nicolet Forest. Hazen's is a northwoods synonym not only for hospitality but also for friendship. (Also see Dining.) (See *WISCONSIN trails*, Summer 1975.)

• North Twin Lodge, on 17 about five miles west, all year. Housekeeping, 13 units (many are excellent new duplexes with attractive furnishings, bunks for kids and queen-size beds for their folks). Pretty setting overlooks an island; sand beach plus an indoor pool! This would make an interesting vacation choice.

CAMPING: NICOLET NATIONAL FOREST

• Kentuck Lake Campground. See Eagle River.

- Lac Vieux Desert Campground. See Land O' Lakes.

- Spectacle Lake Campground, off Highway A via Forest Roads 2196 and 2572, late May–mid September. 40 units.

EVENTS

- Summerfest, July (two days), regatta, dances, exhibits, entertainment.

- Firemen's Picnic, August, games and refreshments.

- Colorama, in color time.

- Phelps Snowmobile Derby, races and endurance run, around February.

INFORMATION

- Phelps Chamber of Commerce, Phelps 54554.

- Phelps Public Library, community center complex on 17 east, in town, is operated by the Woman's Club; a bright new facility!

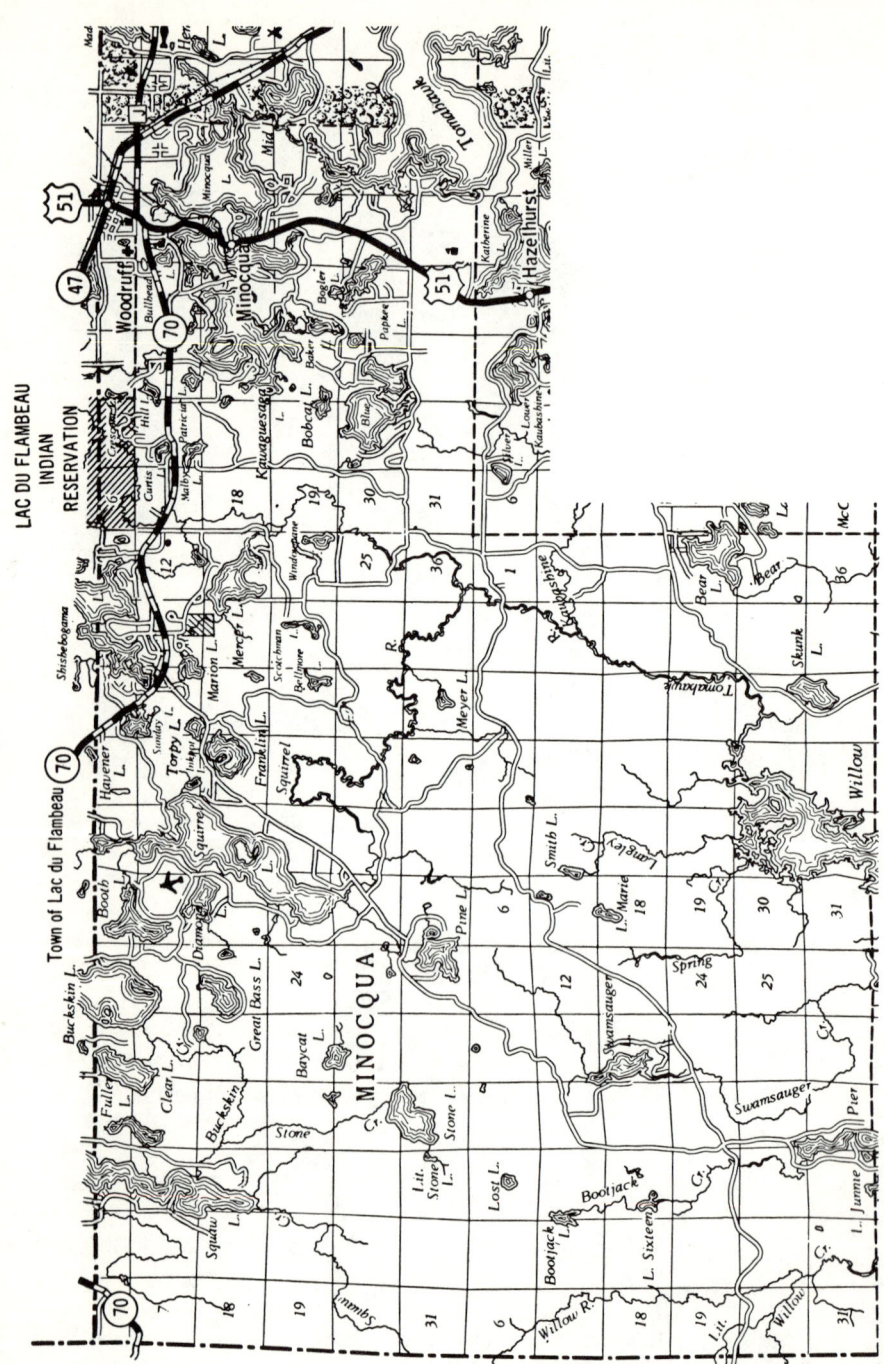

ONEIDA COUNTY

MINOCQUA

If a pageant of Minocqua history were staged and all the characters appeared in one grand finale, log drivers would be mingling with water skiers, pioneer surveyors chatting with resort operators, moccasined Indians rubbing elbows with an ex-president. And somewhere on the stage, as modern merchants watched, "Captain" Stiles Ray would toot the whistle of his little steamboat, the first one on the lakes in the 1890s, while conductor Charlie Carman and engineer Bernard Enckhausen would compare watches for the departure of "Mr. Carman's Train," as the boondock express north to Boulder Junction was called.

Such are the people who have trod the stage of Minocqua history. The Indians ranged the entire area because it was close to their Lac du Flambeau stamping ground and was on one of their canoe routes. Minocqua's name, in fact, is a corruption of the name of an Indian chief, tradition claims.

The loggers came because of timber, some of which they drove down river and some of which they saved to send out two decades later by rail from 1900 to 1915.

The early focus of Minocqua was upon the point of land just south of the second bridge on the old railroad, now the bike trail. An Astor trading post there, we are told, swapped furs with the Indians. Much later a train track reached there in fall 1887 at the cost of several horse and ox teams that the nearby swamp simply swallowed, according to local folklore, while their drivers ran for their lives. An instant tent village grew up, with two tent taverns and a tent store along with a log saloon or two. The first sawmill was situated there, as was one of the first big resorts 13 years later.

Symbolically, the first building near the site that was finally selected for the town, in 1888-89, was a hotel, and the first one in the actual townsite was also a hotel. The new town was a raw one, with maybe 15 houses, half painted, a few stores, and some hotels and some boardwalks in the stumps and mud. Buildings multiplied till a great fire in 1912 and its cleanup gave birth to a business district of brick.

Vacation accommodations more sophisticated than wooden boarding houses along the side streets began appearing by the 1890s or 1900, mostly lodges. Cottage colonies for housekeeping patrons multiplied after 1920. Summer homes appeared during those periods too; many had no original land access, and their owners had to come up by train and travel all summer by boat between town and cottage. Small wonder that boat-building shops were among early Minocqua's most active businesses and their output up to 125 boats a year, that there were elaborate boat liveries, or that the island shore was dotted with private little boathouses.

Farmers did not play a large role in Minocqua history, although resort owners had to be farmers in the early days to the extent that they needed gardens and cows to put food on their lodge tables. Homeowners needed cows too. One estimate claims that the island had 65 cows at one time and all had to be led across the bridge to pasture every morning and back at night.

One of the fruits that a later, greater growth in summer visiting brought was the cluster of interesting shops around Minocqua. Another was the young crew of Min-Aqua Bats who took to the waters in the early 1950s as ski show pioneers. A third was celebrity visitors, with General and ex-President Dwight Eisenhower at the top of the list.

SIGHTSEEING AND TOURING

• Minocqua village and chain of lakes. To most tourists, Minocqua is "the island," the central business and residential area. Stores here are adopting an attractive, timbered Tudor architecture. One of the most interesting businesses would lose all its unique charm if it were remodeled that way: the 1913 popcorn wagon, near the police station (open all summer; a Minocqua landmark since 1947).

A small monument in a streetside triangle near Bosacki's honors war dead from 1914 to 1954.

A drive down the side streets and roads will disclose the charming semi-island nature of the townsite. Lake Minocqua offers a watery playground and the novel scenery of its old, towered boathouses. The lake is connected with Kawaguesaga and Tomahawk lakes to form a chain linked to Lake Katherine via a canal.

Much of Minocqua's population and commerce is now located in residential areas around the chain and shopping districts along major highways north and west.

• Jim Peck's Wildwood, Highway 70 west, May–October. I consider this the nicest of area animal parks: commercially on a low key, exceptionally clean and unsmelly. Wandering animals like deer, pettable babies from farm or woods; caged animals, some unusual like prairie dogs and cute little ferrets; fishponds; little nature trail into a scenic swamp. In many places interpretive signs help make a visit more informative. Moderate admission.

• Squirrel Hill and fire tower, off Squirrel Lake Road (turn east at unmarked dirt road just south of Squirrel Creek and south on paved road at 0.3 mile). Excellent views in most directions; for brave souls craving more, there's the ladder of the tower.

• Cedar Falls, reached most easily via Hazelhurst. See Hazelhurst.

• A note about traveling side roads here: signs have sometimes been turned around by pranksters. Carry a map.

• Squirrel Lake Road, Bo-Di-Lac Drive, Bo-Di-Lac Road scenic loop south of Highway 70 west. Quite varied lake views and deep woods (notably near Diamond Lake). Unusually nice boglet along Jansen Road to west. This loop is area's prettiest.

• Chicago Rod and Gun Club Road, north from 70 west. Short, scenic; esker or similar ridge above lake.

• Mercer Lake Road and Driftwood Road, south from 70 west. Generally pretty.

• Country Club, Thoroughfare, and Mid Lake roads between Highway 51 south and Highway 47 from Woodruff. Typical residential and lake cottage artery, but a scenic one.

• Not accessible to public, the Finnerud Pine Forest state scientific area.

RECREATION AND ENTERTAINMENT

AMUSEMENT PARK
- Holiday Park, Highway 51 north, seasonal. Giant slide, mini golf, and similar activities.

BIKE RENTAL
- Bosacki's Tackle Shop, Highway 51 in town, 356-5292.

BIKING
- Bearskin Recreation Trail. See Hazelhurst. Minocqua access not completed.
- Circle trips on public roads. See Sightseeing and Touring.
- No biking is permitted on the main business blocks of Highway 51 on the island. Use side streets.

BOAT AND CANOE RENTAL
- Bosacki's Tackle Shop, Highway 51 in town, 356-5292.
- Minocqua Marine Mart, Highway 51 north (P.O. Box 31), 356-9411.
- Roberts Sports Center, Highway 70 west, 356-5824.
- Smith Brothers Marine, Highway 51 north, 356-5551. Fishing motors only.

CANOEING
- Squirrel River from Squirrel Lake Road downstream. Pretty at first, quiet.
- Tomahawk River to Willow Reservoir. Check locally on conditions.

GOLF
- Minocqua Country Club, Country Club Road east from Highway 51 south. Nine holes.
- Timber Ridge, Highway 51 south. Members only.

PARK, BEACH, RECREATION AREA
- Torpy Park, in town. Beach with lifeguards in season; tables, tennis.
- Indoor pool sometimes open to public at Lakeland Union High School, on 51 north.

SCUBA
- Bennett's Sport Shop, Highway 51 north, 356-3900. Air, rentals.

SHOOTING
- Minocqua Gun Club, Highway 51 south. Daily in season.

SKIING / CROSS COUNTRY: RENTAL
- Bennett's Sport Shop, Highway 51 north, 356-3900. I rent my skis here.

- Easy Slider Ski Touring Academy, Northern and Kawaga roads off 51 south (P.O. Box 211, Woodruff 54568), 356-2657. Rentals, instruction program, groomed trails.

- North Country Experience/Musical Madness, 313 Chicago Ave. New operation.

SKIING / CROSS COUNTRY: TRAILS
- Easy Slider Ski Touring Academy (see Rentals). Check on fees; groomed trails.

- Schlecht Lake Ski Trail (DNR), Highway 51, onto Leary Road. 2.2 miles; short, challenging.

SKIING: DOWNHILL
- Squirrel Hill, see Sightseeing for directions. Four slopes, three rope tows; weekends and vacations.

SNOWMOBILE RENTAL
- Minocqua Marine Mart, Highway 51 north (P.O. Box 31), 356-9411.

- Roberts Sports Center, Highway 70 west, 356-5824.

SNOWMOBILING
- Bearskin Recreation Trail. See Hazelhurst.

- Local trail network, Lakeland Scenic Trails, groomers.

STABLE
- Circle M Corral, Highway 70 west. Trail riding, pony rides, evening hayrides with marshmallow roast. Clean, responsible, well-supervised operation carefully matches rider and horse. Cute little Saddle Bum shop with horse-related gifts and gear.

SUMMER THEATER
- Northern Lights Summer Playhouse. See Hazelhurst.

TENNIS
• Lakeland Union High School, Highway 51 north, four courts; Torpy Park, in town, two courts.

WATER SKI SHOWS
• Min-Aqua Bats, Aqua Bowl, in town, 8 p.m. Wednesday, Friday, Sunday until Labor Day. Since 1952, the finest in water ski shows. Free; collection.

SHOPPING AND BROWSING

• American Heritage, in town. Showcase of the Indian heritage (jewelry, rugs, gifts) and the folk heritage (primitives, antiques, art).

• Book World, in town, *is* a world of paperback, regional, and hardbound books.

• Cheddar Shed, Old Depot complex, in town. Gourmet foods, cheese, sausage in tiny but cheery shop; silver and jewelry in The Loft section.

• Christmas Chalet, three miles south on 51, May–December. Colorful, fragrant array of Christmas gifts, decorations along with all-season gifts, imports.

• Greenleaf Shoppe, 51 in town. Uncommonly charming and aromatic shop with unusual items among home and kitchen accessories, gifts (especially men's), doll reproductions, and, rarest of all, pipes and tobacco in a cute shop-within-a-shop.

• Little Swiss Village. See Dining.

• Millie's Antiques, 110 Milwaukee, March–December. Need a 1922 Cadillac, in black? Millie has one in the garage at her home and shop, besides a large stock of antiques from small primitives to player-piano-size furniture.

• Mole Hole, 51 just south of bridge, May–December. Here books, toys, home accessories, and gifts cluster in their own different alcoves in a homelike shop.

• Northwoods Nature and Art Center, 8090 Thoroughfare Road (via Country Club Road from 51 south), July and August, or by chance most of year. Books (native American, nature, regional); art (prints, little showings of original art); bells for collectors.

• Olde Minocqua Boardwalk, 51 north. New mini mall begun in 1977; among early shops: Gem Trader (Indian jewelry, kachinas, rugs, sand paintings).

• Popov's Gifts and Gallery, 51 north, May–December. Limited edition prints, carvings, original art, decorative accessories, gifts—chosen and displayed with restraint and taste.

• Schneider's Pottery Shop, Squirrel Lake Road (Fire Number 8441), May–Labor Day. Pottery and textiles created by the owners.

• Vagabond Lover, in town. Unusual art, jewelry, and apparel, much of it imported.

- Wildlife Art Gallery and Gifts, 51 north, mid May–October. Original work by several nature artists; prints; gift area (pottery, pewter, home accessories).

DINING

- Back Bay Inn, off Highway 70, seven miles west; evenings, all year, 356-3228. Uncongested, many-windowed, carpeted dining areas; contemporary appointments; meals here, notably the specials, combine quality, value, and thoughtful touches (almondine vegetables, for instance). Cocktails.

- Bosacki's, in town; noons and evenings, all year, no reservations on Friday (their immensely popular fish night). Lake-view dining room blends Tudor, contemporary, wildlife elements. Wide menu selection even at noon. Interesting old bar.

- Holiday Inn Supper Club, Highway 51 south; daily in summer, short week rest of year, 356-5875. Garden-view dining room. Extensive menu. Salad bar is unquestionably the best in terms of novelty, luxury, and quality that I encountered in northwoods dining. That quality continues to unusual soups, generous entrees. Cocktails.

- Jansen's Squirrel Lake Lodge, Squirrel Lake Road off 70 west; daily, May–November, noons and evenings by reservation only, 356-3442. Resort dining room, one entree, often a roast; family style. Unique in that Mrs. Jansen herself home cooks and bakes everything on huge, half-century-old wood-burning range. Beer.

- Little Swiss Village, three miles west on Blue Lake Road; breakfast and lunch only to 3 p.m., daily, May–October, 356-3675. Delightful Alpine complex of restaurant, motel, shops in pined hollow with flower beds, stone walls. Small knotty-pine dining room. Hearty sandwiches, unusual pancakes, touches like wintergreen garnish. Beer. Motel units are little Alpine-type duplexes, low roofed, wide eaved; nine nicely furnished suites of sitting, bed, bath rooms. Separate clock and gift shops, both tastefully Swiss in merchandise and decor.

- Mama's Supper Club, three miles west on 70; evenings, weekends only in winter, 356-5070. Deservedly popular; carpeted, picture-windowed, lake-view dining rooms; Mediterranean decor; attentive service, a hostess who really listens and cares. American and Italian fare includes the unusual, such as delicious Italian breaded chicken breasts. Limited number of reservations taken 24 hours in advance, a thoughtful courtesy by a restaurant that is almost invariably full. Cocktails.

- Paul Bunyan, 51 north; daily, late May–Labor Day. Faithful logging camp surroundings. All-you-can-eat meals, usually chicken and another entree or two from noon on; served till noon, the big breakfast makes a good brunch. Curios, gifts.

LODGING

AMERICAN PLAN
- Driftwood Lodge, off 70 west via Mercer Lake Road to 8400 Driftwood Place

(Route 2, Box 312), May–October. Lovely grounds on narrow lip of a hilly point; 11 cottages with living room. Modified American plan; bar; swimming pool.

• Jansen's Squirrel Lake Lodge, Squirrel Lake Road off 70 west (Route 2, Box 203), May–November. Spotlessly maintained, full American plan resort stressing quiet and home cooking (see Dining). Pine grounds, sand beach; eight cottages and some rooms with bath; log lobby where fireplace fire glows nightly.

• The Northern Resort Hotel, end of Northern Road off 51 south (Route 3, Box 55), Memorial–Labor days. Modified American plan. Six cottages, 18 rooms with bath. Pioneer resort retaining essence of its 1900 beginnings through careful preservation and judicious updating. Sandy beach, expansive lawns, interesting setting.

HOUSEKEEPING COTTAGES

• Acklam's Hook and Hoof Resort, just off 70 west (Route 1, Box 230), May–October. Six well-appointed, carpeted or hardwood-floored cottages with interesting view high over beach. Fine resort, well kept and attractive.

• Coachlite Resort, Country Club Road off 51 south (P.O. Box 402), May–October. Tasteful example of how an older resort can be revitalized. Everything very compact, precise, tidy: the grounds, the compound itself, the cottages (eight, most overlooking lake), and the exceptional complex of decks, stairs, and piers. Lovely beach.

• Na Hee Ta Pines, on 51 south (Route 3, Box 21), May–October. Six different, cozy cottages, all with carpet, new kitchens, and baths. Appealing pine setting; dock area.

• The Narrows, Narrows Road off Country Club Road via 51 south (P.O. Box 269), Memorial–Labor days. Seven cottages, including five captivating, tasteful, northwoodsy, varnished wood ones with knotty-pine, carpeted interiors. Attractive pine setting and sandy shoreline.

• St. John's Vacation Homes, off Camp Pinemere Road via 70 west (Route 2, Box 105), all year. Eight up-to-date, carpeted cottages in semicircle between woods and lawn. Sandy beach; boat lagoon, rec room; good reputation over the years.

• Van's Mercer Lake Resort, Killawee Road off 70 west (Route 2, Box 255), May–November. Attractive grounds of tall pines and lawn; six up-to-date, well-furnished cottages; rec room; good beach. A very fine resort indeed.

MOTELS

• Aqua Aire Motel, in town (P.O. Box 13), 356-3433. 10 units.

• Back Bay Inn, off Highway 70, seven miles west (Route 1, Box 261), 356-3228. Indoor pool here is a jewel of the northwoods!

• Cross Trails Motel, 51 north (Route 3, Box 442), 356-5202. 19 units.

• Lakeview Motel, in town (P.O. Box 575), 356-5208. Exceptional urban-lakeside motel with dock and swimming.

• Little Minocqua Motel, 51 south at bridge (P.O. Box 560), 356-3288. 21 units, beach and dock.

- Little Swiss Village. See Dining.
- Pines Motel, 51 north (P.O. Box 223), 356-5228. 30 units.

CAMPING

- Patricia Lake Campsites, Camp Pinemere Road off 70 west (Route 2, Box 119), May–September. Over 70 units.

EVENTS

- Lakeland Gem Club Gemboree, late July, show and demonstrations.
- Aquarama, mid August, summer's main event. Ski show, parade, coronation of queen.
- Beef-A-Rama, fall color time. Clever event: downtown merchants grill beef roasts at their shops, parade with them to the chamber of commerce booth in mid afternoon, and then slice them to feed the throng of visitors.

INFORMATION AND TRANSPORTATION

- Greater Minocqua Chamber of Commerce, P.O. Box 113, Minocqua 54548. Office in old railroad station on 51 in town, 356-5266, open daily in summer, closed Sunday rest of year.
- Public library next to chamber of commerce.
- Bus: Greyhound Lines, summer only; Wisconsin-Michigan Coaches, Woodruff, all year.
- Car rental: Lakeland Rent-a-Car, Lakeland Airport, 356-3891.
- Charter air service: Lakeland Airport, 356-3891.

Increasingly these summer visitors traveled by road, especially after improvements like a 1936 reconstruction of Highway 51, which cut almost seven miles off the distance to Tomahawk alone. The Milwaukee Road, as the old St. Paul had come to be called, first took off the Pullman trains, then the little two-coach day train, and in 1972 even the freight train. It left a stronger Hazelhurst than it had found in the late 1880s, and its roadbed became a new recreational trail.

SIGHTSEEING AND TOURING

• Hazelhurst. Yawkey Street has an array of charming little houses, one an old depot, and Lakeview has a walled estate, park, and weathered derelict of the mill hotel (posted against trespassers). The mill stood along this shore. Across 51 on a hillside, a cemetery, shaded by birch and pine, overlooks quiet Alice Lake in one of the prettiest settings in the north (Lower Kaubashine Road).

• Lake Katherine. This picturesque lake, partly ringed with homes, can be circled via scenic Sylvan Shores Drive and scrubbier Mill Road (6.2 miles), with a 1.9-mile side trip on South Shore Drive. Special points of interest: the tree-dwarfed canal dug to allow boat access from the lake to Lake Tomahawk (the land along it is private; respect that fact); and the incredible narrow ridge along Tigertail Point out on South Shore Drive. Maybe an esker but likelier a glacial ridge formed between melting ice blocks, it is heavily wooded and drops sharply from a very narrow road on its crest—a spectacular surprise!

• Cedar Falls, Oneida Road from 51 westward about a quarter mile, then south on rollicking, woodsy Cedar Falls Road, seven miles. In Oneida County's only real waterfall, the Tomahawk River first skids and then crashes down a raw rock channel. (Private complex of tavern and campground surrounds the falls.)

• Blue Lake and Boehm roads, east from 51 three miles south of town. Pretty little summer vacation lake is distinguished by the esker on its west, which carries Boehm Road between the lake and a marsh further west.

• Warbonnet Zoo, five miles south on 51, May–October. Two compounds, one shady, one open; in the former are northern animals in cages; in the latter, a petting area of deer, geese, and the like, plus access to pens of larger or wilder animals like timber wolves. About 100 animals. Gift shop. Moderate admission fee.

RECREATION AND ENTERTAINMENT

BIKING AND SNOWMOBILING
• Bearskin Recreation Trail (DNR), from Baker Lake Road, Minocqua, to Highway K. 16 miles; Minocqua access not completed; Hazelhurst is the ideal access point with travel possible either north or south from Oneida Road near the Hiawatha tavern. No motorized cycles or other vehicles.
Former Milwaukee Road railroad bed, surfaced with "rotten granite" about seven feet wide; 10 trestles have been planked and fitted with railings, one a long, curving structure. Charming little all-weather rest area on shore of Blue Lake, 3.7 miles south of

Hazelhurst: toilets, tables, grills, water. Isolated route gives a grass-roots glimpse of terrain and growth that highway cannot. Special features: frequent proximity to Bearskin Creek; one spring pond, many marshes, but few close-by lakes; one ridgy area north of 51 overpass. I suggest that if you wish to ride one way only with a car at either end, the southbound ride has slightly easier grades. Prettiest stretches: Hazelhurst to rest area or just beyond; Goodnow (or just above it) to Lakeview Road.
The trail is groomed for snowmobiles and ties in with area trails.

- Town roads also offer good scenic biking, see above (some gravel on Sylvan Shores loop); also the Kaubashine roads.

GOLF
- Pinewood Country Club. See Cassian.

PARK, BEACH, RECREATION AREA
- Lake Katherine Public Beach, foot of Oneida Road in town. Beach, lifeguard, tables, toilets, pump, raft, slides (when I visited, kids were giving a crayfish a ride).

STABLE
- Warbonnet Zoo, five miles south on 51.

SUMMER THEATER
- Northern Lights Summer Playhouse, five miles south off 51, opposite Warbonnet Zoo; nightly plus several matinees, mid June–Labor Day. Permanent theater shell, open sides with canvas curtains to admit or close off weather; good acoustics and sight lines. Light comedy, possibly musicals by 1979. Well-acted performances show effective staging and imaginative use of sets. Ample all-weather parking; bring a wrap for cool nights. Phones: 453-3398, day; 356-7173, evenings (box office). Mail: Route 3, Tomahawk 54487.

TENNIS
- Municipal court behind firehouse in town.

HAZELHURST

"Hazel...Hazel...Haze*lhurst*," thought the lumber baron's wife as she considered a name for the new lakeside town and mill site being prepared for her husband's Yawkey and Lee Lumber Company. Thus was the community named, in 1888 or 1889.

The sawmill (and a box factory added around 1891) boomed and its mill village grew to 1,000 people by 1900. Linking the mill complex to its many woods camps were temporary logging tracks and Yawkey's own common carrier railroad, which could also deliver loaded lumber cars either to the St. Paul Road right close by in Hazelhurst or to the Chicago & North Western at Lake Tomahawk, whichever was giving the best rates.

The earlier history of Hazelhurst is harder to pin down; reports that I have read make it possible that the Astor fur-trading empire had a post near Cedar Falls in the early 1800s and that the local word *Kaubashine* may be a corruption of the name *Capuchin* for a missionary order that may have ministered in the area in the mid 1800s.

The whining saws, by now owned by a successor firm to Yawkey and Lee, the Yawkey-Bissell Lumber Company, bit into their last log in October 1911. Even so, the mill's twenty-two-year life was an unusually long one; nearby Garth, whose mill had begun cutting around the same time, had lasted only about five years and its townsite then lay idle until its resurrection as a summer resort (Schwartz's) around 1903.

The sawmill company's store and huge boarding house were turned over to new owners and unneeded mill houses torn down. But the community did not die. Other loggers worked the woods to the northwest till 1914, and agriculture, resorting, even fox ranching and concrete block manufacturing helped take up the slack.

Lake Katherine, already site of some tasteful estates, drew additional summer-home builders, and log bungalow resorts attracted short-term visitors.

DINING

- Jacobi's Hiawatha, Oneida Road just west of 51, in town; noons and evenings all year, closed Monday except in summer. Likeable local tavern with picturesque barroom and separate wallpapered, carpeted dining room; family operated; modest prices, very good food, especially fish and chicken. I like the place!

LODGING

- Black's Cliff Resort, Lower Kaubashine Road, all year. 10 log cottages featuring fireplaces, new remodeling, novel swinging beds on porches, and other thoughtful touches; lovely hilltop site, very northwoodsy; fine waterfront and beach. Sparkling hosts devote much attention to guests via canoe trips, cookouts, etc.

- Parkside Motel (formerly Lee Lake Motel), a mile south on 51, all year, 356-6449. Six units.

CAMPING

- Big Bearskin Lake, Lakewood Road three miles south of Highway D. 18 units.

EVENTS

- Hazelhurst Carnival, late July weekend, carnival, games, water fights, meals.

- Farewell to summer vacationists. Crowd gathers at Whitman's Bar on 51 on Labor Day to wave farewell to departing vacationists...more than a bit superciliously.

- Winter Fun Day, late February, ice-fishing contest.

INFORMATION

- Hazelhurst Chamber of Commerce, P.O. Box 22, Hazelhurst 54531. Information booth, Highway 51 in town, 356-5533, open Friday, Saturday in summer. At other times attendant may be reached by phoning number posted at booth.

THE WILLOW REGION

The Willow Region, named for Willow Lake, River, and Reservoir, is Oneida County's southwest corner, including (for purposes of this book) the southern portion of the Town of Minocqua and the long north-south towns of Lynne and Little Rice.

The area is more interesting than scenic, with its esker-tinged terrain and vast reaches of second-growth forest with nary a house. Nowhere else in the two counties has man's

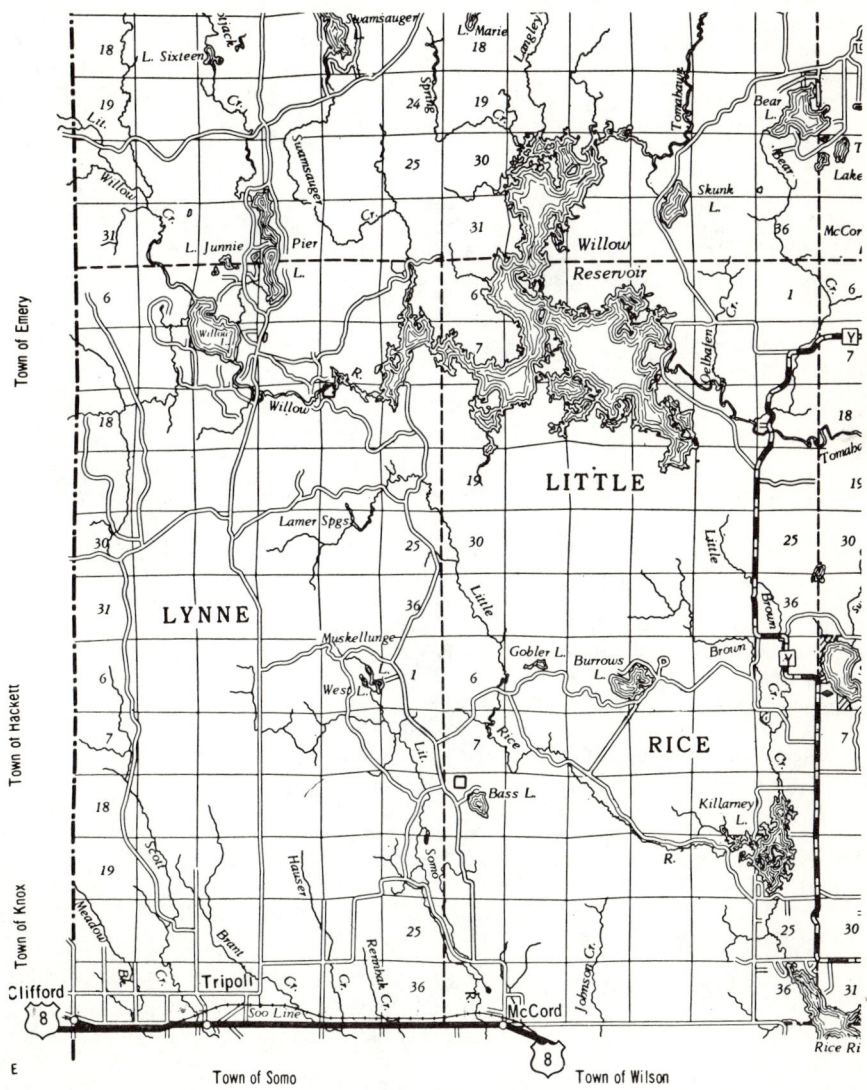

Willow Region/113

touch so altered a whole region, lately with creation of the sprawling Willow flowage, and a generation earlier with removal of majestic forests that were never succeeded by anything else as colorful or interesting as farms, villages, or resorts, and that never bounced back with the grandeur that second-growth forests have attained at many other places in the northwoods.

Its heart was logged by pine loggers in the 1880s, driving their cut down the Tomahawk River. What they left or could not reach was taken by railroad loggers by 1914 or so. The vast number of easterly pointing, newer-fallen trees will be a reminder for decades of another conqueror of trees, the Fourth of July storm of 1977.

Wisconsin Valley Improvement Company built its Willow Dam in 1926 to form a 7,400-acre reservoir; this brought a little resort development. Other development has occurred around Pier and Willow lakes.

In early years the area was not closely knit, and even today there is hardly a road worthy of mention going east or west between Lynne and Little Rice. Instead, traffic moves north and south, in Lynne via the Squirrel Lake-Pine Lake-Willow roads between Highway 70 and Tripoli. In Little Rice, Highway Y between Hazelhurst and Bradley is the main artery.

The southern edge of the area looked to towns along the county line and the Soo Line railroad. McCord was the mill and general store hamlet for the east; its final gasp came with a CCC camp in the thirties. West, four miles, Tripoli had begun in 1900 as a mill town and in 1923 boasted a mill complex big enough to keep 300 men busy in wood camps or on 10 miles of logging tracks. Later it dwindled to a crossroads hamlet.

SIGHTSEEING AND TOURING

• An important note: drive the back roads of the Willow Region *with a map*, preferably the Oneida County Rural Road Directory as well as a copy of the county forestry department's map of the Willow Region unit of the Oneida County forests; that is the snowmobile trail map available free.

• Willow Region eskers. Vilas-Oneida's largest concentration of eskers (snaky ridges, once glacial stream courses). Willow Road rides an esker for 0.4 mile just north of its crossing of the Willow River. Many others, in strings up to four miles long, are hidden off the roads.

• Willow Rapids County Park, 0.9 mile east from Willow Road ball park via Rapids Road; follow signs. Major, scenic rapids somewhat blighted by loss of trees in 1977 storm but still rugged and pretty. Tables, toilets.

• Oneida County Forest, south of a line from Pier Willow to Burrows Lake, is interesting because of the huge area and absence of development.

• Tripoli, Highway 8 at Willow Road. Old concrete-chinked log church with novel belfry next to it; note benches beneath the bell.

• Bass Lake County Park. McCord Road (four miles east of Tripoli) four miles north from Highway 8. Tables on water, and tables, grills, toilets in spotless pine grove; restful and, like all Oneida County parks, very neatly kept.

• Gobler Lake State Scientific Area. McCord Road north 5.7 miles from Highway 8; Kelly Fire Lane 1.6 miles east to fork of Burrows Lake Road (from the left of the fork). Burrows is impassable for most cars; park here and walk as far as you wish on Burrows. The road climbs up and down eskers for over a mile. Road construction and wear, and gravel pit, bare the stony material of the esker. The Gobler scientific area is the muskeg with the spindly tamaracks along the esker's north side. Though hard to reach, this little area is one of the north's great natural surprises. Exit via Kelly Lane 1.3 miles to road right-angling in from left, and take that road to Burrows Lake Road and east to Highway Y.

- Killarney Dam, Little Rice Dam Road 0.8 mile west from Highway Y. Three-gate earth-fill dam creating a lake with pretty shoreline.

- Willow Dam and Reservoir, Willow Dam Road loop off Highway Y. U-shaped three-gate concrete, earth, and riprap dam holds back the flowage. The Wisconsin Valley Improvement Company provides public landings, and the shore can be a good place to search for driftwood.

RECREATION

CANOEING
- Tomahawk River. Five access points between the dam and Lake Nokomis.

HIKING AND HUNTING
- Seeded, mowed habitat trails in the Oneida County Forest. Get map locally.

SNOWMOBILING
- County Forest Trail, two loops, 47 miles, rest area where they meet. Parking at Pier Willow and at Burrows Lake. Map available.

- Trail connections toward Hazelhurst and Tomahawk; Northern Trails Unlimited.

DINING

- Willow Haven, Willow Dam Road; evenings, Tuesday–Sunday at least in summer, all year. Carpeted, attractive dining area, brawny furniture; good salad bar and entrees (e.g., my beef: big portion, perfectly done, on hot platter) but sour cream and hash browns less good. Also cottages; grounds very cluttered. Cocktails.

THE CASSIAN-NOKOMIS AREA

The Cassian-Nokomis area involves three towns, those two and Woodboro, and the other familiar names, Goodnow and Harshaw, once railroad station stops.

The original Cassian settlement was located in what is now the Town of Nokomis, not in today's Town of Cassian at all. It began in the latter 1880s as Casanova Junction, jumping-off point for a logging track from the main line of the Chicago, Milwaukee & St. Paul; a hamlet grew up around the junction, a store, and a mill there; sawing took place into the years just before World War I. Nothing now remains of the settlement proper, though farms homesteaded and laboriously carved out by 1890s and 1900s pioneers like Olaf Olson are still active or commemorated by forest clearings.

Woodboro began only a little later. The George E. Wood Lumber Company built a mill and fifty homes around 1893 and logged along its private railroad till a serious fire around May 1904 shortened its operations.

Harshaw was a railroad station site; it took its name from a former state treasurer and

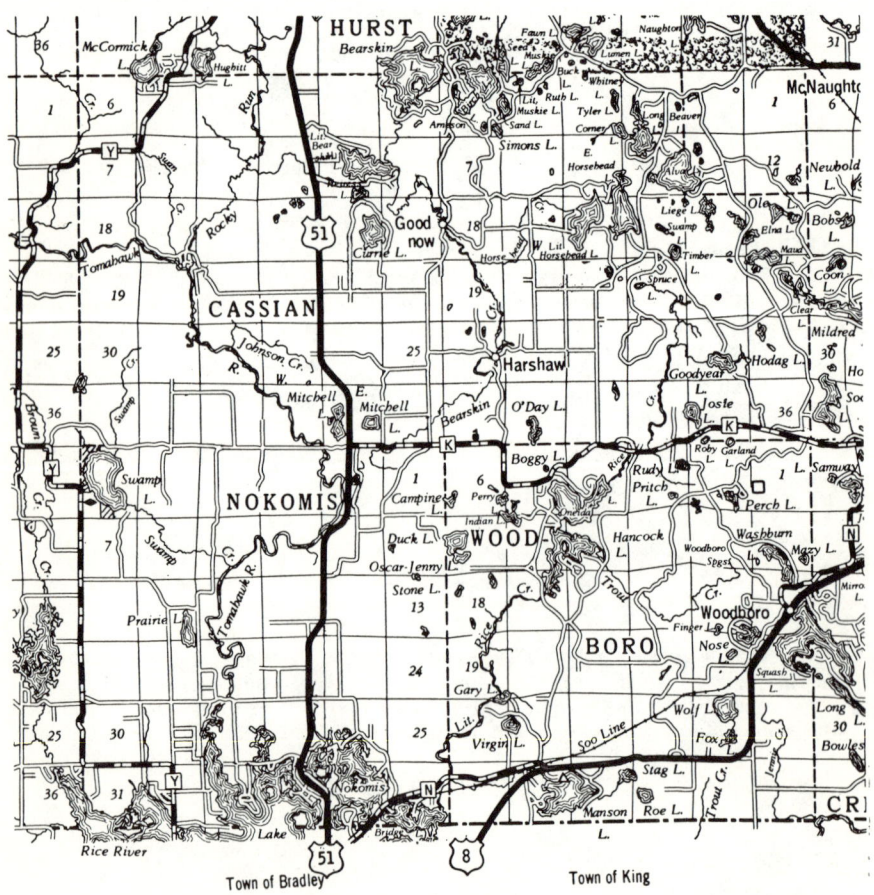

116/Oneida County

was a pine-sawing town by the 1890s. Farming succeeded lumbering, as attested to by the two now derelict potato warehouses where the tracks used to be. **Goodnow** was only a crossing stop north on the line of the St. Paul. The modern site of Harshaw post office is a bit north of there, and one of the area's pioneer resorts is still active, the Idlewild lodge and cottage complex of 1921.

SIGHTSEEING AND TOURING

- Harshaw is a pleasant hamlet in hollows along Church Road and Bearskin Creek.

- Woodboro is just a crossroads with homes, taverns, a supper club, and an occasionally used pulpwood-loading track, but Nose Lake Road west from the rail crossing lilts a couple miles across hill-creased farm and lake lands to pass a tiny, nostalgic family graveyard.

- Chief attraction of the Town of Nokomis is its scenic, sprawling namesake, Lake Nokomis. Bell Road off Highway Y at the county line peeks at it through trees and yards. Highway N passes a pretty eastern section before darting on past woods and farms. The town also has two crossings of the Tomahawk River at attractive bends in the stream, on Swamp Lake Road near 51 and on Prairie Rapids Road, where the bend has mysterious old rock bridge piers and a roadside table.

- Highway 8 through the Woodboro area is the most pastorally scenic stretch of main highway in Oneida County, intermingling long farm vistas with splendid lakes like Manson, Squash, and Crescent.

- Highway K travels woods and farms and offers a few long views ahead from ridges.

- Interior roads lace the region; many are pretty; I suggest, for instance, twisty Sand Lake Road between Fawn Lake Road and Lakewood Road.

- Lakewood Road between highways K and D, while varying in scenic quality and smoothness, is a shunpiking alternative to Highway 51, in fact, its predecessor. Possible bike road.

RECREATION

BIKING
- Bearskin Recreation Trail, from Highway K north; facilities limited; be careful of possible deep sand at the parking lot at this end. See Hazelhurst.

- Town roads for biking. See above under Sightseeing.

BOAT, CANOE, SNOWMOBILE RENTAL
- Tomahawk Sports Center, Highway 51, 453-5373.

- Tomahawk Trailer and Boat Sales, Highway 51, 453-2824.

CANOEING
- Tomahawk River from the northwest. See Willow Region. Possible take-out points: Swamp Lake Road or Prairie Rapids Road, west of 51.

GOLF
- Pinewood Country Club, Lakewood Road between Goodnow and Harshaw, Highway 51 access via Rocky Run Road. 18 holes, daily fee. See Dining.

HIKING AND HUNTING
- Oneida County Forest, Cassian-Woodboro unit seeded habitat trails.

PARKS, BEACHES, RECREATION AREAS
- Perch Lake County Park, south from Highway K, about 0.5 mile east of Perch Lake boat landing. Pretty picnic area (no beach). Tables, toilets, open lawn.

- Sand Lake Public Beach, Sand Lake Road, 1.7 miles west from Lakewood Road. Beautiful sand beach, raft, toilets or changing areas.

- Waysides on Highway 51 at Bearskin Creek and Highway 8 at Crescent Lake are unusually pretty for picnicking; waterfront at Crescent site.

SKIING/CROSS COUNTRY
- Pinewood Country Club, see Golf for location, 282-5500. Trails (fee charged), rentals, refreshments, as of press time.

SNOWMOBILING
- Bearskin Recreation Trail. See Hazelhurst and Biking, just above.

- Oneida County Forest, Cassian-Woodboro Trails, 45 miles, rest areas (two); access from Highway K.

- Trails of several clubs converge in this vicinity.

- Rentals listed above under Boat Rental.

DINING

- Hideaway Lodge, Sand Lake Road, 2.5 miles east of Lakewood Road or 8.6 miles east of 51 via Rocky Run, Lakewood, and Sand Lake roads, or follow signs from Highway 47 or Highway D; evenings, all year, closed Monday and Tuesday in winter,

277-2494. This is Oneida County's "better mousetrap" hiding in the woods. Excellent and generous German specialties and roasts prepared from scratch; steaks, fish. Pleasant dining area overlooks lake and bird feeders. Cocktails. Also lodge rooms and housekeeping cottages.

• Phil's Dinner Club, Highway 51 at Lake Nokomis, turn east at the windmill; evenings, daily, all year. Very popular; waits are a distinct possibility. Substantial fare, vaguely Great Gatsby surroundings; no salad bar. Cocktails.

• Pinewood Country Club, see Golf for location; noons and evenings, late April–October, 282-5500. Handsomely furnished dining room, sweeping view on three sides. Full menu, salad bar. My sampling took the form of a broiled cod dinner, which was delicious and attentively served. Cocktails.

LODGING

• Cedarwood Resort, Highway 51 on Lake Nokomis (Route 2, Tomahawk 54487), all year. Housekeeping, four cottages. Look for details like excellent kitchens (even stainless steel tile), wood paneling of variety reflected in each cottage's name (Birchwood...); sand beach, lawns. Bar draws likeable customers; sandwiches.

• Feases' Shady Rest Lodge, Manson Lake. American plan. See Rhinelander.

• Lakewood Resort, Bell Road east from Highway Y at Lincoln County line (Route 2, Tomahawk 54487), May–mid October. Housekeeping, 12 well-kept, paneled cottages (some with lovely lake view) in a tidy compound that is almost like a little village. All combination baths. Sandy beach; mowed, shaded grounds; rec room, bar.

CAMPING

• The Outpost, Highway N at county line (Route 3, Tomahawk 54487), May–October. 250 units.

• Tomahawk Trailer and Boat Sales, Highway 51 in Tomahawk, 453-2824, rents tent campers, delivers and sets them up at local campsites.

INFORMATION

• Cassian Chamber of Commerce, Harshaw 54529, no booth; Rhinelander Area Chamber of Commerce, Rhinelander 54501, office in city hall, booth adjacent; or Tomahawk Chamber of Commerce, Tomahawk 54487, office opposite hotel, all year, 453-2353.

LAKE TOMAHAWK

Lake Tomahawk is the center of a ring of lakes, forests, and state and civic institutions that give it more than just vacation interest and activity.

The Wisconsin River and Tomahawk Lake were its first focal points. To Indians these meant travel routes. The Wisconsin was a direct but sometimes dangerous artery. The lake was a restful link in an alternative route bypassing a portion of the Wisconsin, and was a link in a route to Lac du Flambeau and on to the Chippewa River. A short portage from the Wisconsin to Tomahawk Lake gave access to the Minocqua lakes; from there the Tomahawk River was the bypass to Tomahawk and the Wisconsin again. Or from the Minocqua lakes, portages to Shishebogama and Fence lakes brought travelers to the Flambeau area and direct river links to the Chippewa. Indian habitation on Lake Tomahawk began back beyond record, continued through the fur-trading era (a post was supposed to have operated here around 1804), and lasted to the 1880s. Mounds along the lake are mute memorials.

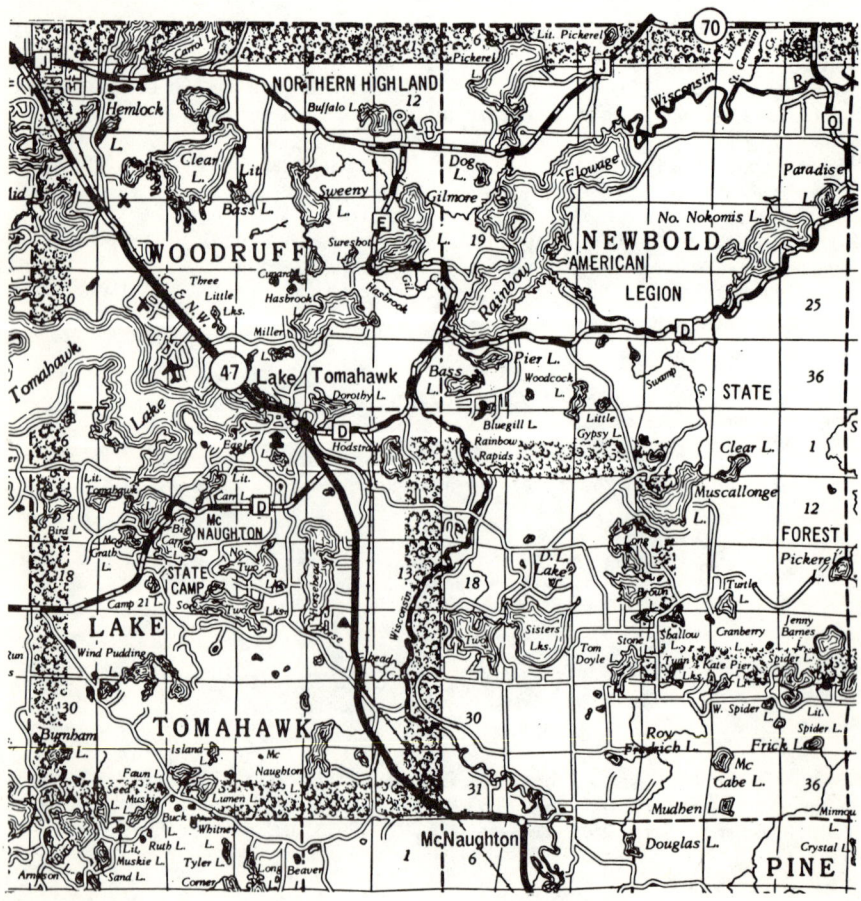

120/Oneida County

Loggers also used the Wisconsin for river drives but the lake mostly for rafting logs to mills or loading points on the lake and a little bit for floating logs for the river trip down the Tomahawk. Many logging firms cut around the lake and deep inland, using the lake to float logs. One had a little mill around 1888, but really only a single firm did large-scale sawing on the lakeshore and that was its name: Lake Shore Lumber Company. It cut from 1890 to 1904. A little village grew up near it; the company sold off its houses for the lumber after it closed down. During that time the town name changed from Rainbow (for a nearby rapids in the Wisconsin) to the name that the railroad had been using since 1888: Tomahawk Lake. The two words were reversed in the 1920s to avoid confusion with Tomahawk.

Its area had a few homesteaders after 1890 but farming was not important. Two early resorts—one a converted summer estate, the Sanders House by 1892, the other the still-remembered Sunflower complex—opened the hospitality era. As elsewhere in the north, it took the dual forms of resorts and private cottages, but the resort growth of the 1920s preceded the summer-home booms of the late thirties and postwar years.

The state's role in Lake Tomahawk came only with tree nursery activity and establishment of a TB rehabilitation camp, both around 1913. State institutions in the neighborhood today include a correctional center on Little Tomahawk Lake. Random cutover forest tracts were systematized into the American Legion State Forest in 1929 and were replanted by the CCC in the 1930s. The forest took the name of another interesting Lake Tomahawk neighbor, for the American Legion had been operating a veterans' camp in the township since 1925.

Since 1962, however, it has been a playing field right in town that brings Lake Tomahawk probably the greatest attention in its history. The sport is snowshoe baseball and modern Lake Tomahawk is its capital (see Recreation).

McNaughton is the familiar Highway 47 corner with the post office-tavern-gas station all in one and settlement around it. The name was recycled to apply to that center when the first McNaughton site was discontinued. It had been a switch along the railroad where a logging line ran out to the mill on McNaughton Lake that D. W. McNaughton was running by 1891 for the Land, Log and Lumber Company.

SIGHTSEEING AND TOURING

● Lake Tomahawk, 3,627-acre lake of many moods. Scenic shoreline, channel to Minocqua chain, and little canal to Lake Katherine.

● Rainbow Reservoir and dam, Highways D and E, three miles north. Five-gate dam built on top of the rapids of the same name in 1936 as part of Wisconsin Valley Improvement Company network of storage areas; 2,035-acre lake.

● Camp American Legion, Highway D south. Short-term convalescent facility and outpatient therapy center for veterans. Public welcome to see therapy facilities, but there's really very little of interest to casual sightseers; it is the role of the institution that brings it honor.

● Rainbow Road-Highway D-Bluebird Road scenic loop. Cross-section of Lake Tomahawk's nicest scenery, south from town and back in a circle. Beautiful woods west of Little Carr Lake; lovely wooded narrows between lakes, along D; varied woods along Bluebird, with lake peeks. Take Kildare east for a mile to Horsehead Lake boat landing to see a pretty lake outlet and tiny dam with only a six-inch drop!

- Highway D south toward Hazelhurst. Pine seed tree nursery, two scenic isthmuses; scenery confined mostly to area between town and McGrath Lake.

- Side roads off Highway D. Fawn Lake Road meanders through generally thick woods all the way to Beaver Lake Road. Off from Fawn Lake Road, Sand Lake Road is pretty (see Cassian), and Big Buck Road west from Fawn to Lakewood has a leafy tunnel and abandoned farm clearing whose rock piles memorialize some forgotten toiler. Lakewood Road south is a shunpike. See Cassian.

- Highways D and E north. Wisconsin River landings, then dull woods, a few lakes on D east to O. E has scenic highlights like Gilmore Lake landing (dam, creek, lakeshore, toilet), scenic side road to Cunard Lake, and a number of hills and curves.

- South of D and back out of easy reach a new Indian Creek Wild Area of 7,000 acres has been proposed; management and development restricted.

RECREATION

BIKING

- No trails; for Sightseeing (above) I selected roads with biking in mind; try those (some gravel on the loop trip).

- Longer loop trip is possible via Rainbow Road, D, Fawn Lake Road, Highway 47 east to Bridge Road (at McNaughton), River Road back to the east edge of town at 47; several lakes, two Wisconsin River crossings; refreshments at McNaughton.

CANOEING

- Small creek between Cunard and Sweeney lakes; road access available to both lakes.

- Wisconsin River. Popular stretches are from landings at Rainbow Dam southward, especially between River Road near town and Bridge Road at McNaughton.

CANOE TRIP SERVICE AND RENTAL

- Canoe Headquarters, on 47 east in town (P.O. Box 143), 277-2549, offers neat package trip between River and Bridge roads on Wisconsin River (canoe, drop off, and pick up) for a reasonable fee; easy, pleasant three- to four-hour float, nice for kids. Also rentals, guide service. An accommodating little operation by an enterprising, interesting woman who also has a unique self-service firewood stand here!

PARKS, BEACHES, RECREATION AREAS

- Indian Mounds Picnic Area, north shore of Lake Tomahawk, off Highway 47 west. Exceptionally attractive picnic grove with real Indian mounds among the tables and grills. Long sandy beach, fine view; boat ramp; toilets, water.

- Big Carr Lake, Highway D. Residents use boat landing as impromptu beach.

SCUBA
- Big and Little Carr lakes have visibility to 50 feet, are popular for diving.

SKATING
- Ice rink and warming house at baseball park in town.

SKIING: CROSS COUNTRY
- McNaughton Lake Ski Trail (DNR), Kildare Road off 47 east. 6.2 miles of trails.

SNOWMOBILE RENTAL
- Recreational Sales, in town, 277-2861. Also outboard motors.

SNOWMOBILING
- Lakeland State Trail. 18.2-mile main loop; access via Hasbrook Drive or Woodruff.
- New-Tom Sno Fleas club grooms local network of trails.

SNOWSHOE BASEBALL
- Yes, players really wear snowshoes during play on a wood-chip field! Matching their giant footwear is a giant ball, 16 inches. Over 700,000 spectators have watched the fun since 1962. In town, 7:15 p.m. Monday, late June–late August. Refreshments.

SHOPPING AND BROWSING

- Buck's Northwoods Sporting Goods, in town. Some gifts and curios in a shop significant for the scale of its outdoor orientation—three guides work out of here.
- Gift and Tackle Shop, in town. Souvenirs, jewelry, moccasins, gifts.
- Lou Gillingham's Eagle Lake Antiques, 8004 Eagle Road; May–October or by chance, closed Tuesday. Lakeside cottage with general line, books, some furniture.
- Prchal's, in town, May–September. Sewn specialties, custom bikinis; handcrafts.

DINING

- Tomahawk Shores, west on 47; nightly except Monday in summer, shorter week other seasons, Sunday brunch, 277-2362. Full menu; very good Friday fish. Cocktails.

LODGING

- Fawn Lake Lodge, Fawn Lake Road off Highway D. Seasonal, housekeeping.

- Lake Tomahawk Motel, west on 47, all year, 277-2330. Six air-conditioned units.

- Tomahawk Shores, on 47 west, all year. Nine motel units, tennis, beach access.

- Wakan Tepe Resort, North Twin Lakes Road off D south, May–October. Housekeeping, five extremely neat knotty-pine cottages, very well arranged and appointed. Woodsy surroundings, excellent beach. One of Oneida's finest little resorts!

CAMPING

- Cunard Lake Campground (DNR), off Highway E. 36 units.

- Indian Mounds Campground (DNR), off 47 west. 43 units.

INFORMATION AND TRANSPORTATION

- Lake Tomahawk Information Bureau, Lake Tomahawk 54539. Information booth, in town, 277-2602, open daily late June–Labor Day.

- Bus: Wisconsin-Michigan Coaches, all year.

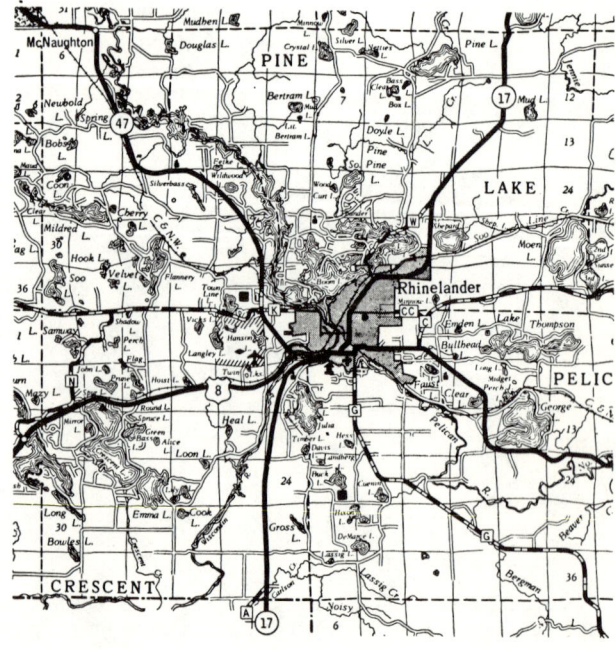

THE RHINELANDER AREA

Rhinelander history can be traced back to landmark events in the 1850s and 1870s. First were the pioneer log drives down the Wisconsin in the late fifties. Their logs went right past the rapids near the Pelican River on their way to mills far downstream. Second was John Curran's choice of a site near the rapids to begin a long, varied career of fur trading, farming, and logging. Third was Anderson Brown's visit by birchbark canoe to the rapids. His imagination pictured the rapids dammed and booms in the resulting lake holding ten or twelve million feet of logs for mills on the site.

Brown's vision came true in the 1880s and 1890s. His family helped induce the Milwaukee, Lake Shore & Western Railroad to the spot, which gave up its old name, Pelican Rapids, in favor of the name of the railroad's president, F. W. Rhinelander, in far-off New York. The trains began arriving in November 1882, and a village sprouted at once. So did mills, the Brown brothers' huge mill among the first, in 1883. An apparent peak came in 1892, when there were 14 different mills or lumber companies in or across the river from Rhinelander, shipping 110 million feet of lumber per year or 30 cars a day. After that some of the little firms were shaken out or burned and the giants got bigger.

River drives fed Rhinelander mills almost exclusively till the mid 1890s, tapering off till the very last drive (down the Pelican) around 1923. A boom company for a while captured logs at a dam (probably built in 1876, surely by the early 1880s); marks put on the logs with hammers by the loggers made sorting possible. By 1895 little logging railroads were necessary to reach upland forests or hardwood stands, since hardwoods would not float for river driving.

Related wood users followed the sawmills, like a screen door or millwork firm, box plant, veneer factory, refrigerator maker, boat works. A supplier of sawmill equipment began here too: in 1889 the Rhinelander Iron Company began making sawmill machinery; it would eventually be erecting boilers and burners even in Canada.

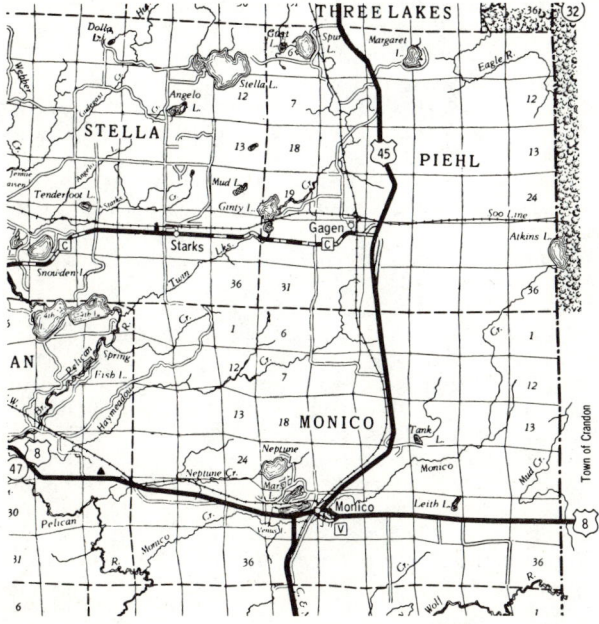

The early 1900s saw two more enduring firms opened. First was the Rhinelander Paper Company whose massive stone millrace, turbine area, and masonry dam and mill were marvels of 1903–4 construction. The mill first made newspaper or butcher paper but saw a future in glassine paper after its first production of that commodity in 1916. St. Regis Corporation purchased it in 1956. Daniels Manufacturing Company opened in 1915 to convert this mill's tissue paper into napkins and crepe paper; now its specialty is packaging, still using locally made paper.

One by one all the great sawmills closed or burned, some taking whole neighborhoods in flames with them, like the 44 houses lost with a mill about 1904. The Brown mill called it quits during World War I and the Browns turned attention to their huge holdings out west.

The lumber business demanded hardy people; so did less swashbuckling fields, like medicine. Pioneer doctors like T. B. McIndoe even used handcars on railroad tracks to cover emergencies; another one, Dr. H. J. Westgate, had moonlighted as a rail post office clerk for three years during medical school to finance his studies, which he completed at age 34.

Brave nuns came into the sawmill town before it was 10 years old to take over a tiny hospital that Doctors McIndoe and A. D. Daniels had started. One way that hospitals met expenses and citizens secured insurance of a sort was through a system of hospital tickets. A ticket bought for a few dollars assured a lumberjack, for instance, of full, prepaid care for a year. Rhinelander's sisters, one of my logger friends recalls, visited the lumber camps to sell the tickets, not even disdaining to eat in the cookshack or sleep in the bunkhouse. A lifetime later, in the 1970s, their hospital is the northwoods's largest.

The maturing city and its visitors enjoyed certain amenities. Wooden hotels had given way by 1916 to the first big, fireproof one, the 66-room Oneida, and moviegoers had a choice between the colorfully named Cozy and Majestic picture palaces. Vacationists could stay at lodges or in cottages by then, or even build cabins of their own on lakes like Lake George that had been subdivided. Children could stay at summer camps by 1916, after rocking all the way up from Chicago by Pullman.

Better roads and the first traffic light (downtown) were contributions of the 1920s; streamlined trains came in the forties, airline service in 1948, a county park system in 1966, Nicolet College in 1968, and shopping centers in 1973 and 1975.

Outside the city proper, farming grew in two waves. Small homesteaders of the 1890s and early 1900s laboriously cleared virgin tracts, notably as dairy farms. Larger scale farmers came behind the loggers to clear cutover tracts, especially for growing potatoes.

Starks was a center of such farm development. Called Pennington (and briefly a Soo Line division point in the 1880s), it next became Hobson and finally took the name of the company that bought 17,000 acres of logged land in 1912 and eventually came to farm about 4,000 acres of it. Potato growing, mainly here and around Sugar Camp, still occupies 3,500 acres of Oneida County farmland.

Gagen, a railroad junction town, lived through two surges in sawmilling: once around 1886 when the lumber business there meant 100 jobs and again in 1920, with a new mill and 15 houses that resurrected the sleepy crossroads of a hotel and four homes. In the 1970s there is even less, just a building or two. Probably the biggest still ever broken up by Oneida County lawmen in the 1920s was hidden in a swamp east of Gagen.

Monico was a pulpwood preparation center from 1883 to 1887, just after its 1882 birth as a railroad junction town. Its dream of a paper mill vanished in the smoke of an 1887 fire. Later it had an excelsior mill and box plant. As late as the 1950s some of the Chicago & North Western's last steam engines worked between Eland, Monico, and Watersmeet, and the town still boasted coal and water towers and a big depot. A leaky steam engine would bring down the branch-line passenger train from Watersmeet and Eagle River, gently hiss away the day at rest in the Monico yard, and chug out at twilight with a fresh set of coaches in tow.

SIGHTSEEING

• First National Bank, 8 W. Davenport, 1911–12 building listed on the National Register of Historic Places and designed by Purcell, Feick, and Elmslie. The Prairie School of architecture and Louis Sullivan influenced details like its arched entry and upper-level terra cotta trim.

• Oneida County Courthouse, east end of Davenport Street, 1908 structure with imposing columns, pseudo-balconies, huge Tiffany glass dome (lovely at night). Elaborate capitaled columns and marble rails on the central open court join with regional murals (upper floors) to decorate this remarkable edifice.

• Rhinelander Logging Museum, Pioneer Park, daily, Memorial Day–late September. Loggers' camps and the means they used to cut and move logs are the theme here. A narrow-gauge logging train (engine and all) leads the list, followed by a steam sleigh-hauling tractor, big wheels, sleds, a log-driving bateau. Not forgotten are saws, axes, and hundreds of related tools and artifacts. Sheltering most of the displays are authentic camp buildings, outfitted as a bunkhouse and a cookshack.

• St. Regis Paper Company mill tours, weekdays almost hourly in summer from plant entrance, north side of Davenport Street east of river. St. Regis's mill makes glassine and greaseproof papers, and everything about it is big, big, big, from three-story supercalender machines that finish the finest of these papers to this plant's big share of the American greaseproof-glassine paper market—up to 40 percent of it! Most dramatic steps that visitors see are debarking, where a 32-foot rotating drum rubs the rich piney-smelling logs free of bark, and the actual papermaking, where a mixture of 200 parts water to one of extra-fine fiber sprays onto an endless belt of madly speeding, extra-fine mesh. This mesh screen drains the pulp into an endless strip of paper. A battery of rollers and dryers have it dry and rolled about 40 seconds and 500 feet after its birth!

• Historical markers. First county zoning policy is commemorated on the courthouse grounds. The Hodag is honored in Hodag Park. Puckish Gene Shepard made the beast out of skins, wood, and steel, gave it electric eyes and wire-manipulated limbs, endowed it with its own folklore, and let it occasionally be viewed in dim light. The mythical beast came to be both a Rhinelander legend and symbol.

• Holmboe Conifer Forest State Scientific Area, Pelican River opposite Shepard Park (Highway 17 south). Handsome hemlock-pine stand rising from river bottomland.

• Nicolet College and Technical Institute, off Highway G. Community college and vocational-technical center. Campus of 280 wooded acres shelters a handsome set of harmonizing buildings. Buildings are open to public and often feature art exhibits, plays, lectures, and other special events. Tours: 369-4410.

• North Central Forest Experiment Station, Highway K. U.S. Forest Service laboratory, studying how tree growth takes place and how the culture of trees and the species themselves can be improved. Because this is essentially a huge working indoor, outdoor, and greenhouse laboratory, it has no tourist facilities and programs (except for educational groups). I do not encourage a visit; its very existence is what makes it important to the northwoods.

TOURING

- Consolidated Papers Industrial Forest Tour. 12-mile, 19-stop self-guided drive through private timberlands, beginning just north of Monico on Highway 45 and exiting on 45 just north of Highway C; open mid June–mid October; get 24-page guide booklet (free) at area chambers of commerce or Consolidated offices in Monico or Rhinelander.

Three things make this tour significant: first, the help of a booklet, tour stops, and even extra foot trails in helping visitors understand the woods in general; second, a look at a managed forest (a bit like a huge wood farm); third, careful explanations of what forest management does—and how and why. Visitors see natural phenomena like a forest-type line and a deteriorated forest; man-engendered features like clear cuts, tree plantings, comparative experiments with regular and "super" trees (Stop 17), and even admitted mistakes (Stop 15). They can have the fun of a tree identification quiz (Stop 13) of trees already identified along the way. (Quiz sheets are provided; 10 trees are signed; correct identifications are hidden under a flap on each sign.) Both tour and interpretive booklet are excellent!

- River Road between Highway W in town and McNaughton (via Bridge Road at the last). Forest, old farm clearings, many views of Wisconsin River.

- Loop drive south of city via Highway G, Lassig, Hat Rapids, River, Firetower, Crescent, and Wausau roads and Highway 8; about 20 miles. Interesting cross section of area farming, from crop farms in corn to dairy farms to potato fields (east to west), and of terrain from uneven to river bottom to absolute level (at the short jog along River Road; note the lovely view south and west, where ridges rise again).

- Side roads from above tour. S. River Road following river up to Highway 8. Firetower Road for two miles west of junction with Crescent Road is almost like a New England painting in places; keep a sharp eye out to south at first.

RECREATION

BIKE RENTAL
- Mel's Trading Post, 25 S. Brown, 362-5800.

BIKING
- No formal bike routes. Try town roads and county highways.

- Variation of loop described above, via River, Firetower, Crescent roads, crossing Highway 8 and returning via Highways N and K.

- River Road to McNaughton, described above.

BOAT AND CANOE RENTAL
- Adventure Center, 1935 N. Stevens, 369-4884.

- Boom Lake Marine, 1520 Eagle at Highway W, 362-6519. Also rubber rafts.

- E-Z Rentals, Highway 8 west at River Road, 369-2600.

CANOEING
- Pelican River from points along former Highway 8 to the Wisconsin.

- Wisconsin River from Eagle River or south toward Tomahawk and Merrill. The latter is a popular group trip, with camping available at Bradley Park, Tomahawk, or at Camp New Wood downstream or on islands.

HIKING AND NATURE TRAILS
- Almon Recreation Area trails, via Lassig and Hixon Lake roads, 2.1 miles south from Highway G. Gift tract from Dr. Lois Almon; 0.6-mile wetland trail looping along lake and inland past low areas, and 1.4-mile woodland trail. No interpretive signs but a phone number to call is posted when guide service is available.

- Holiday Acres Resort Long Lake Trail off South Shore Drive.

PARKS, BEACHES, RECREATION AREAS
- Hodag Park (city), Boom Lake off Thayer Street. Beach, lifeguard, and related facilities; fishing area; tennis, athletic fields; picnic area, rest rooms.

- Pioneer Park (city), Kemp and Oneida streets. Logging museum; tennis, playground, athletic field; picnic area, rest rooms.

- Shepard Park (city), Boyce Drive at Pelican River. Playground equipment; picnic area, rest rooms.

- West Park (city), Maple and Phillip streets. Playground, athletic field, tennis.

- Almon Recreation Area (county), via Lassig and Hixon Lake roads, 2.1 miles south from Highway G. Very pretty, well-equipped, fastidiously maintained park; play fields, shaded picnic area, shelters, water, toilets. Flawless sand beach. Trails (see above).

- Town Line Park (county), two separate areas: beach area with changing building, right along Highway K one mile west of Highway 47, and picnic area on opposite shore, entry a bit east. Excellent little park, clean, nicely developed on shady, irregular point; tables, shelter, toilets, graveled paths, benches.

- Lake George beach, provided by Lake George Improvement Association.

RECREATION PROGRAM
- Rhinelander Parks and Recreation Department has a summer program, 362-7380.

SCUBA
- R. S. Diving Supply Company, 833 Lincoln. Air, rentals.

SHOOTING
- Hodag Sports Club, Highway C (Fire Number 4460). Trap; lighted areas.

SKATING
- Ice skating in municipal parks; also see Fort Wilderness under Skiing, below.
- Roller skating at Crystal Rock Roller Rink, on 8 west, weekends. Rentals.

SKIING / CROSS COUNTRY: RENTAL
- Fort Wilderness. See Trails, below.
- Holiday Acres. See Trails, below.
- Mel's Trading Post, 25 S. Brown, 362-5800.
- See's Sportmart, Sunrise Plaza, Highway 8 east, 369-2000.

SKIING / CROSS COUNTRY:TRAILS
- Almon Recreation Area. Some skiers use the nature trails.

- Consolidated Papers, Leith Road Trail, Leith Road south from Highway 8, 10 miles east. Two loops, beginners and intermediate, 5 miles. Map available at company offices, Rhinelander and Monico, or at chambers of commerce.

- Fort Wilderness, off 47 via McNaughton. Trails (fee), rentals; skating.

- Holiday Acres, South Shore Drive east off Highway 8 via jog at Faust Lake Road. Five trails, novice to expert, 11 miles, no charge; rentals. Resort facility.

- McNaughton Lake Ski Trail. See Lake Tomahawk.

- Oneida County Forest, Enterprise Ski Trails. See Pelican Lake.

SKIING: DOWNHILL
- Camp 10 Ski Area, 10 miles south via Highways 17 and A. Seven runs; tows, lifts, rentals; Wednesdays and weekends, but check locally.

SNOWMOBILE RENTAL
- Adventure Center, 1935 N. Stevens, 369-4884.
- E-Z Rentals, Highway 8 west, 369-2600, has been advertising rentals.

SNOWMOBILING
- Rhinelander is hub of the many trails groomed by the four United Trail Groomers clubs. For connecting county trails, see Cassian and Pelican Lake.

STABLES
- Fort Wilderness, off 47 east from McNaughton. Winter riding; sleigh rides.
- Holiday Acres Holiday Stables, north Lake George Road.
- Little Ponderosa, Highway 8 east.

TENNIS
- Rhinelander Junior High, Rhinelander Senior High, Hodag Park, Pioneer Park, West Park.
- Rhinelander Tennis Club, Menominee Drive north of 17 north, private club open to tourists by reservation, 369-3445; fee.

ENTERTAINMENT

CULTURAL EVENTS
- Baroque Music Festival, annually in August, St. Joseph's Church.
- Nicolet College Theatre, 369-4410. Program includes some summer offerings.
- Northern Lights Summer Playhouse. See Hazelhurst.
- Rhinelander Symphony Orchestra, check locally for concert dates.

SPORTING EVENTS
- Off-road vehicle racing has taken over the race course used by now-defunct Hodag 50 snowmobile races; check locally for annual schedule at Off Road USA.
- Rocking Horse Ranch, Highway K, welcomes visitors, particularly for special events like annual Dressage and Horse Trials. Ranch is a school training both riders and horses; no public riding. Saddle and tack shop; public welcome.
- Water ski shows at Hodag Park, 8 p.m. Sunday, Tuesday, Thursday, June–August.

SHOPPING AND BROWSING

- Book World, 33 W. Davenport. Books about the area; paperbacks, best sellers.

- Happiness Card and Party Shop, 16 S. Brown. Browse among the books (regional and hardcover) or look for kitchen, bath, and household decorative accessories, crystal, dinnerware, and gifts.

- Leather Plus, 18 W. Rives. Rustic shop with interesting leather goods.

- Second Hand Rose, opposite City Hall on Pelham. Good headquarters for most types of antiques: a whole house full of them, with even a bargain basement.

- Shy Violet Shoppe, in a home near Holiday Acres, follow signs from there. I suggest a call to 362-7405 before a long drive out. Handcrafts, collectibles.

- John Tupa, artist, Island View Drive off Highway 8 east (Fire Number 4269). Lakeshore studio open during normal working hours or phone 362-2036. John Tupa paints sensitive studies in northern landscapes and wildlife (notably ducks and deer) and works with special effectiveness in watercolor to create interesting sky effects. His farm or barn landscapes are superb as well.

• Turn of the Century, at Holiday Acres resort (q.v.). Unusual surroundings: an old log farmhouse; gifts, apparel, jewelry, kitchen items.

DINING

• Al Gen Dinner Club, on Faust Lake Road just north from Highway 8 east; evenings, all year, 362-2230. Full log, red-carpeted decor; always reliable for fine meals like fish, prime rib, smorgasbord. Cocktails. No Friday, Saturday reservations.

• Fireside Inn, a mile west of 47 on K; nightly except Thursday, all year, 369-4717. Modest-size inn; bar. Rustic and western touches. Good food, creative salads.

• Holiday Acres, South Shore Drive via Faust Lake Road off 8 east; all meals year round, 369-1500. Big, tall, handsome raw wood and stone dining room, carpeted. Full table linens. Professional, varied, tasty meals match this pleasing milieu; big salads (salad bar at times). Cocktails. Surely worth a visit.

• Northwestern Lounge, 119 S. Brown; noons and evenings, all year, 362-5080. Cocktail bar specializing in sandwiches, some unusual like two-meat, two-cheese, onion monster on rye called the Hemlock!

• Pied Piper Supper Club, Highway 8 east; evenings, all year, no reservations. Cocktails, hearty fare, splendid salads.

• Pinewood Lodge, south end of Lake Thompson Road via North Shore Drive off Highway C; evenings, all year, 362-4779. Low, carpeted, lake-view dining room where I enjoyed delicately butter-broiled scallops. Cocktails.

• Rhinelander Cafe and Pub, 33 N. Brown; all day, year round, 362-2918. Rich, mellow brick-and-wood decor with nautical effect. Supper club fare at night; wide variety at noon. Efficient service; cocktails. The title *cafe* understates an unusual, fine downtown restaurant.

LODGING

AMERICAN PLAN

• Feases' Shady Rest Lodge, 14 miles west on Highway 8 (Route 4), June–September. Modified American plan; 22 carpeted units with bath (11 cottages, some with fireplace; nine lodge rooms, two apartments). Interesting lake setting includes narrow point with lodge at tip, some cottages on crest. Sand beach; tennis, many activities. I am impressed by the two-generation family that runs this fine resort.

• Millers' Shorewood Vista, west Lake George Road off 8 east, May–October. Full American plan; 36 carpeted cottages (42 units), many with fireplace, pine decor. Very compact compound fronting sandy beach; tennis, many sports and activities, some competitive. Caters to families. Bar.

HOUSEKEEPING

• Blue Waters Resort, Lake Mildred Road off 47 west (Route 1), all year. 10

cottages or condominiumlike units, some with upper levels, fireplaces, carpet. Pretty, northwoodsy lake, sandy beach. Considerable personal attention and organized activity. A thoughtful operation and one that's a little bit different.

• Brekke's Fireside Resort, right on Highway 8 east (Route 6), seasonal. 12 carpeted cottages (11 with fireplace) in two sets: diminutive ones back from lake, larger ones on hill above water; sand beach, play area; tennis. Bar.

• Engstrand's Idlewood Cottages, Crescent Lake off 8 west (Route 2), May–October. Nine northwoodsy units set between forest and sunny lawn, facing long sand beach, individual piers. Pleasant hosts, good privacy.

• Holiday Acres, South Shore Drive off Highway 8 east via short stretch of Faust Lake Road (P.O. Box 460), all year. 36 cottages, some lakeside and many with one or more features like fireplaces, dishwashers, combination baths. 18 very attractive motel-type units. Grounds vary from lawn to woods. Sandy beach, tennis, indoor pool, hiking trails; cross-country skiing, snowmobiling with rentals. Appealing dining room, bar, gift shop. I don't think any resort in these two counties puts so many things together so well as Holiday Acres.

• Kafka's Resort, Lake George Road off Highway 8 east (Route 6), all year. Eight cottages, most set in a neat lakeside row and all nicely outfitted, many with carpet and combination bath. Sandy beach. Professionalism evident everywhere, but especially in maintenance and in spotless, extensive lawns. Bar.

• Pine Point Resort, Lake George Road off 8 east (Route 6), May–October. Seven little vacation homes, most carpeted, amid tall, whispering pines; sand beach. Bar.

• Pinewood Lodge, south end of Lake Thompson Road (Route 5), all year. Combination of housekeeping cottages and 16-unit stone motel (nicely furnished); mowed grounds, sand beach. Bar, dining (q.v.).

MOTELS

• Claridge Motor Inn, 70 N. Stevens, 362-7100. 81 units, indoor pool; cocktail lounge, dining room.

• Downtown Motel, 15 E. Anderson, 362-7171. 31 units.

• Holiday Acres. 18 motel-type units. See Lodging: Housekeeping.

• Holiday Inn, Highway 8 west (P.O. Box 675), 369-3600. 103 rooms, indoor pool; cocktail lounge, dining room.

• Pinewood Lodge. 16 motel units. See Lodging: Housekeeping.

CAMPING

• The Bronze Wheel, Highway 17 north to Pine Lake Drive west, May–September. 40 units. Prettiest campground I found in these counties.

- Holiday Acres Camping Resort, South Shore Drive off 8 east via Faust Lake Road, all year (advance notice in winter). 71 sites.
- Lake George Campsite, Highway 8 east (Route 6), seasonal. 35 units.
- The Outpost. See Cassian.

EVENTS

- Oneida County Fish for All, countywide contest, all summer.
- Hodag Holidays, late June into early July, the year's main observance. Parade, carnival, athletic competition, Drums in the Night pageant, horse shows.
- Upper Midwest Laboratories of the Arts (Rhinelander School of Arts), early August. Week-long program of seminars, workshops, individual sessions in the arts and writing. Usually open to public are traditional evening events: lectures, banquet, autograph party, entertainment programs. For information write UW Extension, P.O. Box 695, Rhinelander.
- Rhinelander Antique Show, early August.
- Baroque Music Festival, mid August.
- Festival of the Leaves (Colorama), fall color time.
- Oneida County Winter Festival, winter-long, varied local events.

INFORMATION AND TRANSPORTATION

- Rhinelander Area Chamber of Commerce, P.O. Box 795, Rhinelander 54501. Office, city hall at Stevens and Pelham streets, 362-7464, open Monday–Friday all year. Information booth, city hall grounds, 362-4711, May 20–October 15, daily in summer.
- Rhinelander Public Library, new location to be announced.
- Air transport: North Central Airlines.
- Buses: Greyhound Lines and Wisconsin-Michigan Coaches.
- Car rental. In town: Budget, at Winquist Oil Company, Highway 8 east; at airport: Hertz, National; opposite Holiday Inn: Avis, Highway 8 west.
- Taxis: Courtesy Cab, 369-2323; Yellow Cab, 362-3100.

THREE LAKES AND SUGAR CAMP

Three Lakes's contemporary appeal comes from its unusually scenic woods and chain of lakes. No other portion of the two counties has forests of equal beauty around so many of its lakes.

It was the combination of woods and waters that drew the first loggers into lands previously known only to the Chippewas and their occasional rivals. Streams like the Pine, east of the chain of lakes, made it possible to float logs down to Marinette, and the chain itself made possible log driving down the Wisconsin, thanks to the loggers' new dam where Burnt Rollways is now and the technology of tugs, rafting, and even running tap ditches to outlying lakes. Maybe half a dozen outfits were logging pine east of the Three Lakes townsite in the 1880s, and one firm built a big mill and village known as

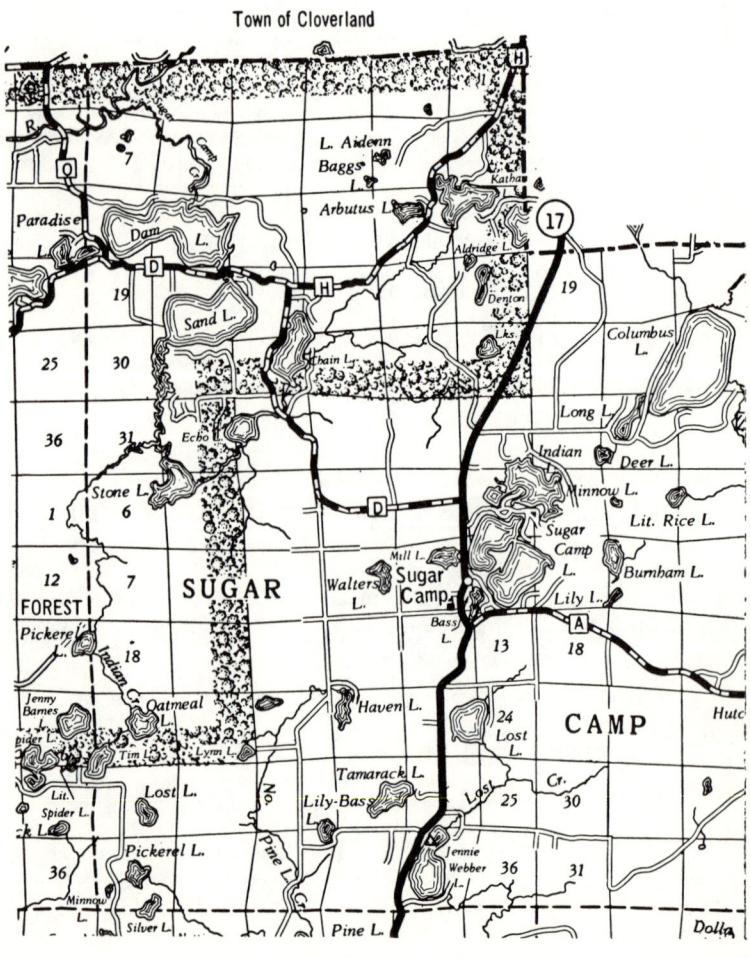

Buckwheat just to the north of the present settlement. The firm was Woodruff & McGuire, which remained till perhaps 1904. The region had one late logger: the Thunder Lake Lumber Company cut along its narrow-gauge logging railroad east of town and up into Vilas and Forest counties till 1940.

The waters also proved to be a highway for early residents, who had no road network. To reach other lakes or shop by boat they even rearranged the landscape by digging canals or dredging channels between lakes. It took till after World War II to get the levels all properly interrelated again after some lakes all but whooshed away down new or altered passageways. Meanwhile mail boats, passenger launches, freight scows, and even farmers regularly peddling produce made routine use of the Three Lakes chain.

The waters were a playground as well, and by 1910 two fishing clubs, several resorts, and a couple score of summer homes dotted the lakes.

Lodges with outlying cabins were the dominant resorts in the early years, until the ease of automobile travel enabled people to choose housekeeping cottages that required frequent shopping jaunts by car. The Northernaire of 1947 was the last big food-and-

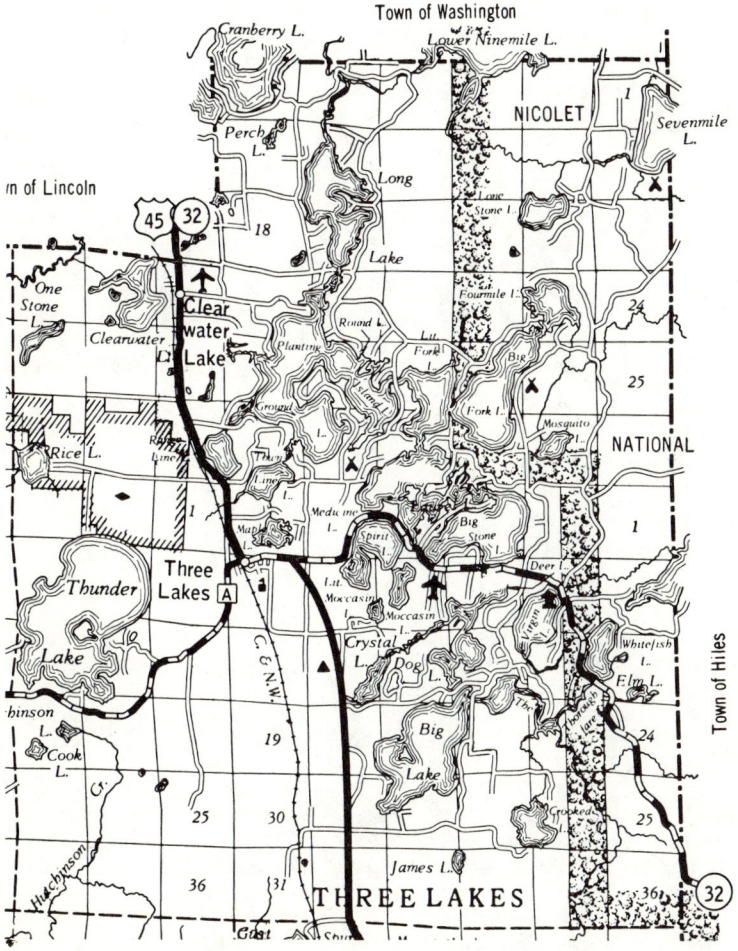

lodging resort built in Vilas and Oneida counties.

All this time farmers had been working cutover and freshly cleared lands, ever since the initial surge of homesteading in the 1890s. Potato planting grew very important, and in 1947 cranberry growers started their marshes.

The village was developing all this time too, from just one structure, the new railroad's section house, in 1882. Its first decade brought stores, hotels, and attempts at a newspaper. Around town children's camps were developing by 1916, and in 1933 the word *camp* took on yet another meaning as CCC camps in the area provided workers for replanting cutover forests like the brand new Nicolet.

Sugar Camp shares elements of Three Lakes's history like logging, farming, and vacationing, though lack of an equivalent to Three Lakes's chain of lakes kept its history from being quite so glamorous.

Its first loggers cut light pine too, for mills at Rhinelander, muscling the logs overland to Mud Lake from which a series of lakes and creeks afforded a water route to Rhinelander. Frustrated by water too low for driving in 1893, the lumber company bypassed the offending stream by building a little railroad into its woods near Pine Lake. A few years later the company extended it east and north to Sugar Camp Lake, where there was already a little store and resort of 1891 homesteader Frederick Tripp. Soon a mill and settlement joined Tripp's pioneer complex. On promising sites south from there the lumber companies began farms to provide food for both man and beast in their huge lumber camps, beginning a trend that has never been reversed.

The hamlet was called Robbins at first, for the lumber magnate whose name was also borne by the railroad. It was a narrow-gauge line but a common carrier; it seldom hauled passengers except for special excursions, like trips to bring city folks out to see the Indians at Indian Lake campsite or to picnic in the woods. One excursion was a benefit for the Catholic church at Sugar Camp about 1900 or 1902. Hundreds of dollars in voluntary fares from riders were donated to the church.

The area's logs all gone, Sugar Camp/Robbins lost its little trains too, in 1920, but it still had hospitality and farming. New resorts grew on Dam and Sand lakes, where there is still a modest resort business. As anyone can see who rambles off the beaten track around the vicinity, potato production has kept farming a factor in modern Sugar Camp's existence—more than in most other places around the northwoods.

SIGHTSEEING AND TOURING: THREE LAKES AREA

- Three Lakes village is both residential, principally to the south of Highway 45, and commercial, with some buildings in a harmonizing Alpine style suggested as a townwide theme by local architect Cy Williams. Gentle touches range from an apple tree in a vacant lot opposite Northland Marine ("No one owns it; it's a town tree," kids told me as they climbed it for red apples) to two ancient cast-iron, cross-topped tombstones in the cemetery, their raised wording in Polish.

- Edward U. Demmer Library, in town. Rarely is a library a landmark or a symbol but this one is. The sparkling building is a memorial gift but its spirit is local; no small community in the north can match it for facilities, collections, congenial librarians, community service, and public use. (Daily except Sunday.)

- Three Lakes Chain of Lakes. 20 lakes, 7,657 acres, made more scenic by islands and 80 miles of unusually wooded shoreline. Boat lift at Burnt Rollways allows travel to Eagle River chain too. See Eagle River.

• Water mail route. A carry-over from days before roads knit the shoreline of the chain, when a mail-passenger-package boat ran, this very rare summer-only mail route serves boxes on piers along approximately 35 water miles. (No riders.)

• Nicolet Forest historical marker, Forest Road 2178, commemorates first land acquisition in 1928 from Thunder Lake Lumber Company and Nicolet's creation in 1933.

• Cy Williams historical marker at chamber of commerce recalls the National League's first hitter of 200 home runs, later a Three Lakes architect.

• Sam Campbell historical marker and memorial tree plantation, Forest Road 2207, honors the naturalist, conservationist, inspirational writer, a longtime summer resident who did much of his writing at his island retreat.

• Thunder Lake Marsh, west from Highway 45 north (partly a state scientific area). Careful watching will reveal wildlife (deer, coyotes, beaver, eagles) and history (the ditching was part of a grand scheme to drain and farm the marsh).

• Cranberry marshes. Commercial marshes at several points; visitors welcome if they park at designated points and sightsee on foot. Get list and locations locally.

• Nicolet National Forest. Extensive, often scenic tract east of Three Lakes. Among its special sightseeing treats are these marked facilities:

• Giant Pine area and trail, Road 2414 via 2183. Swamp, hemlock ridge, hardwood forest, a few big pines, along two-mile trail used for hiking and skiing (qq.v.).

• Scott Lake Hemlock Grove, on 2183, interpretive map sign and half-mile path through beautiful growth. A scenic must.

• Shelp Lake, just opposite Scott Lake on 2183. Little boardwalk to bog pond. Excellent cross section of encroaching vegetation stages that turn a quiet kettle pond into a northern bog. First (from pond back toward shore), floating pondside mosses; second, intermediate brush and tamarack; third, "Christmas tree" types taking root on older, now solidified bog area nearer to shore. Fourth is the original shore itself with its typical dry land forest growth. Scenic and informative.

• Highway 32 southeast. Scenic road skirts lakeshores past older cottages, cuts into deep forests, passes Virgin Lake where Hi Polar's 1850s trading post provided first area hospitality and Military Road passed (where Holiday Haven is now). Next to the onetime general store of the Thunder Lake Lumber Company (now Don's) can be seen the abandoned right-of-way of the narrow-gauge logging tracks removed in 1941 (posted against trespassers).

• Highway 45 north goes up to **Clearwater Lake,** farming and vacation hamlet and once a sizable Seventh-day Adventist settlement, which even boasted a denominational boarding school, 1907–16. Clearwater Lake General Store has had its tiny post office and pressed tin ceiling since 1912.

• Highway X north from Three Lakes is my candidate for most scenic county road or major town artery in the county. It ties together a few farm clearings and lake views with mile upon mile of splendid forest.

• Side roads from X can add more beauty: Wheeler Island Road passes summer homes and circles the lovely island. Russell and Burchmore-Sugarbush roads are woodsy. Scholmann (also shown as Schomann) soars up a ridge before easing down to become a beach drive. Reed Road grows rustic to the east. An offshoot, Sam Campbell Road, is unspoiled. (If you have never seen a government section corner and bearing tree, you can see one about 50 feet east of the turnback and gate that close the road to further travel.) Preacher's Point Road off Reed Road is quaint and densely wooded. Beside it is the tiny, belfried Chapel in the Pines built in 1924 by families that for 20 years or so had had no road access to Sunday services and had held services in their homes.

• Forest Road 2178, Military Road, is well wooded. Map sign 0.3 mile north of Highway 32. Road 2207 loops west past Sam Campbell plantation, rejoins 2178.

• Highway 32 side roads are wooded and restful, like Chicken in the Woods and Leatzow roads, north, or Col. Himes Road, south.

• Seaplane rides offer a different view. Highway 32 east at Big Stone Lake, 546-2313.

SIGHTSEEING AND TOURING: SUGAR CAMP AREA

• Highway A is the main artery between Sugar Camp and Three Lakes, sweeping effortlessly past a few farm clearings and through quiet woods.

• Sugar Camp is not a concentrated village cluster but a loosely scattered community along Highway 17. It is a significant agricultural area.

• Indian Lake Road east from 17 is a short, amazingly pretty road through well-inhabited but still virgin-appearing forest between Sugar Camp and Indian lakes. Many little side roads add even further to the richness of this very short side trip. A DNR stairway-type fire tower stands in a loop of Tower Road.

• Votive cross, Highway D, Cross and Pine Lake roads intersection. White, hewn-log cross about 18 feet tall and so old, I was told, that few know its past. I am sure its establishment was a devotional or vow-fulfilling gesture, for many devout Poles settled the area and gave Sugar Camp one of rural Oneida County's earliest Catholic churches. Nowhere else in northern Wisconsin have I seen a roadside cross like this.

RECREATION AND ENTERTAINMENT

BIKE RENTAL
 • Northland Marine, in town, 546-2333.

BIKING

- Nicolet Bikeway. 70-mile loop linking Three Lakes and Phelps, with abundant scenery and possible rest stops. Map is necessary and widely available.

- Try the side roads and county roads listed above under Sightseeing.

BOAT AND CANOE RENTAL

- Aero Marine, Highway 32 east (Route 1), 546-3407.

- Northland Marine, in town and Town Line Lake, 546-2333. Sailboats too.

- Shorewood Marine, Highway 32 east (Route 1), 546-3633.

- Watercraft Sales, Highway X (Route 1), 546-3351. Sailboats too.

CANOEING

- Lake canoeing on the chain; campsites on some islands

- Crystal Creek and Lake between the chain and public landing on Big Lake Loop.

- The Thoroughfare and Eagle River southeast, off Big Lake.

- Sugar Camp Creek to the Wisconsin.

FIRE TOWER
- Tower Road loop off Indian Lake Road, Sugar Camp. DNR stairway-type tower.

GOLF
- Northernaire, Highway 32 east. Nine holes.

HIKING
- Nicolet Forest trails: Giant Pine, Scott, and Shelp sites (two-mile trail at Giant Pine) and a pretty little trail at Sevenmile Lake campground. Seeded trails in Kimball Creek and Alvin Creek game areas.

PARKS, BEACHES, RECREATION AREAS
- Three Lakes municipal beach (Maple Beach), in town near chamber of commerce. Sand beach, lifeguard in season, lessons; changing area; tables.
- Sevenmile Lake Picnic Area (Nicolet Forest), Road 2435. Beach, picnicking.

SKATING
- Town ice rink near high school.

SKIING / CROSS COUNTRY: RENTAL
- Northland Marine, in town, 546-2333.

SKIING / CROSS COUNTRY: TRAILS
- Giant Pine Trails, Forest Road 2414. Frozen swamps make six miles of ski trails from hiking trail.
- Sheltered Valley Ski Area, off Road 2182.

SKIING: DOWNHILL
- Sheltered Valley Ski Area, off Road 2182. One lift, two rope tows, short runs on nice little hills. Also runs for inner tubes.

SNOWMOBILE RENTAL
- Aero Marine, Highway 32 east (Route 1), 546-3407.
- Northland Marine, in town, 546-2333.
- R&M Sales and Service, Military Road (Route 1), 546-2576.
- Shorewood Marine, Highway 32 east (Route 1), 546-3633.

SNOWMOBILING
- Northern Lights Snowmobile Club trails and Nicolet trails.

STABLES
- Russ's Lazy N Stable, Highway 45 north.

- Samuelson's Stables, at Northernaire, Highway 32 east.

TENNIS
- Three Lakes school grounds, in town.

WATER SKI SHOWS
- Three Lakes Ski-Bees, 7 p.m. Sunday and Wednesday at the Northernaire.

SHOPPING AND BROWSING

- Red Shed Antiques, on 45 north (Fire Number 529), May–September. General line.

- Redwood House, Highway 45 north, April–Christmas. Looks in several directions: to living and dining rooms with decorative accessories; to the den, with books, notably all the Sam Campbell books by Three Lakes's own author, and other local books; to the whatnot shelf with Hummels and collector plates; and to givers themselves with jewelry, personal and Christmas gifts. Gracious service; wheelchair access.

- Sugar Camp Antiques, Indian Lake Road off Highway 17, May–October. General line.

DINING

- Bronkalla's, Highway 17, Sugar Camp; daily (closed Monday, September–June), all year, 272-1033. Combined bar and dining area with divider; windows over lake—it's pretty if you catch a sunset as I did. Full menu; dinners include the rarity of a cuplet of sherbet. I found good soup, unusual potatoes, meat generous and cooked as ordered.

- The Chalet, downtown Three Lakes; evenings (closed midweek in slow periods), all year, 546-3443. Alpine-Old English dining area; full menu; Friday fish fry. Cocktails. Also rooms above, some with bath and some newly and attractively redecorated.

- Lola's, on 45, Three Lakes proper; nightly, all year. Bar with hearty sandwiches.

Three Lakes-Sugar Camp/143

• Northernaire, on 32 east of Three Lakes; all meals, year round, 546-3331. Full course meals; attentive service. Cocktails.

• The White Stag, Highway 17, Sugar Camp; nightly, all year, no reservations. Mellow decor with old masters-type artworks; somewhat limited fare; cocktails.

LODGING

• Evensen's Resort, Maple Lake Dam Road off 45 north, Three Lakes, all year. Housekeeping. Respected resort of seven beachside cottages, several with furnace and combination bath. All with porches, wood-finished interiors.

• Motel Maple, downtown Three Lakes, spring to fall, 546-3540. 12 units.

• Northernaire, on 32 east of Three Lakes, all year. American plan (hotel, primarily); many facilities. Current brochure, which I picked up at desk, still shows a 1950 Packard in one photo, a metaphor, perhaps, for the resort in 1977.

• Oneida Village, downtown Three Lakes, all year, 546-3373. Motel, 47 big units. Dining room, cocktail lounge.

• Rustlewood, Russell Road off X, Three Lakes, May–October. Housekeeping; seven knotty-pine cottages make fine use of hilly point; appealing waterfront with tiny islet.

• Sunset Shores, off Chicken in the Woods Road, Three Lakes, most of year. Housekeeping, five cottages; the strong point here is the appealing pine site. Beach.

• Van Kirk's Lake Breeze Resort, on X, Three Lakes, all year. Full American plan, summer; housekeeping rest of year. 15 carpeted cottages or units set among tall trees on mowed, flower-planted grounds. Rec room, waterfront with much to do. A nice resort.

CAMPING

PRIVATE
• Huey's Idlewild, on 17 south, Sugar Camp, May–October. 18 units.

• Olson's Campground, on 32 east, Three Lakes, seasonal. 40 units.

• Running's Campground, off King Road east from 17, Sugar Camp, all year. 60 units.

NICOLET NATIONAL FOREST
• Laurel Lake Campground, off 32 east, Three Lakes, short season. 13 units, no beach.

- Sevenmile Lake Campground, Road 2435 off 2178, short season. 22 units.

EVENTS

- Arts and Crafts Fair, July, Demmer Library, Three Lakes.
- Three Lakes Horse Show, late July.
- Firemen's Picnic, early August, Three Lakes; contests, games, refreshments.
- Polka Festival, latter part of August, Sugar Camp.
- Flower Show, late August, Three Lakes.
- Fall Festival, fall color time, Three Lakes; merchants' promotion, cookout.
- Ice Fishing Jamboree, early February, Three Lakes.
- Cross-Country Snowmobile Race, mid February, both communities, and Three Lakes Sprints snowmobile races, usually same weekend.
- Ice Box Derby, mid March, Three Lakes; a soap box derby for sleds! Cute event.

INFORMATION

- Three Lakes Chamber of Commerce, P.O. Box 276, Three Lakes 54562. Information booth, Highway 45 in town at the park, open daily Memorial–Labor days and Friday-Saturday to mid October.
- Sugar Camp has no chamber of commerce or booth. The nearest chambers to contact are those in Three Lakes, Rhinelander, and Eagle River.

PELICAN LAKE

Pelican Lake was a favorite Indian site long before tourists popularized it. Not far away, near Mole Lake in the early 1800s, a violent Sioux-Chippewa battle took place, and tradition has it that two brother chiefs right on Pelican Lake engaged in hostilities when one wanted to go on the warpath against Uncle Sam's forces and the other did not. But otherwise its history has been a peaceful one.

The Indians settled on three points on Pelican Lake, eventually, and a trading post on the present Chicago Point took their furs; another, more important post stood on Post Lake, catering not only to the Indians and early white settlers but to crews building the Military Road past that point. Government policy after the Indian treaties of the mid 1800s was to move the native Americans onto reservations; some lingered long around the lake, but eventually even they had to leave, only their mounds or corn hills remaining behind to remind the first resort or cottage builders of their predecessors.

No huge sawmills whined at Pelican Lake after the logging era dawned. There was a pulp mill at Pratt Junction, just down the track, in the 1890s, but the main logging followed the railroad branches as they were pushed east to Post Lake (around 1885), west toward Harrison and Parrish in 1888 or 1889, and up to Crandon in 1901. The hamlets to the west rocked with the play of the loggers, from the usual saloons to a bawdy house over Parrish way.

The first lake cottage was built perhaps a year before the first train arrived in 1882. A lad named Grosskopf hiked up from Antigo in the company of an Indian guide, liked what he saw, bought land, and put up his cabin. The earliest flurry of fishermen's visits came

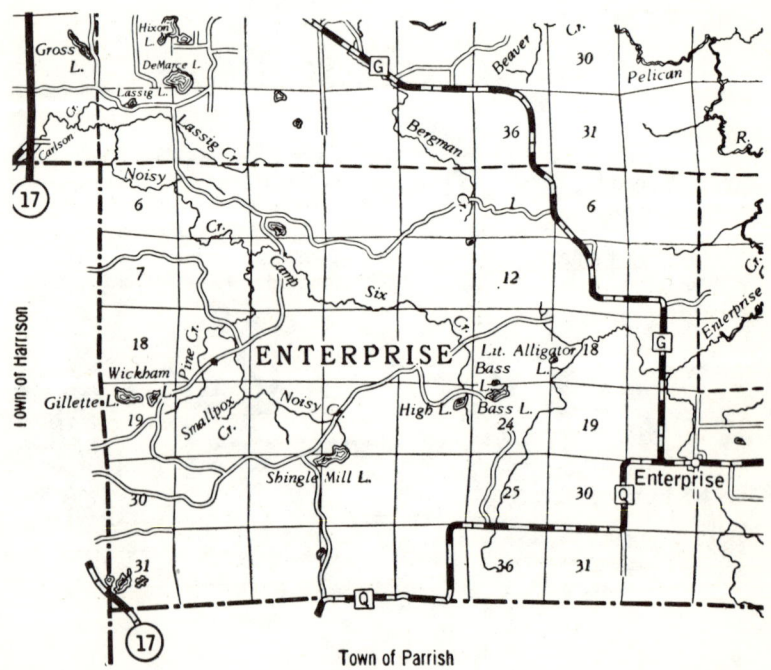

Town of Parrish

146/Oneida County

soon after 1890, but serious efforts at accommodating visitors waited till a hotel was built in town in 1898–99, and outlying resorts were begun in 1900 and 1905. There had been enough settlers, though, to justify cutting roads to Post Lake by 1885 and other towns soon after. Cottage resorts were mostly part of a second wave of resort building after 1913.

Lake levels had been raised about 1899 and reset by a new 1906 dam. Lake travel was very important. Even into the 'teens the only access to many cottages and resorts was by water, and a 20-passenger launch delivered tourists as well as mail. Scows carried freight and building materials. Only in the mid 1920s was a road completed around the lake and lakeshore mail delivery shifted to roads.

The main development of the half century since has been the continuous growth of vacation properties around the lake. There are still over 17 resorts on its banks, most small with modest cottages along and then back from limited shorefronts. Many resorts or old camps and clubs have been subdivided, and especially tasteful summer-home areas line the roads on the three points of the earlier Indians.

The central Pelican Lake area saw little farming. **Enterprise,** just west, saw more, as industrious Germans, among others, homesteaded from 1891 on; the first carried in their belongings on their backs. One old-time Enterprise farmer in 1923 was reportedly the last fellow in the county still using oxen. Not everyone had such high values; a huge still was broken up there in 1927! Today Enterprise is a hamlet with a tavern-store, a few homes, and one city block with all four streets carefully signed.

More Germans settled at **Lenox** in 1900, where a man named Wolfgram built a village (now gone) of 11 homes, a creamery, hotel, and store. Poles settled at **Jennings,** a mile to the south, which took its Irish-sounding name from a land colonizer who got them there about 1900. Of their village two businesses remain, besides a few homes and a remarkable stovewood derelict (see Sightseeing).

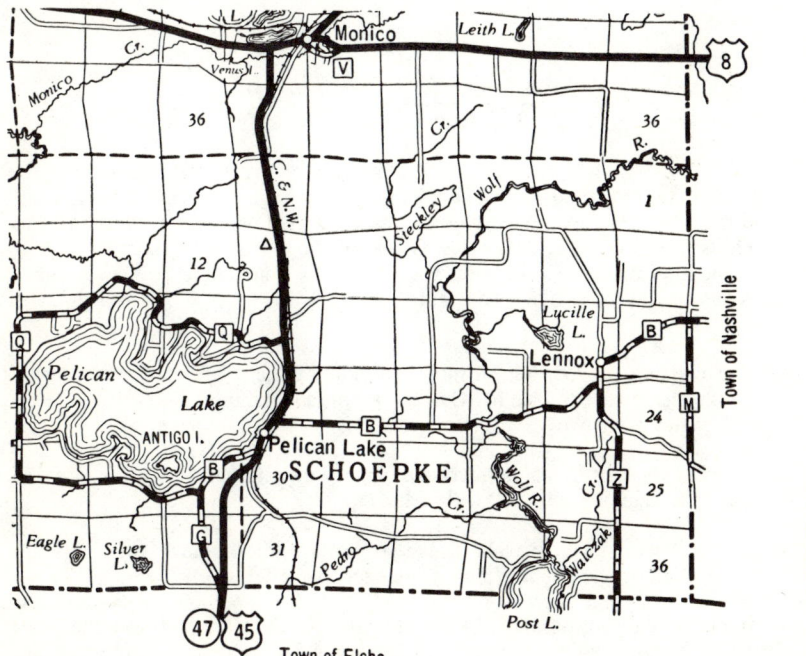

SIGHTSEEING

• Pelican Lake and village. The village stands on the east shore of 3,585-acre Pelican Lake, second largest natural lake in Oneida County. It is two-thirds spring fed, has two islands, and drains from an outlet on the north shore at the dam into the Wisconsin River system. Five public landings offer good lake views.

• Old cemetery, Cemetery Road east from 45 north of town. Touching, tree-shaded, deeply ferned hill. Wild roses, a few stones from 1906 to 1940, simple boards, and sunken hollows mark the graves.

• Mecikalski Saloon, southeast corner of Highway B and Z, Jennings; 1895–1900 example of stovewood construction. Two-story sidewalls are stacks of 16-inch firewood filled in with mortar. Unoccupied, posted against trespassing. Listed in Historic American Buildings Survey.

• Oneida County Forest, Enterprise unit. Though some areas are cut, the forest is still a huge and generally lovely wilderness occupying almost a full township.

• The landscape of this area is unusual. For one thing, lakes are very few: only 20 lakes or ponds in the 108 square miles. For another, the south edge of the area is rough end moraine; if you could hike into sections 31 and 32, the county forest's southwestern corner, you would find the 41 kettles indicated on the definitive soil survey map that records such features. Finally, the third novelty is the cigarlike ridges in the eastern end of the area, running northeast into southwest, probably part of a drumlin trend beginning in Forest County. (There are also eskers between the village and the ridges, following the same direction.)

TOURING

• Highways B, G, Q, and 45 around the lake. Loop begins with small resorts and then a big old inn (converted now to other uses) whose clearing was farmed and dairied to feed lodge guests; more farm clearings line G toward the Germans' church. Along Q deeper woods and industrial forest shade the road; lake views and homes are few because most cottages are on lakeshore side roads. The Pelican River, crossed by Q, is the lake outlet.

• Side roads from the loop reveal more resort and cottage life and lake scenery: South Shore (with Meckinac off from it), Chicago Point, and Sabinois Point roads. Deep woods line part of the latter two.

• Highway G south of B is a premier road for viewing trilliums in season, while G west of the lake is a shunpiking route to Rhinelander.

• Highway Q west from the lake is the scenic and often bumpy route through forgotten farms and along the county forest's boundary, to Highway 17.

• Within the county forest lands, I suggest taking North Road west from the intersection with G at the snowmobile trail parking lot, going 5.6 miles to Camp Six Road;

then Camp Six 0.8 mile to snowmobile rest area. Highlights: total solitude, well-drained forests, a possible esker at mile 2.6, and the beautiful Noisy Creek bottomland at the snowmobile rest area. Backtrack or continue to Highway 17 via Camp Six (4.3 miles total) and Gravel Pit (1.3 miles) roads. Carry a forest map of the variety planned for snowmobilers.

• Highway B, Highway 55, and Forest County S between Pelican and Highway 8 at Crandon. Most scenic route is west to east. Within two miles of Pelican Lake, B leaves wetlands to mount ridges with a long view east; it crosses the Wolf River and dodges hills into Jennings (note the egg-shaped small one on farm on left). Eastward it crosses the interesting succession of ridges and hollows, some of them farmed. Along 55 side roads like Lemke Road present an almost Swiss prospect. About 13.4 miles from Pelican Lake Highway S leaves 55. Around Fire Number 5195 look for Cemetery Road. A charming little graveyard on the western ridge, burial site for many a pioneer and many an infant, tells a story of hardship and acceptance even if one sentiment is misspelled: "Weep not for us, dear children/For we are angles now." Making my already moving visit a bit more so was the tinkle of cowbells from the farmyard next door. Highway S meets Highway 8 a short distance ahead.

RECREATION

BIKING
• Try the roads and loop listed above under Touring.

BOAT AND CANOE RENTAL
• Zander's Pelican Lake Garage and Marine, in town, 487-5435.

• Resorts such as Sabinois Point Resort (Lake Number 608), 487-5272, or Weaver's Resort (Lake Number 481), 487-5217, for canoes, pontoon boats, sailboats.

CANOEING
• Wolf River from Jennings or above (Highway B), down to Post Lake.

SAILING
• Pelican is an unusually nice sailing lake.

SHOOTING
• Chamber of commerce sponsors summer trap shoots.

SKIING / CROSS COUNTRY: TRAILS
• Oneida County Forest trails, off Highway G northwest. Extensive network of trails, up to 20 miles, much of it actually used for the first time this year. The oldest loop is routed along an esker at one point.

• Local skiers frequent the industrial forestlands of Consolidated Papers in the area; get local advice on whether any formal trail has been set up. Also ask about trails and rentals by a private party near Jennings.

SNOWMOBILING
• Oneida County Forest trails, off G. About 40 miles of trails, the first public snowmobile trails in Wisconsin! Two rest areas.

DINING

• Knight's Inn, in town, evenings. This has been an off again, on again spot but from summer 1977 hoped to stay open all year. Slightly schoolroomlike dining room with fireplace, lake view, pleasant accessories and table settings. Our meal was very good throughout: excellent prime rib, unusually seasoned chopped sirloin. Cocktails; handsome bar. Also hotel rooms above.

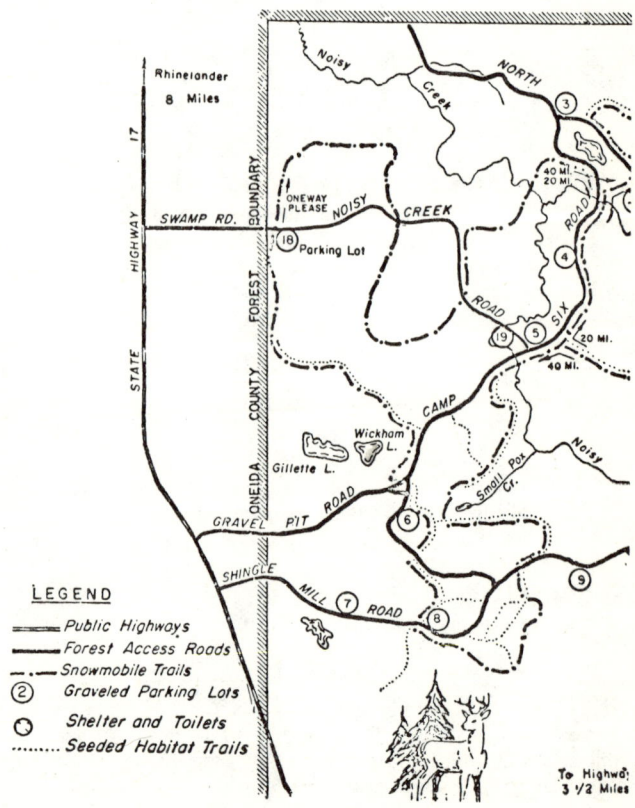

LODGING

- Trail-Inn Motel, on 45 in town, all year, 487-5280. Six units.

- Weaver's Resort, Chicago Point Road, Lake Number 481. Represents over 50 years of hospitality. Well-kept grounds on a point, sandy beach; five housekeeping units, 15-unit campground, mobile home park. The Weavers' daughter operates Sabinois Point Resort nearby (Lake Number 608) with two additional cottages.

INFORMATION AND TRANSPORTATION

- Pelican Lake Chamber of Commerce, Route 1, Box 328, Pelican Lake 54463. No information booth.

- Bus: Wisconsin-Michigan Coaches.

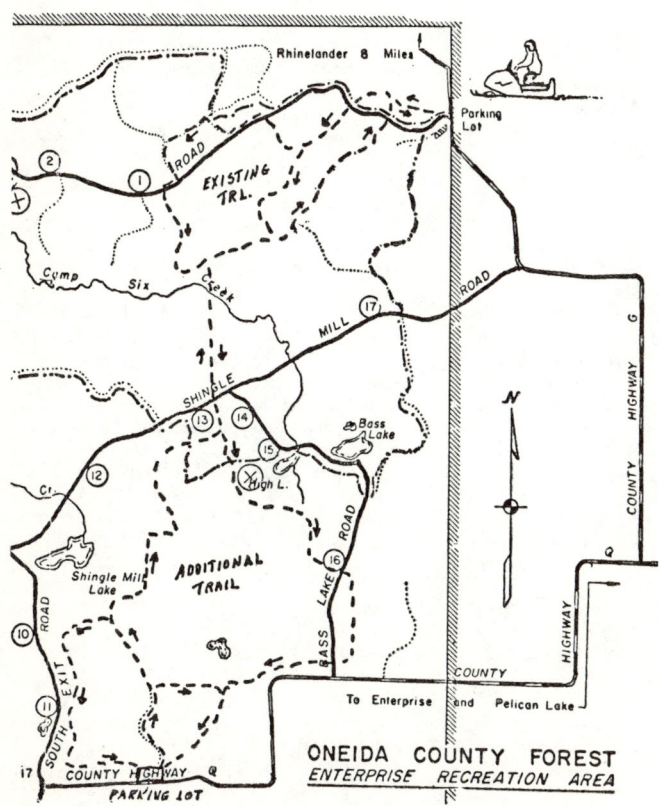

INDEX

Airline and charter, 45, 53, 81, 93, 108, 135
American Legion State Forest, 41, 121
Animals, species and descriptions, 14-16
Animal watching, 14; also see Zoos.
Arbor Vitae, 39-45
Artists/Studios/Galleries: Fred Aman/Aman's Gallery & Gifts, 84; Art Long, 43; Bob Schwartz/The Hangup, 77; Tony Staroska/Eagle River Pottery, 77; John Tupa, 132; John Wons/Wons String Instrument Shop, 77
Ballard-Partridge Lake Portage, 61
Beaches, 24, 30, 36, 42, 49-50, 64, 74-75, 88, 90, 97, 103, 111, 118, 122, 129, 142
Bearskin Recreation Trail, 110, 117
Biking: 24, 41, 49, 55-56, 73, 83-84, 89, 96, 103, 110, 117, 122, 128, 141, 149; Nicolet Bikeway, 73, 83, 96, 141
Birds, species and description, 16
Black Jack Springs, 73, 96
Boat and canoe rental, 24, 29, 42, 49, 63, 73, 89-90, 103, 117-8, 129, 141, 149
Boating, 6
Boat landings, 6 and *passim*
Boat trips, 74
Bogs: explanation, 12; examples, 63, 139
Boulder Junction, 11, 18-19, 46-53
Burnt Bridge Tavern, 84
Burnt Rollways boat lift, 72, 139
Bus service, 32, 45, 108, 124, 135, 151
Buswell, 35
Camp American Legion, 121
Campgrounds/Trailer/RV Parks: Arbor Vitae, 45; Benedict's, 93; Birchwood, 53; Bronze Wheel, 134; Camp Holiday, 53; Car-Lee, 38; Coe's Deerskin, 80; Eagle Crest, 58; Fox Fire KOA, 45; Hiawatha, 45; Holiday Acres, 135; Huey's Idlewild, 144; Indian Shores, 45; Kairis, 80; Lake George, 135; Lofty Pines, 58; Lynn Ann's, 58; North Shore, 93; Olson's, 144; Otter Lake, 80; Outpost, 119; Patricia Lake, 108; Pine-Aire, 80; Pondorosa, 38; Running's, 144; Wa-Swa-Gon Park, 26; Weaver's, 150
Campgrounds, public: American Legion State Forest, 45, 112, 124; Chequamegon National Forest, 26; DNR canoe campsites, 29, 49, 69; Nicolet National Forest, 80, 93, 98-99, 144-5; Northern Highland State Forest, 53, 66; Sylvania, 93
Camping equipment rental, 49, 75, 93, 119
Canoeing (routes/services), 24, 29, 35, 42, 49, 56, 63, 74, 84, 90, 97, 103, 115, 118, 122, 129, 150
Car rental, 45, 53, 81, 93, 108, 135
Cassian, 116-9
Cathedral Point, 48-49

CCC camps, 28, 73, 114, 121, 138
Cemeteries, 23, 28, 35, 47, 60, 62, 89, 110, 117, 138, 148
Chambers of commerce or information offices, 26, 32, 38, 45, 53, 58, 66, 81, 85, 93, 99, 108, 112, 119, 124, 135, 145, 151
Chapel in the Pines, 140
Chequamegon National Forest, 23-24
Clearwater Lake, 139
Cloverland, Town of, 70-81
Clubs, fishing and hunting, 18, 95, 137
Conover, 67, 82-5, 95
Consolidated Papers Forest tour, 128
Continental Divide markers, 72, 89
Courthouses: Oneida, 127; Vilas, 71
Cranberry marshes, 29, 139
Cranberry Winery, 77
Dams: Bear River, 23; Burnt Rollways, 72, 136; Fishtrap, 49; Gilmore Lake, 122; Horsehead Lake, 121; Killarney, 115; Lac Vieux Desert, 88; Long Lake, 96; Manitowish River, 47; Otter Rapids, 72; Pelican Lake, 147; Rainbow, 121; Rest Lake, 28; Rhinelander, 125-6; Willow, 115
Department of Natural Resources (DNR): 14, 16, 17, 29, 35, 47, 49, 61, 63; Trout Lake Headquarters, 48
Drumlins, 11, 40, 47, 148-9
Eagle River, 19, 20, 70-81
Eagle River Recreation Association, 72, 76
Enterprise, 147
Eskers, 11, 47, 49, 63, 69, 102, 110, 113-5, 148-9
Events, 26, 32, 38, 45, 53, 58, 66, 80, 85, 93, 99, 108, 112, 135, 145
Farms and farming, 27, 33, 34, 40, 54, 71, 82, 83, 87, 95-96, 101, 109, 116-7, 121-2, 125-6, 128, 138-40, 147-9
Fire towers, 23, 35, 47, 102, 142
First National Bank, Rhinelander, 127
Fish, species and management, 16-18
Fish hatcheries, 17, 23, 28, 41
Fishing: 6, 16-18, 24, 48; fee fishing, 35, 48
Forests: trees, forest types, and management, 12-13; tour, 128; unusually scenic forests, 23, 61, 69, 73, 139, 140, 148-9
French settlement and activity, 22, 86
Gagen, 126
Garth, 109
Glacial spillway, 11, 68
Glaciers and glaciation, 9-11, 47, 62-63
Golf, 42, 63, 74, 90, 97, 103, 111, 118, 142
Goodnow, 111, 116-7
Harshaw, 116-9
Hayrides, 97, 104
Hazelhurst, 40, 109-12
Hiking trails, 42, 49, 56, 64, 74, 90, 115,

152

118, 129, 142
Historical markers: Sam Campbell, 139; First Forest Patrol Flights, 47; First Rural Zoning, 127; First Snowmobile, 62; Forestry Beginnings, 47; Hodag, 127; Lac du Flambeau, 24; Lac Vieux Desert, 88; Military Road, 72, 88; Million Penny Parade, 40; Nicolet Forest, 139; Cy Williams, 139; Thirty Second Division Highway, 88; Wisconsin River, 88
Hodag, 127
Holiday (amusement) Park, 103
Howard Young Medical Center, 41
Hunting, 6, 16, 115, 118
Ice, for sale, 43
Indian Powwows (modern), 23
Indians: 21-23, 27, 28, 59-60, 67, 88, 101, 120, 138, 146; battles, 21, 23, 146; mounds, 120, 122; tribes: Chippewas, 21-22, 136, 146; Potawatomis, 59, 67; Sioux, 21, 146
Industry, 71, 87, 95, 126, 127
Jennings, 147, 148
Kames, 11, 63
Kettles and kettle landscapes, 10-11, 35, 41, 55, 63, 89, 148
Lac du Flambeau, 11, 19-26, 28, 101, 120
Lakes, origin, 11
Lakes, by name: **Oneida County:** Carr Lakes, 18, 121-3; Katherine, 102, 110, 121; Minocqua chain, 102, 120; Nokomis, 117; Pelican, 146-8; Rainbow Reservoir, 16, 121; Sugar Camp, 138, 140; Three Lakes chain, 72, 136-9, 141; Tomahawk, 110, 120-1; Willow Reservoir, 113-5; **Vilas County:** Boulder chain, 17, 49; Cisco chain, 87-88; Crab, 34-35; Devil's 89-90; Eagle River chain, 72; Escanaba Lake and Five Lakes Project, 17, 48-50; Flambeau chain, 17, 23; Indian, 60, 67-68; Lac Vieux Desert, 17, 19-20, 86, 88, 90, 96; Manitowish chain, 17, 19, 27-28, 49; St. Germain Lakes, 17, 54-56; Trout, 11, 15, 18-19, 29, 40, 46-49; Twin Lakes (Phelps), 18, 82-83, 95-97
Lake Tomahawk, 19, 120-4
Lakota, 83, 95
Land O' Lakes, 11, 19-20, 35, 67, 86-93
Leinenkugel's beer, 37
Lenox, 147
Libraries, 38, 66, 81, 93, 99, 108, 135, 138
Lincoln, Town of, 70-81
Logging, historic, 22, 27, 28, 33-35, 40, 46, 54, 59-60, 67-69, 70, 82, 87, 94-95, 101, 109, 114, 116-7, 121, 125, 136-7, 146
Logging camp sites, 27-28, 61, 68-69
Lost Region, 67-69, 89
Manitowish, 27, 29
Manitowish Waters, 16, 18-19, 27-32
Maps, advice, 6-7, 102, 114, 149
Marshes: explanation, 12; Powell Marsh, 12, 16, 23, 28-29, 32; Thunder Lake Marsh,

12, 139
McCord, 114
McNaughton, 121
Mecikalski Saloon (landmark), 148
Memorial Grove/Caro Woods, 23
Military Road, 18, 72, 86, 88, 95-96, 139, 146
Minnow stand (Art Holt's), 98
Minocqua, 11, 19, 40, 101-8
Missionaries, 22, 86, 109
Monico, 11, 126, 128
Monuments, 35, 55, 88, 102
Moonshining, 34, 126
Moraines, 10-11, 33, 41, 68, 95, 148
Motels/Motor Lodges: **Oneida County:** Aqua Aire, 107; Back Bay Inn, 107; Claridge, 134; Cross Trails, 107; Downtown, 134; Holiday Acres, 134; Holiday Inn, 134; Lake Tomahawk Motel, 124; Lakeview, 107; Little Minocqua, 107; Little Swiss Village, 108; Motel Maple, 144; Oneida Village, 144; Parkside, 112; Pines, 108; Pinewood Lodge, 134; Tomahawk Shores, 124; Trail-Inn, 151; **Vilas County:** Arbor Vitae Motel, 44; Bel Air, 92; Braywood, 79; Buckhorn Lodge, 45; Char Rose, 65; Chic-A-Dee, 79; Country Lane, 45; Edgewater, 45; Gira, 79; Hiawatha, 79; Holiday Court, 58; Jolin's, 52; Lakeside, 93; Meadow Lark, 80; Northern, 45; Northern Highland, 53; Northland, 85; Persian Paradise, 80; Pineaire, 93; Riverdale, 80; Rustic Manor, 58; Shoreline, 80; Sportsman's, 38; Tower, 26; Traveler's Inn, 80; White Eagle, 80
Museums: Antique Phonograph, 40; Henkelmann's, 40; Rhinelander Logging, 127; Shrimp's Wildlife Displays, 48; Vilas County Historical, 62
Music: Baroque Festival, 76, 131; Rhinelander Symphony, 131
Muskellunge Hill, 11, 62
Musky Jamboree, 53
Nature trails, 23-24, 42, 49, 61, 63, 73, 129, 139
Newspapers, 7
Nicolet College and Technical Institute: 126-7; theater, 131
Nicolet National Forest: background, 138-9; main attractions, 72-73, 88, 96, 139
Nokomis, Town of, 116-9
North Central Forest Experiment Station, 127
Northern Highland, 9-10
Northern Highland State Forest: background, 40, 48, 61; attractions, 48, 49-50, 61, 63
Northern Wisconsin National Canoe Base (BSA), 47
Nuns, St. Mary's Hospital, Rhinelander, 126
Oneida County Forest, 16, 114-5, 118, 148-151
Ottawa National Forest, 89
Parks, 36, 42, 64, 74, 84, 88, 90, 97, 103,

153

111, 114, 118, 129
Partridge Lake Wilderness, 11, 67-69
Pelican Lake, 11, 146-51
Personalities: John Dillinger, 31; G. L. Draper, 86; Carl Eliason, 50, 62; Dwight Eisenhower, 101; Pere Rene Menard, S. J., 86; Dr. Kate Newcomb, 41, 47; Chief Sharpened Stone, 21; Peter Vance, 18, 28; William F. Vilas, 70
Phelps, 19, 72, 94-99
Picnic areas: 23-24, 30, 36, 42, 49-50, 55, 64, 74-75, 88, 90, 97, 122, 142; waysides, 24, 50, 88, 90, 97, 118
Pioneer Lake Lutheran Church, 82-83
Playgrounds, 30, 50
Pleasure Island, 74
Plum Creek Fishing Grounds, 55
Plum Lake, Town of, 59-66
Popcorn wagon, 102
Powell, 16, 23, 27
Presque Isle, 11, 33-38, 88
Racing: auto, 76; off-road, 131; snowmobile, 81, 145
Railroads/Trains/Abandoned grades (common carrier and logging), 22, 27, 33-34, 40, 46, 49, 54, 59-61, 67-70, 82-83, 86-87, 94-96, 101, 109-10, 114, 116-7, 121, 125-7, 137-9, 146
Rearing ponds, 13, 35, 61
Resort development and history, 18-20, 22, 27-28, 34, 40, 47, 54-55, 59-60, 70-71, 82-83, 86-87, 95, 101, 109, 114, 121, 126, 137-8, 146-7
Resort evaluation guidelines, 7-8
Resorts: **Oneida County:** *American plan lodges:* Driftwood, 106; Feases', 133; Jansen's, 107; The Northern, 107; Northernaire, 144; Shorewood Vista, 133; Van Kirk's, 144; *Housekeeping cottage resorts:* Acklam's, 107; Black's Cliff, 112; Blue Waters, 133; Brekke's, 134; Cedarwood, 119; Coachlite, 107; Engstrand's, 134; Evensen's, 144; Fawn Lake Lodge, 124; Holiday Acres, 134; Kafka's, 134; Lakewood, 119; Na Hee Ta Pines, 107; The Narrows, 107; Pine Point, 134; Pinewood Lodge, 134; Rustlewood, 144; St. John's, 107; Sunset Shores, 144; Van's Mercer Lake, 107; Van Kirk's, 144; Wakan Tepe, 124; Weaver's, 151; **Vilas County:** *American plan lodges:* The Bear, 37; Cardinal's, 44; Chanticleer, 78; Coon's, 44; Deer Park, 31; Dillman's, 25; Eagle Waters, 79; Forest, 52; Froelich's, 65; Hazen's Long Lake, 98; Lost Lake Resort, 65; Motel in the Woods, 52; Musky Inn, 57; Resort of the Woods, 52; Sunrise, 92; Voss' Birchwood, 31; Wildcat, 52; Zastrow's Lynx Lake, 38; *European plan inn,* The Gateway, 92; *Housekeeping cottage resorts:* Afterglow Lake, 98; Aschenbrenner's, 31; Bazso's, 31; Birchwood Cove, 52; BranAnn's Colonial, 92; Brown's Point, 37; Butler's, 44; Connors, 57; Copp's, 52; Coun-Tree Acres, 31; Cox's Estrold, 57; D-Bar-D, 26; Deerpath, 85; Dittman's, 92; Four Seasons, 85; Gasper's, 52; Helminski's, 44; Hemlock Haven, 26; Heulla Lodge, 85; Hiller's, 57; Holiday Harbor (houseboats), 79; Holzinger's, 44; Johnson's Millpoint, 31; Jung's, 52; Kangle's, 44; Knotty Pine, 79; Lake Aidenn, 79; Lehor's, 58; Lofty Pines, 58; Luetzow's, 26; McPartlin's, 92; Maplewood, 79; Meander Post, 79; North Shore, 85; North Twin, 98; Perveiler's Dor-Way, 58; Pride o' the North, 58; Saunoris', 44; Schmuecking's, 26; Schrock's, 79; 7-mile Pinecrest, 79; Shelter Bay, 52; Shorewood, 38; Silver Beach, 26; Silver Muskie, 65; Simon's Sunrise, 38; Sleight's Wildwood, 31; Smith's Birch Lane, 58; Tall Timbers, 65; Thomson's, 85; Timberlands, 79; Twin Waters, 58; Voss' Breezy Point, 32; Wah-Wah-Taysee, 65; Watson's, 26; West Bay, 92; Wildcat Lodge, 52; Wittig's Point, 52; Woody's, 52; Worthen's, 58; Zastrow's, 38
Restaurants / Supper clubs / Lodge dining rooms: Al Gen, 133; Ar-Ber, 78; Archdale's North, 92; Back Bay Inn, 106; Bill and Holly's, 65; Blink Bonnie, 57; Bosacki's, 106; Bronkalla's, 143; Captain's Galleon, 43; Chalet, 143; Czecho, 78; Darton's Char' Lou, 78; Dillman's Lodge, 25; Ehrich's Bavarian Inn, 30; Eliason's Someplace Else, 57; Fence Lake Lodge, 25; Fireside Inn, 133; Froelich's Sayner Lodge, 65; Gateway, 92; George's Steak House, 51; Golden Eagle, 78; Hazen's Long Lake Lodge, 98; Headwaters Resort, 51; Hideaway Lodge, 118; Holiday Acres, 133; Holiday Inn Supper Club (Minocqua), 106; Holiday Lodge, 98; Idle Forest Inn, 65; Jacobi's Hiawatha, 112; Jansen's Squirrel Lake Lodge, 106; Keep Schmil-Inn, 31; Kelly's, 43; Knight's Inn, 151; Little Bohemia, 31; Little Swiss Village, 106; Lola's, 143; Lost Lake Resort (Gabe's), 65; Mama's, 106; Mint Bar, 78; Molgaard's Indian Lodge, 57; Musky Inn, 57; Napoli, 78; North Twin, 98; Northernaire, 144; Northwestern Lounge, 133; Paul Bunyan, 106; Persian Paradise, 78; Phil's, 119; Pied Piper, 133; Pine Cone Inn, 44; Pine Gables, 78; Pinewood Country Club, 119; Pinewood Lodge, 133; Plantation, 44; Rhinelander Cafe and Pub, 133; Skyview, 37; Spang's, 57; Thunderbird, 44; Tomahawk Shores, 123; Tower, 25; Turtle Lake Lodge, 37; Voss' Birchwood Lodge, 31; White Spruce Inn, 78; White Stag, 144; Willow Haven, 115; Zastrow's Lynx Lake Lodge, 37
Retreat Bar, 37

Rhinelander, 125-35, 145, 148
Rivers: Bear, 22-24; Deerskin, 18, 72, 74, 97; Manitowish, 18, 27-29, 46-47, 49, 68, 90; Pelican, 17, 125, 127-8, 148; Tomahawk, 17, 103, 110, 114-5, 117-8, 120; Wisconsin, 16-17, 54, 56, 68, 74, 82, 84, 86, 88, 90, 120, 122, 125, 128-9, 136, 148; Wolf, 149
Roads, scenic, 24, 28, 35, 41, 48-49, 55, 61, 63, 68-69, 72-73, 83, 88-89, 96, 102, 110, 117, 121-2, 128, 139-40, 148-9
Roadside cross, 140
Rocking Horse Ranch, 131

Sailing, 95, 97, 150
St. Germain, 20, 54-58
St. Regis Paper Co. mill tour, 127
Sauna, 75
Sayner, 11, 19, 59-66
Scientific areas (state), 40, 48, 61, 63, 102, 114, 127
Scuba, 64, 104, 123, 130
Seaplane rides, 48, 140
Section corner and bearing tree, 140
Shooting, 30, 36, 42, 50, 64, 75, 84, 91, 104, 130, 149
Shops: **Oneida County:** *Antiques:* Gillingham's, 123; The Mill, 43; Millie's, 105; Red Shed, 143; Second Hand Rose, 132; Sugar Camp Antiques, 143; *Gift/Specialty:* American Heritage, 105; Book World (Minocqua), 105; Book World (Rhinelander), 131; Buck's Northwoods, 123; Cheddar Shed/Loft, 105; Christmas Chalet, 105; Gift and Tackle Shop, 123; Greenleaf Shoppe, 105; Happiness Card and Party Shop, 132; Leather Plus, 132; Little Swiss Village, 105; Mole Hole, 105; Northwoods Nature and Art Center, 105; Olde Minocqua Boardwalk, 105; Popov's Gifts and Gallery, 105; Prchal's, 123; Redwood House, 143; Schneider's Pottery Shop, 105; Shy Violet, 132; Turn of the Century, 133; Vagabond Lover, 105; Wildlife Art Gallery and Gifts, 106; **Vilas County:** *Antiques:* Arvilla's, 50; Hackley House, 97; House of Antiques, 77; Stonehouse, 57; Treasure Chest, 92; Village Shop, 77; Ye Olde Workshop, 43; *Artisans/Workshops:* Artisan Industries, 37; Cousin Willy Woodsculpture, 51; Steincraft, 37; Uncle Dick's Workshop, 51; The Wooden End, 37; *Gift/Specialty:* Arrow Gifts, 78; Bernadette's, 91; Big Barn, 78; Bluebird Doll House, 77; Bookworm, 51; Camera Shop, 77; Christmas House, 77; Cranberry Gift House, 77; Cricket Cove, 30; Crossroads Sports and Gifts, 84; Denton's Sports and Gifts, 84; Elf Hut, 43; The Gateway Gifts, 91; Gebic Shop, 25; Hartshorne Sport and Gift Shop, 64; In Stitches, 51; Junction Country Store, 51; Lehner's Jewelry and Gifts, 77; Mabel's Gift Shop, 25; Meadow Ruh, 77; Moccasin Shop, 78; The Ox Yoke, 30; Pop and Ole Dean's, 65; Red Apple, 57; Red Wing Trading Post, 78; Ronbach Shop, 51; Spiess Sporting Goods, 78; Strawberry Patch, 77; Totem Trading Post, 25; Trading Post Internationale, 91; Yankee Studio and Gifts, 30
Skating: ice, 50, 75, 84, 123, 130, 142; roller, 130
Skiing, cross-country (including rentals), **25**, 30, 36, 42, 50, 56, 64, 75, 91, 104, 118, 123, 130, 142, 150
Skiing, downhill, 76, 91, 104, 130, 142
Sleighrides, 97, 131
Snowmobile, first, 60, 62
Snowmobiling (including rentals), 6, 25, 30, 36, 43, 50, 56, 64, 76, 84, 91, 97, 104, 115, 118, 123, 130-1, 142-3, 150
Snowshoe baseball, 121, 123
Squirrel Hill, 102, 104
Stables, 56, 76, 104, 111, 131, 143
Starks, 126
Star Lake: 13, 19, 48, 59-66, 67; Forestry Plantation, 61
State Line (Land O' Lakes), 11, 20
Sugar Camp, 136-45
Summer home development, 22, 28, 34, 46, 55, 71, 87, 95, 101, 109, 121, 126, 137, 146-7
Swamps: explanation, 12; examples, 28, 72
Sylvania, 89-91, 93

Taxis, 81, 135
Telephone hotlines, 6
Tennis, 25, 30, 43, 50, 56, 76, 91, 105, 111, 131, 143
Theater (live): Nicolet College, 131; Northern Lights Summer Playhouse, 111
Three Lakes, 20, 136-45
Trading and trading posts, historic, 18, 22, 86, 101, 109, 120, 125, 139, 146
Trees for Tomorrow Center, 72
Tripoli, 114

Washington, Town of, 70-81
Waterfalls: Cedar, 110; Willow Rapids, 114
Water mail route, 139
Water ski shows, 30, 64, 76, 91, 101, 105, 131, 143
Wild areas (proposed): Frank Lake, 48, 63; Indian Creek, 122; Lost Region, 67-69
Wildflowers, 13, 96, 148
Wild ricing, 47
Willow Region, 11, 16, 113-5
Winchester, 11, 16, 19, 33-38
Winegar (Presque Isle), 11, 18, 33-34
Wisconsin-Michigan state line, 88
Woodboro, 116-7
Woodruff, 20, 39-45
Zoos: Aqualand, 47; Buck & Doe, 74; Peck's Wildwood, 102; Pleasure Island, 74; Warbonnet, 110; Weber's Wildlife Farm, 63

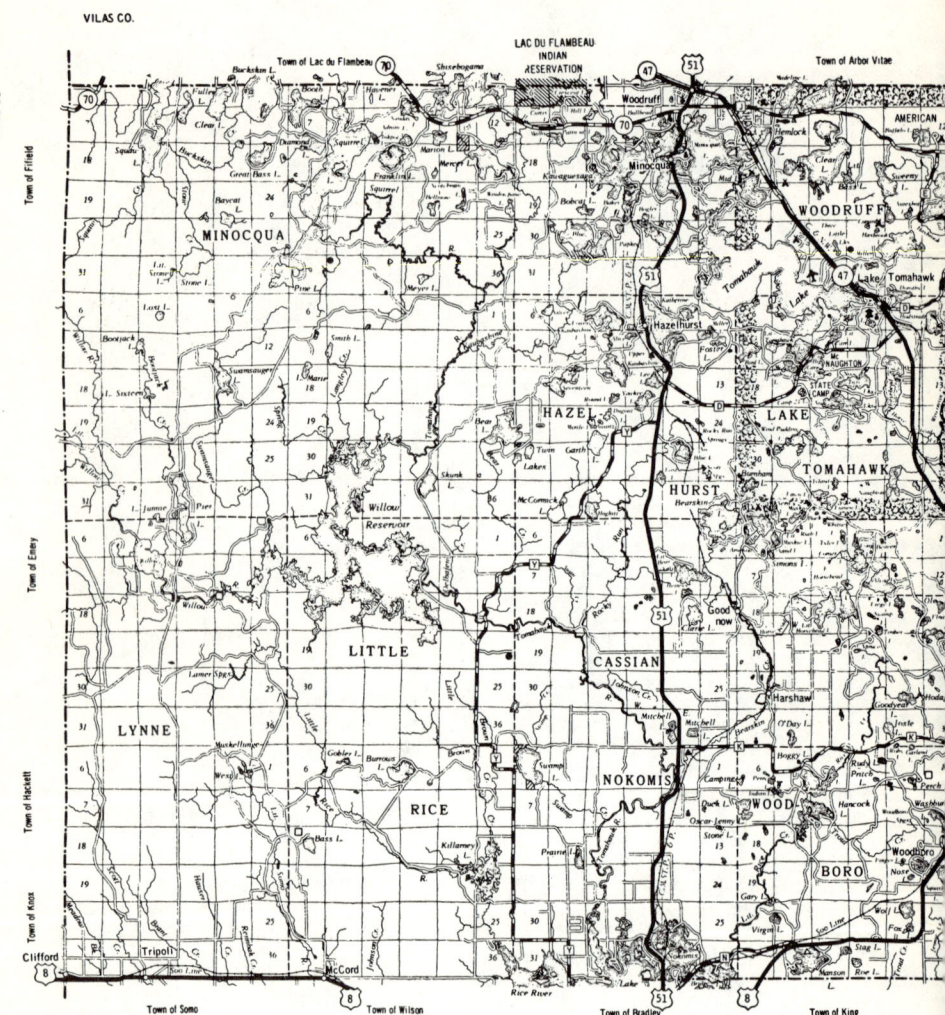

ONEIDA CO.